K

LANGUAGE AND EMOTION

Language is a means we use to communicate feelings; we also reflect emotionally on the language we and others use. James M. Wilce analyzes the signals people use to express emotion, looking at the social, cultural, and political functions of emotional language around the world. The book demonstrates that *speaking, feeling, reflecting*, and *identifying* are interrelated processes and shows how emotions such as desire and shame are attached to language. Drawing on nearly 100 ethnographic case studies, it demonstrates the cultural diversity, historical emergence, and political significance of emotional language. Wilce brings together insights from linguistics and anthropology to survey an extremely broad range of genres, cultural concepts, and social functions of emotional expression.

JAMES M. WILCE is Professor of Anthropology at Northern Arizona University.

DATE DUE

Brodart Co.   Cat. # 55 137 001   Printed in USA

STUDIES IN THE SOCIAL AND CULTURAL FOUNDATIONS OF LANGUAGE

The aim of this series is to develop theoretical perspectives on the essential social and cultural character of language by methodological and empirical emphasis on the occurrence of language in its communicative and interactional settings, on the socioculturally grounded "meanings" and "functions" of linguistic forms, and on the social scientific study of language use across cultures. It will thus explicate the essentially ethnographic nature of linguistic data, whether spontaneously occurring or experimentally induced, whether normative or variational, whether synchronic or diachronic. Works appearing in the series will make substantive and theoretical contributions to the debate over the sociocultural-function and structural-formal nature of language, and will represent the concerns of scholars in the sociology and anthropology of language, anthropological linguistics, sociolinguistics, and socio-culturally informed psycholinguistics.

Editors

Judith T. Irvine
Bambi Schieffelin

Editorial Advisers

Marjorie Goodwin
Joel Kuipers
Don Kulick
John Lucy
Elinor Ochs
Michael Silverstein

A list of books in the series can be found after the index.

LANGUAGE AND EMOTION

JAMES M. WILCE
Northern Arizona University

CAMBRIDGE
UNIVERSITY PRESS

CAMBRIDGE UNIVERSITY PRESS

Cambridge, New York, Melbourne, Madrid, Cape Town, Singapore, São Paulo, Delhi

Cambridge University Press
The Edinburgh Building, Cambridge CB2 8RU, UK

Published in the United States of America by Cambridge University Press, New York

www.cambridge.org
Information on this title: www.cambridge.org/9780521682824

First published 2009

Printed in the United Kingdom at the University Press, Cambridge

A catalog record for this publication is available from the British Library

Library of Congress Cataloging in Publication data
Wilce, James MacLynn, 1953–
Language and emotion / James M. Wilce.
p.   cm.
(Studies in the social and cultural foundations of language; 25)
Includes index.
ISBN 978-0-521-86417-6 (hardback) – ISBN 978-0-521-68282-4 (pbk.)
1. Language and emotions.   2. Laments.   3. Anthropological linguistics.
I. Title.   II. Series.
P325.5.E56W55   2009
306.44–dc22
2009005332

ISBN 978-0-521-86417-6 hardback
ISBN 978-0-521-68282-4 paperback

CONTENTS

FIGURES

TRANSCRIPTS

ACKNOWLEDGEMENTS

I would like to thank the many patient and helpful souls who spent precious time reading and commenting on all or part of this book at earlier stages: Laura Ahearn, Mara Buchbinder, Nick Endicott, Cre Engelke, Neill Hadder, Paul Iverson, Michael Lempert, Elizabeth Owens, and Maggie Ronkin. Whatever quirks and errors that remain in the book are my sole responsibility. Finally, to Sarah, whose enthusiastic support kept me going, my warmest thanks and love.

INTRODUCTION

Feelingful language

Last year I met an exchange student I'll call Hussein, a man with a laptop, and a heart, full of songs. These were not just any songs, not secular songs, but Shia Muslim **laments** – songs of mourning. These songs and their compelling lyrics, along with tears and other public signs of grief over a particular set of historic martyrs, help to define Shia Islam vis-à-vis other forms. In the process of interviewing Hussein it became clear that, for him, language and feeling – the subject of this book – came together in the context of Shia religious practices that pervade his life and in many ways define what anthropologists call culture (his, in this case). That is, this coming together, this fusion of language and feeling, is the very stuff of culture.

Hussein's laptop contains perhaps hundreds of mp3 files of these Shia laments. But that is not where they live; Hussein has made them a part of his life. When during the course of our interview there was a dull moment as we waited for a file to download, I found him humming. What was he humming? Another lament. *This book explores language and feeling: feelingful language, like Hussein's.*

Both Arabic and English versions of many Shia laments are available as downloads from Shia devotional websites. (This is a cultural story in itself but one that I will not pursue.) As Hussein played for me the English version of a lament by the popular Iraqi lamenter (composer, performer), Basem al-Karbalai, the **genre** ceased to be merely the object of study as its power began to move me. Throughout our meeting, Hussein's devotion – his quiet and steady affect centered on these recent productions combining word, melody, and a vocal quality intended to resemble weeping (Feld and Fox 1994) – disturbed my secular sensibilities, touched me, and reminded me that language and emotion, for the linguistic anthropologist, are not only linked together, nor are they ends in themselves. They are linked to cultural ends.

Shia laments aim to commemorate the death of another Hussein, the grandson of the Prophet Muhammad and son of Ali. Shia Islam embraces Ali, and Hussein ibn Ali, as Imams (the third and first, respectively, of a canonical list of

1

twelve divinely authorized leaders of faith). Language feelingfully harnessed
in the task of honoring God, his Imams, and his martyrs – this makes sense
to Shia Muslims. Lament cut off from these moorings does not. Hussein was
providing for me the rich contextualization on which ethnography, the anthropologist's approach to studying social and cultural life, thrives. He was demonstrating that the link between language and affect passes through the *process
of identification*, his identification with the suffering of the Imams (an identification that I fleetingly experienced).

Let's trace the backstory behind my meeting with Hussein. A friend had
described him as someone who would be interested in helping me understand
Shia Islam, and laments. And just before that, I had heard a feature story on
National Public Radio (Tarabay 2006) that had highlighted the role newly
composed laments were playing in Iraq's Shia community. The story compelled me to learn what I could about such laments from someone to whom
they were personally meaningful. NPR's Jamie Tarabay presented the laments
in her story as social or political commentary on the current scene in Iraq,
and on Sunni–Shia tensions in particular. And thus I was primed to raise this
sort of function with Hussein. Although he is not from Iraq, he is a Shia Arab,
and I guessed he might have a lot to say about these moving songs. From the
start, however, Hussein redirected my attention. The first sign that I was, in his
view, off track, was when he did not quite understand what I meant by calling
the laments political. Very soon I realized that for him and others who made
the songs part of their lives, these songs served primarily to focus and inspire
religious attention and practice.

Why this book? Why now?

Cultural stories of the hot-as-molten-metal fusion of language and emotion
need telling, and this is my task here. World-class scholars such as Ochs,
Schieffelin, Abu-Lughod, Lutz, and Besnier (to name but a few) have explored
this territory, making my task immensely easier, shedding light on the social
(and discursive) construction of emotion. They pioneered the study of the **pragmatic meaning** of emotion talk, i.e., what it *does*, not just what it is "about"
(Lutz 1988: 8; compare Ochs 1986, Ochs and Schieffelin 1989). Yet the time
is clearly right for such a book as this, and not only because of such historic
events as the resurgence of Shia Islam, a religion of lament. As Woodward
felicitously notes, it is a time of "academic warming" toward the subject of
emotion, some emotions in particular, and affect (Woodward 1996). In describing postmodernity, Frederic Jameson has pronounced the death of the centered
subject, and with it, the waning of affect – "The end of the bourgeois ego, or
monad, no doubt brings with it the end of the psychopathologies of that ego –
what I have been calling the waning of affect" (Jameson 1991: 15). Such pro-
nouncements notwithstanding, Brian Massumi (and others) have declared this

postmodern age to be one of affective intensity.[1] Today one can even read profoundly scholarly, articulate arguments for an emotion-based approach to law and international relations.[2] At the same time, however, I dare say there is often more warmth than light, at least in the areas I address. In particular, the time is right for an anthropological treatise on language and emotion that takes a strongly historical, processual, semiotically informed approach. (In order to communicate more clearly the complexities involved in such an analysis, I have provided a glossary of the terms you see in **bold**.)

All speaking and writing is inherently emotional to a greater or lesser extent; objective, distant coolness *is* an emotional stance. Emotion is not confined to the outskirts of linguistic civilization but pervades its core (we could say, *Extra adfectum nullam salus*),[3] by which I mean that nearly every dimension of every language at least potentially encodes emotion, and that this language-emotion relationship is crucial to what we call "culture." But encoding is an inadequate concept to capture the constant and significant shifts in the way we enact or perform emotion with words, in different contexts,[4] across different historical eras – not to mention across cultural boundaries. These are the themes I explore in this book.

One can imagine a number of books on language and emotion. Mine takes a particular approach to the subject informed by my disciplinary home – anthropology – and my conviction that the method anthropologists use and offer to other disciplines, namely *ethnography*, is a way to grasp our topic in its full cross-cultural and cross-linguistic diversity, with a good sense of real people feeling in real situations. Ethnography offers the potential to collapse distances; it can give readers a sense of being present – alongside the writer. Granted, since I will often be summarizing the first-person accounts of other ethnographers, much of the white-hot, or red, heat (as in warm, blushing face) of intimacy will be lost.[5] But I hope to retain some of it. For even an account of passions should itself move readers and not only appeal to their minds despite our Cartesian **ideologies**.

But I write, as well, as a critic of anthropology's tendency, at least until the 1980s, to neglect history (a tendency that may have been particularly marked among linguistic anthropologists, with important exceptions).[6] I am convinced that local and global histories of the culturally mediated relationship between language and emotion ought to be central to any analysis of emotion, as they are, for example, to Erik Mueggler (1998, 2005). And I am also critical of a sort of flat earth approach to semiotic processes that collapses complex layers or orders of signs or sign relations in which one co-occurring element points to another[7] into simple notions of language pointing to identity – as though, for example, one points to one's Apache identity by speaking Apache or engaging in traditional Apache speech acts when (as I explore in later chapters) identifying with, and emotionally performing, certain **genres** of apparently Anglo-American music turn out to be central to being Apache these days (Samuels

2004). There are significant advantages, as I hope to make clear, in focusing on **identification** processes rather than writing about identity as though it were a thing. In fact emotion, and emotional language, enters into the process of **identification** in complex ways, which I will explore in later chapters. Even when scholars recognize identity as dynamically constituted, I find that changing the subject – focusing on identification – is a very useful reminder of process. This historical, semiotically informed, processual perspective sets my approach off from previous approaches to language and emotion within linguistic anthropology.

Anthropologists sometimes analyze myths. Let me instead offer some at the outset of this book – myth-like narratives that help situate emotion and affect (defined for now as a term that encompasses not only emotion but identifications and sensibilities, for example) in relation to language, culture, and history. I use the myths as a means to clarify some possible meanings of a (linguistically mediated) relationship being defined by emotion. For one of the things that sets my account of language and emotion apart from earlier accounts is its attention to histories and stories of other kinds.

Imagine a baby, far too young for words. The baby cries, and is immediately soothed. This happens often, teaching the infant a lesson about the power – perhaps even the magical power – of certain expressive forms. At some point in the child's life, she or he has a very different experience, leading to different inferences. In one version of the myth I am telling, the disappointed crying child – always a boy in this version – has already become verbal, old enough to make repeated requests that his older sister share her food with him; when she refuses his final request, the little boy in the myth is transformed into a fruit dove and flies away into the forest, where the dove's plaintive cries remind the people, in perpetuity, of the fateful interaction. This version of the myth (negatively) reminds the Bosavi people in Papua New Guinea of the giving and the emotion that should structure this relationship between younger brothers and older sisters, the *ade* relationship, a relationship that is defined by affect – dependent feelings on the brother's part and pity on the sister's (Feld 1990, B. Schieffelin 1990; compare Doi 1973).

If in this version "relationships defined by affect" amount to dyadic kin relations, the next version should indicate the scope and global sociopolitical significance of such relationships. I present a fuller discussion of the real history that forms the basis of this mythic retelling elsewhere (Wilce 2009).

Imagine a population of children and adults in full, active, and unequal relationship to another such population living with them. Imagine yourself a woman of the *bhadralok*[8] in Kolkata (the former Calcutta), Bengal, ca. 1850 – that is, a member of the *bhadra* 'gentle/genteel' classes, the "literary-minded sections of the **Bengali** middle classes" (Chakrabarty 2004: 654–655). You have grown up in this complex society, immersed in its particular emotional atmosphere – the bhadralok's "emotional regime" (its "normative emotions and the official rituals, practices, and **emotives** that express and inculcate them," Reddy 2001: 129). But this emotional regime has been shaped by the engagement of the British with Bengalis, particularly the bhadralok, in Kolkata. The British-bhadralok relationship was a close if problematic one, producing at least superficially similar public emotional habits.

Imagine yourself a bhadralok woman in Kolkata who happens upon the performance of a 'folk' song. This **genre** – which combines discourse (lyrics) and music – resonates yet offends. For generations, *viraha* 'longing' songs have been performed in the area. Among the themes the genre can take up is the love between the god *Kṛṣṇa* (Krishna) and his consort, Radha. This theme is sacred to you and others. The language of Krishna and Radha's love has for centuries stirred sacred emotion in your native Bengal, and all of India. Yet you feel that today's performers, these rustic women whose viraha songs are typically frankly and playfully erotic, should go back to the countryside whence they came! You feel "shame" over the song's "uninhibited debunking of Hindu deities" (feeling that British Orientalists view the song, you, and contemporary Hinduism as degenerate). The voices of rustic women performing in Kolkata seem to you shockingly bold. They "rend the air like the cuckoo." Yet you hear another voice speaking *to* and *of* you, the voice of the New Kolkata Woman. This inner voice laments the fact that your voice "has become … the mew of a pussy."[9]

There is a final act to this narrative. To some extent, you and your family have learned to see 'Hindu' history as the British do – to see that the Hindus (your ancestors, epitomized also in the corrupted version of Hinduism of which the bawdy viraha song is a representative example) lost their way some time long before the British arrived. Your **identification** with this Hinduism shifts in a subtle way since you may begin to perceive the form your generation inherited as a pale version of the original, full reality. This colors your sense of yourself at least as you relate to colonial officers – but also *as you speak*, and thus it colors *how you speak*. For the sense of a fall from the golden age touches off not only religious reform but linguistic reforms. These reforms – including 'purifying' **Bangla**[10] of 'foreign' (Muslim) taint, in and of themselves – have strong affective overtones.

The point of this story is to provide an example of the complex processes we must examine in order to grasp language's relation to emotion. This book invites you to look not only at the eons of evolution that led to the contemporary language-emotion nexus; not only at strictly cognitive-linguistic issues or universal emotional scripts (see Wierzbicka's "Natural Semantic Metalanguage," Wierzbicka and Harkins 2001) said to underlie "emotion labels"; but at the cultural-historical contexts in which even academic talk of emotion takes place

(Wilce 2009). The story also neatly illustrates the multilayered nature of the culturally and ideologically mediated relationship of language and emotion. Such relationships entail apparent sociolinguistic facts (e.g., that rural women's performances are embarrassing, or bawdy – such facts being themselves the product of **ideological** reflection, at whatever degree of consciousness) – that become the occasion for further stages of reflection. And those reflections in turn produce new facts (such as self-conscious shifts in what became 'gentle' or 'bhadralok speech'), in never-ending cycles.

Writing about emotion: who does it, and how?

For an academic, or perhaps a linguistic anthropologist in particular, to write of emotion has, at least in the recent past, been to take some amount of risk. Over the years it has been a labor some consider the concern of a few. The few, at first – Margaret Mead and Ruth Benedict – were women at a time when women were rare in anthropology. Oddly, later work on emotion (by Lutz, White, Ochs, and Schieffelin) was often associated with Oceania (Abu-Lughod's important work being an exception). Some (e.g., Lutz and White) who did this work were practitioners of a subdiscipline – psychological anthropology – that some find problematic. Since linguistic anthropology is another subdiscipline within the tribe of anthropologists, the area of overlap of these two circles of interest – psychological and linguistic anthropology – might appear small. These facts in themselves may **index** male dominance, and the dominance of concerns associated with men as analysts and actors (power), despite some strong evidence to the contrary. Whatever risk was attached to writing about emotion or affect in the past has apparently receded of late as the subject has attracted more and more debate (reflected in this book) and interest.

The cool and distant emotional stance in most academic writing is striking, and this may be particularly true of those who write about language. There are examples of ethnographic writing that contrast sharply. Renato Rosaldo began to think, and write, about grief very differently when his wife and ethnographic field partner, Michelle Z. Rosaldo, died in an accident during fieldwork in the Philippines with the Ilongot people. Without claiming to have become Ilongot, the widowed Renato Rosaldo could reasonably claim to have understood things that Ilongot individuals had been telling him about grief. The comparative absence of any writing like Rosaldo's (in the passage below) from linguistic anthropology was forming itself as a problem in my mind as I set about writing this book:

I experienced the deep cutting pain of sorrow almost beyond endurance, the cadaverous cold of realizing the finality of death, the trembling beginning in my abdomen and spreading through my body, the mournful keening that started without my willing, and frequent tearful sobbing (Rosaldo 1996: 488).

I know of no passage in linguistic anthropology that packs the same emotional punch.

The turning away from feeling in academic writing at times becomes an explicit theoretical statement. Consider the work of Lauren Berlant (1999), whose jaundiced analyses of the invocation of emotion in public discourse have inspired other feminist critiques of the role of emotion in the public sphere (Povinelli 1998). Others note the absence of feelings even from some feminist accounts of affect. For example, Sedgwick and Frank (1995b) critique Cvetkovich (1992) on the grounds that her constructionist approach is blind to large domains of affect, but also because distinctions among particular affects are lost in her account. "Affect is treated as a unitary category, with a unitary history and unitary politics. There is no theoretical room for any difference between, say, being amused, being disgusted, being ashamed, and being enraged" (Sedgwick and Frank 1995: 17). Recently, **cultural studies** scholar Elspeth Probyn sounded the same note: "So let A-ffect rest (in peace), so we can put our energies into motivated analyses of the constitution, the experience, the political, cultural and individual import of many affects" (2005b).

I have been troubled by the popularity of a certain emotion-distant style in linguistic anthropology, and by the dominance of arguments that derive from a certain reading of Wittgenstein, famously skeptical of "private languages," and of Merleau-Ponty, who once wrote, "Truth does not 'inhabit' the 'inner man,' or more accurately, there is no inner man, man is in the world, and only in the world does he know himself" (Merleau-Ponty 1962: xii). Skepticism about private languages has spilled over into skepticism about language's expressive function (Jakobson 1985 [1960]). These issues were brought to a head for me several years ago when I was asked to provide a published commentary (Wilce 2003) on an article disputing the classical view that interjections either manifest emotions or (at least) mental states. In many ways, I owe this book to the brilliant linguistic anthropologist who wrote the original article, Paul Kockelman. In another sense, my commentary – asserting that there is a late-modern cultural influence behind the skepticism this paragraph describes – was only incidentally targeting Kockelman's argument. It was intended far more generally.

In a nutshell, here is the argument I objected to, but which felicitously provided the impetus for this book: "When we focus on internal states ... the situational, discursive, and social regularities of interjections are all too easily elided" (Kockelman 2003: 479). I have no objection to recognizing the social significance of interjections or any other forms commonly analyzed as emotive, and welcome what fellow commentator John Haviland calls Kockelman's "**indexicality**-based account." The problem Haviland and I have is with Kockelman contrasting that account with, as Haviland writes, "one focusing on 'subjective emotional states.' But there is no contrast if 'emotion' is intersubjectively and interactively constructed" (Haviland 2003: 481). Indeed, Haviland raises the proper question: Why construe emotions as purely personal and subjective, problematize them, and then feel compelled to divorce them from language, even those linguistic forms that have been most closely associated with emotions? Why not view emotions as shared **intersubjective** states, performed in complex multimodal contexts involving, yes, interjections, and nearly every dimension of language *and* visible **semiosis**,[11] etc.?

I thank Kockelman, Haviland, and others for starting such a compelling discussion. It is to offer a more nuanced, comprehensive, and theoretically rich version of the argument I offered in 2003 that I write this book.

Overview of the argument and chapters

My argument shares much with other anthropologists' work on emotion, and it is worthwhile stating some of that common ground before distinguishing this work from theirs. Forms of human emotion are not, and never have been, purely personal or biological. Always social in context, emotions and the semiotic forms that help bear and reproduce them are responsive to the forms of our shared life. More than straightforwardly revealing psychological processes, forms of discourse – and more specifically, genres of so-called emotional expression – help constitute social understandings and apparently internal processes. To be a person is to belong to a group; participation in all human communities entails sharing genres of performance and cultural sensibilities guiding reflections on them. Through history, altering emotion, semiotic forms (genres), or social life has meant altering the others, too.

Although you will easily perceive this book's debt to a wide range of other work, it differs from previous treatments of language and emotion in many ways. As I touch on all of the particular arguments that distinguish this work from its predecessors, the perceptive reader will realize that many if not most of them pertain to reflexivity. This book not only calls for greater critical reflection across a number of issues; it also insists that local actors constantly engage in reflection, and that the function of many signs is also reflexive. In fact, all humanly produced signs (from tears, to languages [objectified], to arguments, e.g., that the speech style of some class of persons is naturally more emotional than some standard of comparison) fall under the influence of reflexive (or meta-) signs. **Identification** (Fuss 1995) is an inherently reflexive process. **Language ideologies** (Kroskrity 2000) – culturally particular ideas about language and its relations to the world, ideas always significantly linked to forms of power – are inherently reflexive. The study of linguistic ideologies – "sets of beliefs about language articulated by users as a rationalization or justification of perceived language structure and use" (Silverstein 1979: 193), or "shared bodies of commonsense notions of the nature of language in the world" (Rumsey 1990: 346) – has proven to be one of the most productive areas of linguistic anthropological research since the early 1990s, not least because language ideologies are always about more than language.

Scholarly approaches to the study of culture or language, my own included, exemplify reflexivity (being cultural reflections on culture) as well as its limits; i.e., our reflections may well be just as ideologically driven as any local model of culture, etc. Anthropologists and anthropologies are cultural products, and deserve critical reflection (Wilce 2009). Starting with the next chapter, this book devotes such reflexive attention to the emergence and cultural/historical particularity of the category, emotion. Although some linguistically sensitive anthropologists have debated what to call the first element in their work on the pair emotion and language (e.g., Abu-Lughod 1985 preferring "sentiment"),[12] few have subjected the integrity of the category emotion itself to radical questioning (for an exception, see Beatty 2005). It is an odd oversight – and perhaps indicates the grip the category has on us all, as folks and academics.

Perhaps the explanation for the oversight is that previous approaches to emotion by linguistic and psychological anthropologists have tended to be ahistorical on the one hand or, on the other, to ignore the microtemporal order of interaction, manifest in the close coordination of turns at talk. Indeed, the larger argument into which my questioning of the category emotion falls is a call to historicize our treatment of the language-culture-emotion nexus. On the microlevel, linguists (in contrast with linguistic anthropologists) who have worked on linguistic affect or stance have not consistently located it within the flow of **naturalistic** (inter)action.[13] On the other hand, historians of emotion have quite exclusively focused on macroforces – those, for example, that shaped French emotion-talk around the time of the Revolution (Reddy 2001) – to the neglect of fine-grained analyses of language deployed in real-time interaction.[14]

The tendency (until quite recently) to neglect history does not mean emotion scholarship has neglected time. Some of those concerned with cognition (including emotion) and language focus on their evolution. In fact, anthropological treatments of emotion typically break down according to apparently creedal loyalties to either a universalizing approach that takes biology and evolution seriously (and downplays cultural variability), or a cultural-relativist approach that is apparently allergic to arguments based on evolution, biology, and neuroscience. Nor am I a neutral player on that field of conflict. But this book does represent some of the 'hard science' findings, in part because I share the concern of many anthropologists (who are not so biologically oriented) with embodiment (Csordas 1990). Embodiment, as a paradigm for the study of culture, is typically defined as the development and manifestation of embodied sensibilities, tastes, postures, and practices that are *historically particular*, and specific to some society or social class, i.e., some *habitus*, rather than a reflection of eons of evolutionary development. Sociologist Pierre Bourdieu's (1977a, 1977b) notion of the *habitus* represents an attempt to capture the implicit presence of the social and historical in the embodied dispositions of a sociological fraction, be it one of the contemporary French social classes, or a Berber village in Algeria, or *Homo academicus*.

Directly related to the argument for history is a second argument distinctive to this book, and it pertains to a third element bearing a relation to language and emotion: I problematize the **indexical** relationship that is said to exist between language and (a reified vision of) **identity**, and between emotion-talk and emotion – the latter being the relationship Kockelman also problematized. The relevance to this book of the relationship between language and identity becomes clear when identity is replaced with *identification*, a dynamic process that has, since Freud, been connected with affect. The process of identification, and its many objects, are social and not merely personal.

In order to understand the argument over **indexicality** in particular, it is best to clarify what's meant by calling a sign (more accurately, a sign rela- tion) 'indexical.' This discussion reflects the influence of American philoso- pher Charles S. Peirce and his theory of *semiotic* (more commonly referred to as semiotics.) Peirce was by no means a linguist; he understood his theory of signs to be applicable in every academic discipline, and indeed every corner of the universe. By **indexicality** we mean – following Peirce – a kind of pointing, as when a weathervane indexes the wind's direction (Peirce 1931–1958: 2.276, π 286, p. 161). An index involves a sign (or sign-vehicle, i.e., the material entity that carries the significance) – e.g., the weathervane – that somehow co-occurs with its object. Its meaning radically depends on that co-occurrence-in-context. The weathervane becomes an index *only because it is attached*, grounded in a visible context that someone can share, i.e., looking at the weathervane during a moment when the wind is blowing. Smoke points to a fire, but is an effective index only if you are relatively nearby, and only because it always occurs near the fire. Speakers use words like 'here' and 'now' to point, figuratively, to the spatio-temporal context of speaking. A novelist uses them to point to the time he or she is creating at a particular point in a narrative. An effect also indexes its cause; however, all scientific history can be characterized as an attempt to clarify such relationships.

So, what is wrong with speaking of language straightforwardly indexing identity or emotion? I do not claim that any representation of talk as emotional erases our insight into its indexicality. I object, instead, to common representa- tions of indexical relationships. Many anthropologists question what the lin- guistic sign (specifically, *emotion-talk*) actually points to, debating whether or not we can assume there is any 'there there,' whether the talk can be presumed to point to any actual emotion underlying it. Though that is one problem bear- ing some relation to debate over interjections discussed earlier, this book takes the problem of indexicality further.

It turns out that, unlike weathervanes responding to natural causes, i.e., moved by a natural force that is immune to what we call it (the wind), indexicality in the human world always involves relationships that are subject to change through conscious focus.[15] In the human world, there are many examples in which the index exists before its object. No relationship of indexicality involving humans is a given, an objective fact. Consider the case of Japanese utterance-final particles. Is it the case that "men use *ze* and women use *wa*" and that the first indexes "coarse intensity" while the second indexes "gentle intensity" (Ochs 1992)? The social distribution and semiotic function of these particles appears to be a simple and straightforward instance of indexicality. Yet it turns out to be the result of particular, human, historical **agency** that called the apparent index itself into existence. (Agency is "the socioculturally mediated capacity to act" [Ahearn 2001b: 112] and thus to "affect other[s']" actions, a capacity that makes agents liable to others' evaluation [Duranti 2004: 453]).

Linguistic anthropologist Miyako Inoue demonstrates that "Japanese women's language" – today commonly invoked as an objective category, and inextricably associated with sentence-final particles – was an invention of nineteenth-century Japanese literary modernists and linguistic reformers in the *gembun'itchi* movement (2006: 83). In Japan as elsewhere, the emergence of the novelistic genre was a sign but also an instrument of modernity, crucial to the creation of the modern nation-state; the late Meiji-era *gembun'itchi* writers invented the genre on the model of the Western realist novel. These writers, however, had no good Japanese literary model for representing women's speech. They found their model in the already constructed category of the Japanese schoolgirl, whose speech ostensibly included the sentence-final particles that now, according to many, index femininity – particles that previous generations of intellectuals had judged not feminine, but vulgar! Thus, what is now accepted as a social fact – the existence of a women's language in Japanese – was a creation of late nineteenth- and early twentieth-century Japanese intellectuals as part of the same project that created the Japanese nation-state. The construction of the index – a set of linguistic forms, and the gendered context those forms ostensibly correlated with – involved bringing linguistic forms and 'modern women' into being simultaneously.

The very term 'sociolinguistic' involves a simple vision of indexicality, i.e., of a correlation between a speech form and some social entity, such as Japanese sentence-final particles and women. To complicate this vision, we must recognize that every lower-order sociolinguistic index becomes, in its turn, the object of reflection, if not in everyday life then in scholarship (otherwise we wouldn't know of it). Such reflection constitutes a higher-order index that may transform the correlational 'fact' to which the first (or "first-order") index points (Silverstein 2003a). Hence Japanese literary reformers' invention of 'women's language' in Japan had real-world effects on talk, notions of gender, and relations between citizens and the state (Inoue 2006: 106).

A third way in which this book departs from previous treatments of language and emotion is the way it complicates the one-way reading of the relationship between language and emotion. The capacity of language itself (that is, a code or **register**, as locally conceived) to serve as an affect-laden index – as the epitome of some identity, and thus the object of emotion (e.g., nationalist passion) – has been neglected in works explicitly devoted to language and emotion per se, or has been dealt with in literatures completely cut off from the sophisticated analytic strategies that characterize linguistic anthropology.[16] In explicating how linguistic forms come to be objects of culturally significant affective processes, this book first asserts the pre-eminence of processes of identification over reified notions of identity. It thus invokes Kenneth Burke's synthetic study of "motives" (not excluding certain Freudian notions thereof) against the backdrop of his materialist understanding of society and specifically social divisions, the matrix in which identification occurs. And this book explores particular case studies in which forms of language become the object of various forms of feeling. For example, I discuss Ramaswamy's work on "language passion" (1997), but also reinterpret the notion of "linguistic insecurity" (Labov 1972) as an under-theorized way of describing language as affective object. I integrate these cases, as well as many other cases in which emotion is the **referential** or **indexical** object of language, into a more coherent and comprehensive model of language and emotion. Note that **referentialism** (the **ideology** that reduces the function of language to reference and predication), the critique thereof, and any process that makes language (or emotion) the object of reflection share a common feature – reflexivity.

To reprise the essential arguments just mentioned and place them alongside others I make herein, this book asserts the following:

1. All social facts, including those pertaining to language and emotion, involve a fundamental reflexivity, layer upon layer of potential reflections on 'facts' of practice ("orders of indexicality," Silverstein 2003a). Any such 'fact' is thus inherently unstable. That is, reflections (i.e., **ideologies**, **metapragmatic** discourse [discourse on the pragmatics of speech]) on such facts shape them now and in the potential moment of their reproduction. This demands that we examine various language-affect connections in all of their semiotic richness, and that we recognize the place those connections have in layers or orders of indexicality. In keeping with this, we find something like emotion throughout what we know as language, indexed or performed by means of a plethora of linguistic structures, and in many genres (far beyond **lament**, which I happen to study, to encompass genres of angry rhetoric, or of love). And these genres themselves *are structures of expectation* governing the production and reception of discourse (Bauman 1999), and are thus inherently reflexive. Because it is the object of reflection that has real influence, emotion cannot be an essence. In fact the English word emotion is itself a somewhat arbitrary, historically particular category label, deserving much more academic reflection than it has received. Flowing

from the same insight into reflexivity, we find there is meaningful variation (built, of course, on our biological heredity) not only in the obvious ways languages (and writing systems, including emoticons) differ in encoding emotion (including, but not limited to, words for various emotions), but also in [reflexive] concepts of feelings and of the larger contexts they index and best fit into (e.g., social life, private life, etc.).

2. Whatever degree of hardwiring of human emotions (and of language) there might be, much is to be gained in analyzing their social-interactional and local-cultural contexts. From the dawn of anatomically modern *Homo sapiens*, we have deployed emotion signs (including linguistic ones) in actional/interactional contexts. Thus, emotion talk – like all talk – is a form of action that does things to the world, including the subjective and **inter-subjective** worlds of experience, a form of action that is prototypically collaborative rather than expressive of an essentialized individual self. Nor are group identities essences. Among the acts performed by talk are iden-tificatory acts, the proper focus of an adequate theorization of language as emotional object. Such linguistic-identificatory acts exemplify the pro-foundly interactive nature of emotion-in-talk. Variations in language, and in cultural concepts of both language and feeling, are socialized, learned from infancy in the context of culturally particular events of speaking. And finally,

3. We gain much, as well, by examining not only local contexts of the rela-tionship between language and emotion (from the micro-interactional to the 'cultural'), but also the globally social context of this relationship. There are **political economies** of language and of feeling, and of their variously envi-sioned connections. Cultural concepts of feeling and language are partial, interested (not disinterested) representations, often linked with the political economy and thus can be usefully described as **ideologies** (Woolard 1998). And these concepts and political economies are historically particular. This book thus explores real historical shifts in local and global ideologies of language-and-emotion. But it also breaks new ground in analyzing the cul-tural and historical particularity of academic theories of language-and-emo-tion (our ideologies), including those concerned with pathological relations between language and emotion, i.e., the language-affect relations said to be indicative of madness or mental illness.[17]

There are several implications of taking a global, historical approach to the relationship between culture, language, and emotion. Rather than accepting the primitivist, Otherizing use of ethnographic research in which anthropology's agenda was to collect exotic(ized) heads – including simple stories of how Others feel and speak – we analyze such histories of representation in relation-ship to imperialism (touched on above, vis-à-vis Bengal). We also see, finally, that producing histories, like any other form of representation – including the practice of linguistics or anthropology – affects the very objects of study both in the moment of inquiry and in moments of publication, dissemination, reception, and response.

The book is divided into four parts, discussing language and emotion in relation to theoretical concerns, issues of power, issues of identification and identity, and histories.

Part I: Theory

Chapter 1: Defining the domain clarifies the object(s) of study. What are language and *emotion*? Why not 'affect' or 'sentiment'? How does an anthropologist get at this sort of thing, for that matter? *Chapter 2: The relationship of language and emotion* answers the question, Where shall we locate emotion vis-à-vis language? Emotion is in some sense indexed in and through almost every dimension of language. But I devote particular attention to aesthetically charged ways of speaking, and to the relationship of affect, language, and embodied interaction. *Chapter 3: Approaches to language and emotion* presents four contemporary theories of the relationship between emotion and language – developmental, cognitive, phenomenological, and materialist. *Chapter 4: The panhuman and the particular* reviews three philosophical debates: (1) whether emotion(s) themselves and emotion language are universal or culturally variable, (2) whether or not the emotions form a natural class, kind, or category as some assert, and (3) the nature and source of the self or subject.

Part II: Language, power, and honor

Chapter 5: Language, emotion, power, and politics explores the relationship of emotional discourse to power, both in and beyond political rhetoric narrowly construed. *Chapter 6: Status, honorification, and emotion for hire,* mines Judith Irvine's work on affect and honorification for general principles in the relationship between language, emotion, status, and ideology, and for insights into the global distribution of symbolic capital.

Part III: Identification and identity

Chapter 7: Language as emotional object develops an aesthetic theory of the language-emotion relationship. Here I review the history of "language passion" Ramaswamy (1997) among Tamils, and reconsider models of **indexicality** based on Samuels' model of the role of affect in new formulations of San Carlos Apache performances and ethnic **identification**. *Chapter 8: Language, affect, gender, and sexuality* compares a number of cases, including the less-often-studied gendering of men's discourse and emotion. The relationship between language, gender, and emotion is the playground of stereotypes or linguistic ideologies, but the ideologies differ across cultural contexts.

Part IV: Histories of language and emotion

Chapter 9: A history of theories returns to some of the theoretical terrain explored in earlier chapters, casting a critical eye on important strands of academic thought both Western and classical Indian, and even on linguistic anthropology. *Chapter 10: Shifting forms of language and emotion* analyzes local case histories of global shifts in "structures of feeling" (Williams 1977). Such a perspective clearly differs from all-too-frequent assertions about emotions and the language of emotions in (reified) 'cultures.' In considering these case histories vis-à-vis globalization, we must avoid teleological thinking; however, such cases do tell a bigger story of shifting metasentiments or "**metacultures**" of the emotions (Urban 2001, Wilce 2009).[18] *Chapter 11: Language and the medicalization of emotion* surveys the global spread of the human sciences and the birth and development of psychiatric registers of language as anthropological issues.

Chapter 12: Conclusion synthesizes the book's arguments in relation to reflexivity; language ideologies related to emotion; processes of identification that link language, emotion, and social structure; and the relationship of local stories of language and feeling to globally circulating ideas and practices.

PART I

THEORY

I

DEFINING THE DOMAIN

> When you describe the miserable and unfortunate, and want to make the reader feel pity, try to be somewhat colder – that seems to give a kind of background to another's grief, against which it stands out more clearly. Whereas in your story the characters cry and you sigh. Yes, be more cold….The more objective you are, the stronger will be the impression you make. – Chekhov

Emotion in language: we know it when we hear it, and when we read it. The expert author or playwright – like Chekhov[1] – carefully controls the dosage of emotion she or he produces in her or his writing in order to maximize its effect. This, at any rate, represents a dominant sensibility in the West. Perhaps to many Western authors, emotion is like revenge – best served up cold.[2]

Look back at the previous paragraph. I have used no emotion vocabulary at all, no words **denoting** particular emotions. Yet words like "we" in the previous paragraph have perhaps drawn readers into a cool form of intimacy at one level, while the general tone is academic and thus maintains its emotional distance. Note that even that is one possible relationship between language and emotion, one form of "affective stance" (Biber and Finegan 1989) – a cool, distanced stance. (Note, too, that university lectures share more in common with conversation than they do with academic writing, when it comes to markers of involved stance, Barbieri 2008.) And the first paragraph hints that this book points to cultural and historical differences in the ways speaking or "languaging" (Becker 1991) – a term signaling that we are talking about process, not thing – hooks feelings. It reveals that I take a "you'll know it when you meet it" approach, more than an analytic approach, to emotion. The scope of what "emotion" might mean varies immensely across cultures and histories. The remainder of the book illustrates that defining or delimiting "emotion" is itself a cultural activity. The term itself has a rich social life.

Emotional meaning is not radically separate from denotative-referential meaning (i.e., sense and **reference**; semantic – as opposed to pragmatic – meaning). We cannot consign it to what is popularly called "connotation." Emotion in language is encoded in the same features that encode denotative-referential meaning. Before describing the range of ways language can

19

express emotion, the possible loci of emotion in language (primarily the concern of Chapter 2), we ought to clarify what we mean by "language," and then "emotion."

What is language?

Defining key terms betrays one's context, affiliations, and loyalties. I write as one who has worked in psychological and medical anthropology, but whose primary identification is with linguistic anthropology. Our profession regards language (we might say Language with a capital L indicating we are not referring to one form in particular) as both a "social tool" and a "cultural resource." We regard speaking as "a form of social action" (Duranti 1997: 1–2). This definition encompasses all particular (small-l) languages, whether spoken or signed – be their users deaf (Senghas and Monaghan 2002) or hearing.

Language may be written as well as spoken. We sharply contrast writing and speaking at our peril, as Derrida has shown. Derrida sought to expand our notion of "writing," and to trace the emergence of the "speech/writing binary"; the broader concept of writing includes "all processes of trace-formation, deferral, and delay, the crossing of presence with absence, etc." (Morris 2007: 357). If we assert, as we should, that "writing and reading are ... practices that induce and invite new layers of metapragmatic reflexivity" (Jan Blommaert, personal communication, March 2008), we might wish to follow Derrida at least to some extent. Perhaps one experiences writing's extra boost to reflexivity not only in written discourse but in moments of speaking involving quotation, repetition, and marked forms of poetic (parallelistic) structuring, i.e., speech that has undergone marked **entextualization**. This may be a matter of degree.

We often read that language is a communicative, informational, or representational system that makes extensive use of symbols, and is governed by **syntax**. Linguistic formalists and scholars of the evolution of language prefer this definition (Davidson 2003). But what is meant by "communicative," "informational," and "representational"? Under these terms, the definer often smuggles in a **referentialist** ideology of language, i.e., the view that language is about **reference** (picking out something$_a$ in the world) and predication (saying something$_b$ about that something$_a$), or **sense** and reference, or reference and denotation. Together with their emphasis on the symbolic function, such definitions obscure language's indexical and **performative** functions, as when my **voice**, or **dialect**, or **register** both indicates something of who I am trying to be (or what I am doing, or what my stance is) and effectively constitutes (a sign of) that identity, or more accurately, that process of identification. These indexical signs or signals are precisely *not* part of sense, denotation, reference, etc.; rather than referring, pure indexes mean by pointing (to the source of the utterance, or a target social identification, for example). We might say they are *caught* by listeners rather than (explicitly) *taught* by speakers. And thus we return to the affirmation that, even if language *does* often rely on structures conceivable as grammars, and on symbols (as arbitrary signs); even if a particular utterance *does* refer and predicate; this, too, exemplifies its use as a tool for social actions, one (but only one) of which is predication.

What of the relationship between emotion and forms of language production other than speech alluded to above? How is affect signaled in American Sign Language, or in written genres around the world? Reilly, McIntire, and Seago (1992: 113) locate affective information in both of the two "channels" used in signing – facial and manual – but demonstrate that signers can at times perceive affect from the manual channel alone. It is "the tempo, rhythm, and size of sign movements" that convey emotion. Some Iranian bloggers use emoticons to overcome the challenge of reproducing something of the spirit of Shia **lament** in their online writings:

> Devotional blog entries that resemble the lamentations chanted in mourning ceremonies for the Shi'a Imams lose much of the emotional content carried by aural and visual cues in the oral performances. Often, bloggers who produce such texts on their blogs use *emoticons*, borrowed from instant messaging services like Yahoo Messenger, to express such emotions ... during the mourning month of Muharram" (Doostdar 2004: 654).

Doostdar's study of "Weblogestan" (the Iranian blogosphere) points not only to the need for the broadest conception of language (certainly encompassing writing), but to the increasing electronic mediation of communication.

Niko Besnier's pioneering work has done much to disrupt our easy association of written language with the ostensibly unemotional argumentation of the scholarly essay. In fact, one written genre – Nukulaelae Islanders' personal letters – is "*about* affect." The islanders "*define* letter writing and reading as affectively cathartic contexts" (1995: 108, 111; emphasis in original). While I would not want to include photos in a definition of language, these add to the emotional impact of Nukulaelae letters. As an anthropologist who pays admirable attention to history, Besnier argues that this particular form of language – this particular genre – reflects islanders' very active construction of literacy. Their post-contact history is *their* story, not one of external imposition. Although letter writing came to Nukulaelae from outside and something of its form may still betray those origins, Nukulaelae Islanders' epistolary language is their own creation (1995: 114).

Mass mediated communicative forms – newer forms like blogging and instant messaging, and older forms like films and television ads – are often multimodal, combining visual and audible signs. Print and television ads, to the extent that they manipulate our emotions, do so not just with language, but with images whose color and visual grammar are central to their emotional force (Williamson 1978). This book has a narrower focus, however. Although profoundly indebted to semiotic theory, I invoke it primarily in relation to written discourse and to *speech* in its context – and speech-in-interaction is always embodied and thus involves visual as well as audible semiosis.[3]

Let us return for a moment to the term "language." To speak of either "Language" or "languages" concretizes two sorts of abstraction. No one speaks Language. And, to speak of *languages* tends to elide the variation in what passes for, say, English as a language. That is, the notion of "a language" is to some extent a reification, given the dynamism of language processes. Today, various groups of speakers around the world use many Englishes, such as those spoken in India or Australia (Kachru 1997), and there is no evidence that global electronic communication will eliminate this diversity. Even speaking of any national variety of English – or any national language, for that matter – elides tremendous variation among dialects and registers used in various regions and speech situations. Notions of language, or of "a language," are always shaped by **ideologies** (Schieffelin, Woolard and Kroskrity 1998; Kroskrity 2000). This book explores both what is shared across languages (i.e., Language), and rich case stories arising from the particularities not only of a language, but of specific registers of specific languages, used as particular sorts of social tools.

Two implications arise from treating speaking (or writing for that matter) as social action. Both pertain to the inherent temporality of activity. First, I pay special attention to the particular use of linguistic signs in particular events, as in **speech events** – those events defined by the presence of speech. Communicative events (to use a more inclusive term) are activities. They involve both agents and consequences that in some sense both reproduce and (at least potentially) transform both the resources of that action (linguistic forms or structures, including registers and even languages themselves) and the social worlds in relation to which the action operates (Giddens 1979). Speaking is action not in the sense of declaring or enacting private intentions, but as *interaction*. Meaning, **agency**, and emotion are interactively constituted. It is in interactive systems – rather than essentially, radically individual minds – that emotive and other semiotic acts emerge.

Although some (inter)action-centered approaches to language (and emotion) do not take an historical perspective, such a perspective is vital. Rumor has it that anthropologists study "culture." But we no longer understand cultures as isolated entities, or at least that is the trend. Instead, we explore culture as process. The processual view of culture focuses not only on the local production of meaningful signs through the exchange of material items (speech, writing, gifts, bombs) that bear those signs, but on the circulation of those same things across time and space, and transformations in the very processes and products constitutive of culture. One example of the cultural organization of meaning is the production and circulation of categories, joined together to form taxonomies, i.e., classification systems. When those taxonomies entail social labels (such as "partisan," "friend," or "schizophrenic") they constitute what Sacks (1972) called "Membership Categorization Devices" (see Chapter 11). An historical perspective on language and emotion demands that we attend to the reality that "emotion" is a relatively new superordinate category or **hypernym**.

"Emotion" conveys a model of reality related to modern(ist) psychology as it emerged in the UK in the middle of the nineteenth century and now circulates globally. The mere fact of the model's circulation by no means implies that it completely displaces alternative models that may hold sway in particular localities. The emotion model nonetheless appears hegemonic. In focusing on such processes of circulation we keep histories in view.

In the remainder of this chapter, I address the following questions:

- How have anthropologists, including myself, recently approached emotion?
- What methods do we use?
- What is emotion?
- How is it related to affect?
- Is emotion a single, coherent domain (as our inclusive category label makes it appear to be)?
- And last, why is emotion so frequently contrasted with, and subordinated to, cognition, and how can we transcend such dualisms?

Anthropological lenses on emotion

Anthropologists took up the question of emotion in earnest in the 1970s and 1980s. In particular, ethnographers of Pacific Island societies such as Levy, Lutz, White, Brenneis, Schieffelin, Besnier, Ochs, Duranti, and the Rosaldos were early pioneers in the field. One notes, however, that – just as female leaders of our field (e.g., Ochs and Schieffelin) became identified with work on **language socialization**, they and others like Irvine, Lutz, and Abu-Lughod have been particularly identified with the study of discourse and affect or emotion. This work has been exemplary. It is fortunate that the gendered division of anthropological labor is by no means complete, and is breaking down.[4] Still, the weak correlation deserves consideration.

Early anthropological work on language and affect by Irvine (1982), Ochs (1986, 1988), and Schieffelin (Ochs and Schieffelin 1989, B. Schieffelin 1990) was followed by the analysis of "disentangling" discourse – very public, ritualized, emotional sessions of talk that address conflict, yet fall neatly neither in the arena of "conflict resolution meetings" nor "therapy sessions" (White 1990, Watson-Gegeo and White 1990). The upshot of the work on disentangling was to recognize that talk of, from, and with emotion – or emotion rhetoric – functions as much in the social and moral realms as it does in the private personal realm. This book explores the complexities associated with the social and moral grounding of emotion rhetoric. Such complexities – along with phenomenological, embodied dimensions of emotion and affect (Csordas 1990) – are this chapter's topic in particular.

Like other ethnographers in other places, I have done intensive fieldwork. Mine was in Bangladesh, where I lived with a large extended family for a year

(1991–92), following previous work in Bangladesh for four years in the 1980s, when I learned to converse in, and read, **Bangla**. I returned for shorter periods of fieldwork in 1996 and 2000. In part because of the particular, affect-laden ties I developed (and observed) in 1991–92, I began to devote special attention to some of the topics that uniquely characterize my work on language and emotion – topics like **lament** (spontaneous improvised crying-songs) and madness. I also collected video recordings whenever I could. Videotape has enabled me to focus on certain dimensions of speech-interaction that also set my approach apart from some treatments of the topic. For example, I often highlight the visible, embodied dimensions of interaction, believing not only that speaking and writing are always embodied, but that gesture, postural orientation, eye gaze, and facial expression are best treated as part of the semiotic cluster making up speech-in-interaction. Language, in my title, becomes shorthand for social semiotics. Thus my work contrasts with that of some linguists working on stance. And because video recordings allow me to see all the participants captured within the lens, it potentiated consideration of the emotional significance of one actor's visible movement or gesture in relation to another's movement that occurs just before it, or simultaneously. What people do with each other in such emergent act sequences, visible as well as audible, is a crucial context in which speaking, feeling, and meaning-making occur. The challenge is to combine fine-grained ethnographic study of such emergent acts with historical context.

For decades, anthropologists have been pursuing a series of fascinating questions about language that touch the topic of emotion, in addition to the question of what language is. Do we know what "emotion" means, and what it means for language to be emotional? If so, when is silence a more powerful emotion marker than speech (Basso 1990)? How do different communities introduce children simultaneously to the world, to language, and to affect? Then, starting at the other end of such questions, so to speak, what, if anything, about the language of feeling is basic to our human or primate heritage? What does the study of this nexus of language-and-emotion tell us about what it is to be human? One of the great paradoxes about studying ourselves as a species is that, as soon as we raise the topic of what is fundamental to our humanity, the issue of primitivism and thus of the most fundamental division of human groups conceivable arises. It was once acceptable for anthropologists to describe the far-off people with whom they worked as primitive. Of late, anthropologists study people like themselves, and increasingly we turn our lens on our own work. We may ask, for example, how some have made emotion – or its study! – the domain of one group (women, "primitives," etc.), and rationality the proper possession of another. This book tries to avoid the pitfalls of, and instead to thoroughly critique, the tortured histories by which emotion has been attached to whole groups, who have then been judged unable to control or govern themselves.

Readers might be curious about how anthropologists have access to anything so seemingly private as emotions, particularly when they work in societies quite different from their own. The question is a real one, since indeed such matters as being a male anthropologist may limit access to certain genres, as was the case with my fieldwork in a Bangladeshi Muslim village. But it is also important to point out that emotions, as anthropologists now conceive of them, are no more private than language is. Both language and culturally influenced patterns of emotion sink their roots deep inside persons as they develop. Both have their roots in the evolutionary past of the hominin lineage. But the life emotion and language lead today is, as it always has been, a social life. Neither anthropologists nor those we study use emotional x-ray machines. Linguistic anthropologists, in particular, claim no access to the inner world of the self. Visible and audible signs, publicly or at least interactively produced, are our stock-in-trade.

Here again, video recording is important to many linguistic anthropologists. Marjorie H. and Charles Goodwin use videotape to study **naturalistic** "situated interactions." We describe such interactions as naturalistic, rather than natural, because when observers and/or cameras are present those interactions are not quite what they would be in our absence. On the other hand, we are not calling the shots, organizing the interaction as in an interview or experiment. Linguistic anthropologists like the Goodwins study actual recorded interactions, not reports of them – for example, naturalistic moments of girls playing hopscotch and clashing over whose turn it is. Such moments, on tape, provide anthropologists opportunities for viewing (and repeatedly *re*viewing) naturalistic displays of emotion. On the basis of many such observations, M. H. Goodwin argues that popular and scholarly representations of girls striving for harmony over conflict need revising (Goodwin and Goodwin 2001; M. H. Goodwin 2006).

Steven Caton's research on emotion and poetics took him to the Khawlānī tribes of Yemen. Caton was thrown into the fray when a gun battle broke out between a religiously elite community – one of whose young men stood accused of absconding with two young tribal women – and the tribe that ostensibly protected them. Bullets were flying above the rooftop of the home in which he was staying when he was asked to serve tea on that very rooftop. Caton had been studying, and learning to perform, the genres of Arabic poetry that actually play a key role in these conflicts. The tribal ideal is self-control. Caton learned that the warrior who could channel his passions into highly stylized rhyming couplets was regarded with at least as much honor as the crack shot whose self-control meant that the apparent combatants' bullets flew at "a respectful distance of at least two feet" over the heads of Caton and his hosts (Caton 1990: 12). It was in such settings, for which we use the somewhat sanitized adjective "ethnographic," that Caton learned what Aristotle had argued two millennia earlier: "Emotions ... are made governable by their transmutation into aesthetic form or the stylized release of passion" (Caton 1990: 31). Caton learned this by performing, observing, and listening – in short, by engaging in the social life of emotion and language among the Khawlānī tribes of Yemen. Although ethnographies – written descriptions of human communities and their cultural lives – do not always focus on language or speech-in-interaction, it is mostly those that do that concern us here.

The question of how such things as war, poetry, and emotion – or any of the elements of culture – come to make sense, how people come to have the apparently local cultural feelings they do, requires anthropologists to ask developmental questions. Linguistic anthropologists Elinor Ochs and Bambi Schieffelin pioneered the field of language socialization, centered on the question of how communities transmit culture through the use of language, train their children to use language in particular ways, and thus manifest cultural attitudes toward the acquisition of language. In a series of ethnographic studies in Western Samoa and Los Angeles, Ochs has shown how parents model how to speak based on cultural beliefs about when children become persons or appropriate interlocutors. Schieffelin's studies of the Kaluli people and their language, in the Mt. Bosavi region of Papua New Guinea, paint vivid pictures of children becoming appropriate Kaluli speakers through the same processes by which they become appropriate participants in Kaluli society.

The relevance of language socialization to the reproduction of gender relations becomes clear in Kuebli, Butler, and Fivush's (1995) study of "emotional socialization" in the USA. They found that white, middle-class American mothers used more emotion words with daughters than sons, and that the variety of emotion words used with daughters increased over time. Thus, "by the end of the preschool years girls used a significantly greater number and variety of emotion terms than did boys" (1995: 279).

But language socialization studies do not always focus on the enculturation of children. Schieffelin explains, as well, how the almost completely missionized, fundamentalist Christian Bosavi adults, their pastors, and church-based literacy instructors learn how to "to look and act 'modern'" (B. Schieffelin 2000: 196). This transformation included putting an end to "any expression of strong emotion at all" (E. Schieffelin 1981: 19). Longitudinal analysis of Kaluli pastors' sermons reveals their learning, over time, to grapple with new and foreign models of subjectivity through the particular ways they chose to spontaneously translate certain problematic passages of the New Testament (B. Schieffelin 2007).

Ethnographic fieldwork involves what we call "participant-observation" – a delicate and shifting balance in which the anthropologist negotiates how much of her observing can involve joining in. In the immediacies of social interaction on the field, such decisions cannot be ready made. One may lay out a fieldwork agenda, only to see it changed, perforce, by emerging priorities. I went to rural Bangladesh with a plan to study gender and health complaints, expecting that these would have a strong affective component. I did not know that a woman I call Latifa would visit my field site – the extended family compound in which I lived, along with 65 of Latifa's relatives – and perform a series of crying songs or **laments** over a two-week period, culminating in her forcible removal. Although recording (and trying, for years afterward, to understand) spontaneous improvised crying songs had not been on my agenda (nor important in relation to my expectations regarding gender and health complaints), it demanded my urgent attention.

I have presented just a few of the many examples in which anthropologists encounter emotion in the field. You might ask whether, in all of these cases, anthropologists actually join in – do they participate in lament, or just observe it? I *have* participated (in Finland, not Bangladesh), though the circumstances were exceptional. This book will explore debates over just how deep the divides are that separate those who grow up hearing people break out collectively in spontaneous poetic and tuneful laments at funerals from those who might call such loud wordy weeping 'foolish.' Granted, such musical poetic expressions are quite stylized; understanding requires "an enculturated apprehension";[5] yet it is also true that fieldworkers can acquire a level of empathic understanding – and on that basis, I believe, can participate to some extent. I aim in this book to pass on some of that empathy for other cultural worlds.

Let us return to the question of how anthropologists attempt to achieve, and communicate, such understandings. Participant observation and, increasingly (for linguistic anthropologists), videotaping and transcribing **speech events** have been our stock-in-trade. However, a number of anthropologists in the last decade or two have turned to methods associated previously with historians. Linguistic anthropologists Richard Bauman and Charles Briggs's 2003 book, *Voices of Modernity*, for example, pieces together historical sources that reveal the emergence of modern **language ideologies**. They demonstrate, for example, how some of the foundational modern voices in eighteenth-century Europe such as Robert Wood (1717?–1771), invented the modern distinction between oral and literate cultures and associated orality with naturalness and emotionality – traits he distinguished from **modernity**. These early moderns also associated the discourse and poetry of ancient Others with passion, and that of their own contemporaries with dryness. Bauman and Briggs stress that concepts like **tradition** and **modernity** emerged together as ideological constructs, part of Europe's attempt to assert its own uniqueness in the world.

Even today, whole languages become associated relatively more with emotion (Italian? French?) or with reason (Latin? German? English?) and thus with tradition or modernity. Some sources make these associations not through direct statements but through indexicality, the perceived linkage of speech forms with social entities. The 2004 Alejandro Amenábar film *Mar adentro* (*The Sea Inside*) features three languages – Castilian ("Spanish"), Catalan, and Portuguese-Galizan. Linguistic anthropologist Celso Alvarez-Cáccamo has analyzed who uses these codes in the film, in speaking to whom, and for what purposes (2005). He finds Castilian and Catalan used to discuss or represent the future, with a balance of emotion and reason, while Portuguese-Galizan is used more exclusively by rural persons in the film to discuss or represent the past. Galizan is used, in the film, far more for encoding emotion (and indexing speakers' emotionality) than reason. More than this fact alone, the assemblage of associations – rural people, the past, and emotion – constructs a linguistic stereotype, an indexical association (one of co-occurrence) made into an **icon** (a sign relation grounded in perceived similarity – in this case, of speech forms to an 'essence' imputed to their users). The stereotype bears some relation to the image of orality invented by Robert Wood centuries before.

What is emotion? How is it related to affect?

To raise questions about emotion and affect is to open many cans of worms, for they force us to consider the relation of body, action, and mind; of embodiment and society; of biology and culture; of brain, body, action, and cultural meaning. They force us to ask what it is to be human. Any anthropological investigation does that, implicitly or explicitly. That does not make anthropology unique; many disciplines aim to define humanity. Questions concerning emotion – or affect – are driving studies that transgress disciplinary boundaries. The ideal scholar in this area would therefore be well acquainted with findings from various fields, from biophilosophy (Maturana 1997) to neurobiology (Damasio 1995, 2003), personality theory (Tomkins 1995), developmental psychology and psychiatry (Feldman and Greenbaum 1997, Hobson 1993, Schore 2001, Trevarthan and Daniel 2005), political science and international relations (Saurette 2006), law and philosophy (Nussbaum 2004), cognitive linguistics (Harkins and Wierzbicka 2001, Kövecses 2000), history (Reddy 2001), sociology and evolutionary psychology (J. Turner 2000), and the humanities and **cultural studies** (Massumi 1995, 2002).

'Affect' may have a perceived scientific ring. It has long been associated with nature. The *Oxford English Dictionary* demonstrates that, for centuries, affect has denoted – among other things – a "natural tendency." Thus in Shakespeare's *Love's Labour's Lost* (I.i.152) we read, "For every man with his affects is born" (Shakespeare 1938a). Silvan Tomkins, whose work I describe in a bit more detail below, reproduces this naturalization of affect. His view is summarized by Sedgwick and Frank: "There is a kind of affective table of the elements, comprising nine components, infinitely recombinable but rooted in the human body in nine distinctive and irreducible ways" (1995b: 23). Situating the discussions of affect that follow in relation to such a history is consistent with one of this book's central goals.

Neuroscientist Antonio Damasio has effectively distilled the research literatures from his own field, as well as psychiatry and psychology, in his highly readable books (1995, 2003). Like many in the hard sciences and psychology, he emphasizes the universal, evolutionary grounds of affect. Damasio draws on

Spinoza's (1632–1677) theory of affects (or affections and passions) – drives, motivations, "emotions," and "feelings." (You will find his definitions below.) Spinoza, like many who came after him, situated affects in the body. In contrast with Descartes, Spinoza saw the body as the ground and producer of mind.

Following Spinoza, Damasio envisions various factors motivating human activity in a hierarchy which, for Damasio, reflects their emergence on the grand scale of evolutionary time, a scale that permits no close historical analysis of the sort I advocate. Whatever other functions these factors have, they serve the common purpose of maintaining homeostasis (or "homeodynamics") in the organism (2003: 302). Reflexes and "metabolic regulation" form the lowest rung, together with the immune system, now known to be intimately linked with emotion (Wilce 2003). Pain and pleasure form the next rung up, and are the fundamental ingredients of the higher layers – "drives and motivations," "emotions," and "feelings." Damasio uses "emotions" – modeled on Spinoza's "affects" – and "feelings" somewhat idiosyncratically, defining the former as bodily states and the latter as mental representations, states, or images. "An *emotion*-proper [again, read an "affect"], such as happiness, sadness, embarrassment, or sympathy, is a complex collection of chemical and neural responses forming a distinctive pattern," whereas "a *feeling* is the perception of a certain state of the body along with the perception of thinking and of thoughts with certain themes" (Damasio 2003: 53, 86; emphasis added). These thoughtful feelings emerge from physically experienced emotions, both in evolutionary time and in the moment. Damasio depicts all levels of homeodynamic regulation – dynamic because the adjustment targets nothing stable, but rather a shifting sort of balance – as instrumental, serving to position the organism so as to maximize its potential for "survival and well-being" (2003: 53). Feelings in this model are metasigns – signs that reflect on other signs (namely "emotions"): "The contents of feelings are the configurations of body state represented in somatosensing maps" (2003: 132). The role of "feelings" in Damasio's model is thus similar to that of "meta-emotions" in others' models (Gottmann, Katz, and Hooven 1996). Meta-emotions are emotions about emotions, including such phenomena as experiencing shame about what one is feeling (Planalp 1999).

In humans and perhaps higher primates the same sections of the brain mediate these affective processes – the limbic system (consisting of the amygdala, the hypothalamus, and the cingulate gyrus, among other brain regions), and that portion of the frontal lobe called the ventromedial prefrontal cortex (Damasio 2003: 59), and the sensorimotor area (SMA). Jonathan Turner argues that social scientists "need to learn something about the emotion systems of the brain in order to develop more accurate and robust theories of emotion" (2000: 89–90). As the unique human brain evolved, the anterior cingulate gyrus – which Turner calls "the center for playfulness and mother-infant bonding," i.e., for pleasure (2000: 112) – expanded in comparison with other primates' brains. These areas are activated after the higher frontal lobe appraises a stimulus, internal or external. Stimulating some of these brain areas with electrodes produces a strong emotional response, including (in one person) not only weeping, but also depressive speech such as "Everything is useless ... I feel worthless" (Damasio 2003: 67–68).

The longstanding tradition of locating affects in a naturalized body was carried on by psychologist Silvan Tomkins (1911–1991). Tomkins used "affects" not as an inclusive term, but to distinguish a universal set of inherited responses from both "emotions" and "drives." The universalist approach to affects that characterizes neuroscience and psychology (Damasio and Tomkins) has struck many anthropologists as essentializing. Cultural anthropologists tend to be relativists, and have typically taken a **"cultural constructionist"** approach to emotion, asserting that something fundamental about it is culturally, and not just biologically, determined. Thus they see more variability in "the emotions" than universalists do.

In the 1990s Tomkins' 1960s work on affect resurfaced in a surprising quarter, attracting some in **cultural studies**. Despite a history of agreement between anthropology and cultural studies on a constructionist approach to subjectivity, gender, etc., some in cultural studies continue to engage Tomkins' model. Sedgwick and Frank appreciate both the embodiment and the tidy distinctions Tomkins' set of evolved affects captures. For Brian Massumi, the mystery of affect's embodiment cuts it off from language, leaving "emotion" to cover responses that are named and culturally constructed – effectively inverting Damasio's use of "emotion" and "feeling." Despite the positive attention to affect in cultural studies, something like an anthropological skepticism can still be seen, for example, in Elspeth Probyn's work (2005a). Probyn problematizes the statement, "Affect is biology, while emotion is biography" (2004: 342) – formulated by Tomkins' follower Donald Nathanson (1996: 13). The line between affect and emotion blurs, as do biography and biology, or at least biography and bodily experience.

[O]ur bodies and their everyday biographies may be more complicated than we've given them credit for. Conceptually, they challenge any neat division of biological affect and biographical emotion, the social and the physiological (Probyn 2004: 395).

Indeed, there is growing evidence that social life, and perhaps even culture, *shapes* physiological processes.[6]

Affect and emotion: cultural studies, semiotics, and anthropology

Given the recent interest in affect in cultural studies, as well as its titular dominance in previous linguistic anthropological treatments of this book's topic (Besnier 1990, Irvine 1982, 1990), why does my title pair language with emotion? First, American anthropologists have been less convinced of a distinction between affect and emotion. Some sources use them interchangeably; some equate them. Others use affect to denote the innate, biological, or embodied.

Kulick and Schieffelin, linguistic anthropologists with expertise in affect, define that term to encompass "emotion, feelings, moods, dispositions, and attitudes associated with persons and/or situations" (Kulick and Schieffelin 2004: 352). Affect can encompass desires as well. (We will return to "attitudes" and their relation to "ideologies" in Chapter 7.) I have chosen to use 'emotion,' instead of 'affect,' in a broad and inclusive way, while critically examining the history that led to its hegemony. For this linguistic anthropologist, any drive to purify this or that term for a particular purpose is beside the point; it is a "work of culture" (Obeyesekere 1985) I need not contribute to. But my resistance to at least one cultural studies scholar's argument about affect and emotion requires some explaining.

Brian Massumi links affect with sheer intensity, and emotion with cultural signification. Like Damasio, Massumi grounds his work in Spinoza's discussion of affect(s) ("affections"). As with Damasio's "emotions," affects are felt without reflection. What Massumi calls "emotions" are products of reflective consciousness. Thus, from Spinoza to Massumi we have a line of tradition distinguishing the "raw" and the "cooked," unthought-feeling and reflexivity.[7] Massumi's emotions "capture" affect – although a part of the affect always eludes capture. Affect does have a relation to reflection, but this relation is not primarily linguistic. The struggle to name affect (or particular affects) is doomed (and this distinguishes Massumi from Sedgwick and Frank), even though some form of self-reflection notes its escape, its location beyond linguistic reflection. We cannot explain affect in terms of *ideologies*, according to Massumi. Ideologies belong to the realm of language, not affect. "Affect holds a key to rethinking postmodern power after ideology" (Massumi 1995: 104).

What I find objectionable in Massumi's vision lies in the dualities that structure his thinking, despite his protestations to the contrary. Massumi overemphasizes the apparently symbolic (and thus disembodied) nature of language as a bearer of emotion. We could, alternatively, trace Massumi's shortcomings to a vision of language cut off from its primary manifestation – in embodied, co-present speech-in-interaction. Affect *does* appear to be something separate from the linguistically conceived emotions, but only if one holds a model of language as primarily a tool for **reference**, producing the sorts of decontextualized falsifiable statements philosophers usually ponder. Such a view is as far from the reality of multimodal semiosis, i.e., the multiplicity of semiotic channels people use as they communicate in each other's presence, as it is from a view of speech as a social tool good not only for thinking but for acting, and for laying down two sorts of '**text**' simultaneously. Any given occurrence of speech-in-interaction involves talk *about* something – creating a **denotational text** – and the production and reproduction of social identities (the "interactional text" emergent in any such event, Silverstein 2004). Approaches that ground affect or emotion in the speaking, acting, interacting body, conceived of as an always-already social object and subject, avoid the dualism that characterizes

French **structuralism** and its echoes in cultural studies. However, few anthropologists have made the link between such a grounding of affect and language per se (see discussion of Csordas, an exception, below).[8]

Emotion, affect, social life

Infant development

The preceding section mostly overlooked crucial aspects of emotion, presenting the domain as though it were an individual matter. Perhaps you did not take note of this individualist approach, given how such a viewpoint accords with Western folk theories of the self that dominate psychology and related academic fields (with the exception of Vygotskian sociohistorical psychology). In fact, however, sociologists and anthropologists from the time of Durkheim have inquired into the social nature of emotion. We start our examination of the social nature of emotion by revisiting emotional ontogeny, i.e., emotion and child development.

At least since the groundbreaking work of Stern (1985, 2000), a few psychologists have joined with anthropologists in affirming the deeply social, embodied, emergent nature of affect. Child development is a central object of such psychology. Stern uncovered the pervasiveness of intersubjectivity, "interaffectivity" (2000: xxii), or "affect attunement"[9] in infant-caregiver relationships. The central significance of such mutuality becomes clear in Feldman's work on parent-child affective synchrony (Feldman 2007). Feldman and her colleagues have demonstrated a strong correlation between early (i.e., at age three to nine months) mother-infant affect attunement, the emergence (during the same period) of affective self-regulation skills in the infant, and the child's later verbal IQ and, in particular, engagement in symbolically complex play (2007) and use of what Feldman and Greenbaum call "internal state talk" (1997). Of course, early experiences of intersubjectivity and affective coordination reflect some kind of general cognitive ability on the infant's part. However, these early experiences contribute to the child's future general language abilities and, particularly, his or her ability to talk about perceptions, desires, physiological states, emotions, thoughts, and moral judgments (Feldman and Greenbaum 1997: 12, 19, 20).

A different sort of evidence emerges from studies of at-risk infant-caregiver relationships, or at-risk infants, particularly those who may be diagnosed with autism. Only when we recognize autism not as a "cognitive" disorder in the narrow sense, but as a deficiency in "perceptual-affective capacities" – one that severely disrupts affect attunement – can we grasp "the profound importance of personal-affective relatedness for the course of normal child development" (Hobson 1993: 222).[10] In normal development we are learning the role of *mirror neurons* in mediating such behavioral attunement. Mirror neurons, "a functional mechanism of 'embodied simulation'" (Gallese, Eagle, and Migone 2007: 131), "fire" in two complementary situations – during one's own motor activity, and during observation of another's action. Neuroscientists have uncovered how "the shared neural activation pattern [which mirror neurons bring about] and the accompanying embodied simulation constitute a fundamental biological basis for understanding another's mind" (2007: 131). This neural mechanism may potentiate not only the understanding of others' affects but also the development of a healthy affective-cognitive life.

One of the most promising of the social-psychological models of emotion comes from Bråten (1998), whose concept of "e-motion," a complex consisting of "emotion" and "motion," resembles what Gallese would later call embodied simulation.[11] The infant's (or mother's-and-infant's) experience of e-motion reflects the "bodily communion" normatively present in the caregiver-infant relationship. Through a co-enactment of sorts, in which observers (e.g., infants) experience a "virtual moving with the movements of others," infants develop "e-motional memory."

Such virtual co-enactment with the author of the performance, evoking mental simulation of its successful closure even when the model fails, entails a predispositional participatory perception of the model's movements from the model's stance.

Bråten calls this "altercentric participation" (1998: 106). Perception, the argument goes, is not passive but participatory – and not impassive, but affective. Transposing Bråten's psycho-developmental work into the realm of moral philosophy, Rommetveit (1998: 370) argues that 'normal' development not only of language but of moral **agency** rests upon what he calls "response-ability in dialogical encounter." Bråten and Rommetveit's findings indicate the embodied, fundamentally interactional, foundation of human emotion.

Emotion, sociality, and intersubjectivity

Social anthropologist Margot Lyon challenges the "cognitive bias" in recent anthropologies of emotion (2003: 88). Emotion's central role in "the dialectic of social and bodily life" is manifest in such social processes as "conditioning … habit … mimesis and social contagion" (2003: 84). Given the intimate interrelationship between emotion and respiration, any process leading to the establishment of respiratory co-rhythms must have emotional consequences, and vice versa. Emotion mediates between the embodiment of "individual and group **agency** in … social life" (Lyon 1994: 101). Particular respiratory rhythms and their affective consequences reflect the structure of the social relationships in which they occur (Lyon 1994: 100). Lyon's model finds close counterparts in local models of emotion, particularly those held by Pacific Island societies. *Bhaw* – 'feelings,' in Fijian Hindi[12] – are "not viewed as internal states. Rather moods seem to be located in events themselves" (Brenneis 1990: 118). "Emotions are about one's mode of relationship as a total individual to the social and nonsocial environment" (Van Brakel 1993: 48, citing Levy 1984). This is not only the attitude of Pacific Islanders studied by Levy and Brenneis – it is quite generalizable across human societies, as Lyon notes.

Many social and linguistic theorists who treat the topics of language, conversation, and emotion contextualize their discussions of subjectivity in relation to **intersubjectivity**. **Conversation analysts** treat meaning and even social structure as achievements arising in significant measure out of talk-in-interaction. In conversation, gestures, bodily orientations, and facial and verbal expressions of one interlocutor not only become objects of another's close attention, but – in a fractally recursive process – become a hall of mirrors in which signalers are conscious that their signs will be interpreted by others – as affect markers, for example. In response to such mutual awareness, interlocutors *manage* the signs they produce; this is "recipient design" (Sacks, Schegloff, and Jefferson 1974). From this perspective, what emerges is not so much one individual or the other feeling something autonomously, as both attuning to an emergent sense, feeling, meaning, etc. Thus, close attention to embodied speech-in-interaction reveals what might otherwise seem mysterious – the workings of intersubjectivity.

Embodiment, affect, and language

Csordas has long explored embodiment as "a nondualistic paradigm for the study of culture" (1990: 12). He has grounded this study in ethnographic investigations of "charismatic" Christian groups, such as charismatic Catholic intentional communities, which he says are "essentially a form of Pentecostalism," with many of the same practices, "including faith healing and speaking in tongues" (1990: 12). On the level of linguistic **reference**, Csordas argues that charismatic Catholic talk of demons is really about an excess of certain emotions. Emotion labels become the names of demons to be exorcised, such as a "spirit of anger" – or Anger, the proper name of the particular, responsible demon. But these believers have other emotions in mind when they speak of evidence of divine, healing power.

According to Csordas's intriguing analysis, glossolalia – speaking in tongues – unites emotion, body, and language. To speak in tongues is a communicative *and* emotional experience, given positive emotional significance by its representation as a divine gift, and a special tool for intimate communion with the divine. Like all speech, glossolalia is best seen as verbal gesture. Unlike other speech, it lacks denotative-referential meaning, and thus the verbal gesture has only "immanent" meaning qua gesture. Glossolalia manifests "the preobjective" (but *not* precultural) developmental stage, a stage from which we never quite graduate. That is, glossolalia draws on our potential to return to this mode of bodily experience: "In glossolalic utterance … the utterance takes place at a phenomenological [and developmental] moment prior to distinction between body and mind" (Csordas 1990: 26).

Anthropologists speak of ritual's ability to create a social state of being that is apart, and quite distinct, from the norms of social structure that typically govern human action. Victor Turner calls this state *communitas,* which "breaks in through the interstices of structure, in liminality; at the edge of structure, in marginality" (1969: 128). Communitas entails an experience of sociality in an undifferentiated fashion, one that rejects hierarchy; rituals of inversion create such a state. Although it would be a mistake to reduce this communitas – or its antecedent term, "effervescence" (Durkheim 1965[1915]) – to feeling, positive feeling is nonetheless crucial to both concepts. Glossolalia offers "a positive statement about expressivity ... its critical force is enhanced by the moral force of its claim to be pure communication" (Csordas 1990: 27). Charismatics thus experience glossolalia as a pure expression of divinely inspired feeling. Normal speech cannot be this, in part because of the weight placed upon it by the necessity of sense and reference.

Csordas's phenomenologically inspired vision of embodiment contrasts sharply with work on embodiment, affect, and talk by Charles and Marjorie H. Goodwin. I review their work in Chapter 2.

Ghosts of Descartes

Apparitions of René Descartes haunt popular and academic discourse in the West. For this and other reasons, it is difficult to think of emotion on its own. Instead we tend to juxtapose feeling and emotion with thought and reason. These are, in turn, related to dualistic thinking about mind and body. It has been relatively easier for Westerners to imagine emotion than thought as embodied. Echoing Spinoza, William James wrote that bodily changes in response to a stimulus give rise to emotions – that we feel some "emotion" insofar as we sense the bodily changes, rather than experiencing an emotion that causes bodily sensations. "My theory is that the bodily changes follow directly the perception of the exciting fact [i.e., the stimulus], and that our feeling of the same changes as they occur IS the emotion" (James 1890/1918: 449). These pairs are internally ranked, consciously or unconsciously, and the emotional and the bodily have long come out losers in relation to their purported opposites.

Until recently, few have claimed that bodily changes *are* thoughts, or that bodies think or are mindful (Farnell 1995). But Damasio writes, "Emotion, feeling, and biological regulation all play a role in human reason. The lowly orders of our organism are in the loop of high reason" (1995: xiii). And in recent sociology and anthropology, Bourdieu, Csordas, and Farnell have offered models of the embodiment of culture, cultural sensibilities, and language.

Large bodies of scholarly discourse (e.g., archaeology) still presuppose a sharp divide between the symbolic and the material. Within the limits of such a dichotomy, language appears to be a symbolic phenomenon, one of culture's symbolic manifestations. Yet we produce speech and writing with our bodies. The sounds of speech only arrive in our ears because of their physical effects, carried through the air or some other vibratory medium. Nor is language the exclusive product of the brain's neocortex (and particular Broca's and Wernicke's areas), associated with abstract thought and reason rather than instinct. New research on brain, language, and evolution indicates a greater role for subcortical regions of the brain in speech production (Lieberman 2007). One of the implications of this is that it grounds in neuroanatomy the anthropological assertion (Duranti 1997: 1–2) that speech is action (social action). What happens during speech production involves many areas of the brain working together, some of which are associated with sensorimotor activity – again, neurological-research-based encouragement for nondualistic models. There is "a cortical sensorimotor auditory-vocal circuit which was probably present in the monkey and which served as the precursor for the cortical language circuits in the human brain," and "neural mechanisms adapted for motor control are the basis for syntax and human creative behavior" (Garcia and Aboitiz 2007: 54; Lieberman 2007).

Work on linguistic stance bears discussion here, both because it has been so fruitful and because it has tended to reproduce Cartesian dualism. Biber and Finegan pioneered the contemporary study of stance, which they defined as "the lexical and grammatical encoding of both evidentiality and affect" (1989: 94). It is not difficult to connect evidentiality to cognition. Biber (2006) has shifted toward ever more sophisticated quantitative methods in the study of stance in general, and away from sharply distinguishing affective from epistemic stance. Meanwhile, only one scholar, to my knowledge, has explicitly returned the metaphor ('stance') itself to its embodied origins. Matoesian (2005) breaks new ground in exploring simultaneous deployments of linguistic and "embodied stance." For Matoesian, linguistic stance includes prosodic as well as grammatical and lexical stance markers. "Body posture, facial expression, and gestures" (2005: 168) can all function as markers of embodied stance. Matoesian reconnects speech and affect not only to bodies, but to interaction:

Stance ... emerges interactively and incrementally in the embodied multimodal projection and negotiation of participation frameworks – through the sequentially organized rhythms of language and the body (2005: 169).

Matoesian maintains Biber and Finegan's distinction between affective and epistemic stance, but in other ways disturbs the Cartesian representational economy.

Emotion: a single, coherent domain?

Affect and emotion, gesture and speech, material and symbolic, embodied and discursive – we must transcend these dichotomies and demonstrate the intimate ties between apparent opposites. Still, questions remain about the integrity of the domain we call 'emotion,' and critiques of dualism do not address them. What if we cannot presume the universal integrity or salience of categories like 'emotion?' Anthropologists of emotion, despite their cultural relativism, have tended to treat the encompassing category (under its English label) as though it were present and equally elaborated in all societies. Beyond scholarly squabbles, a variety of cultural perspectives raise concerns about the category 'emotion.'

Recently, Griffiths (1997), Wilce (2004b), and Beatty (2005) have questioned whether there is a single, coherent domain, or one recognized as such in a globally consistent fashion (though the grounds of their doubts differ). "There is no rich collection of generalizations about this range of phenomena [commonly labeled 'emotions'] that distinguishes them from other psychological phenomena," according to Griffiths (1997: 14). He proposes to split the domain into three parts. There is, first, what he calls "the affect program," i.e., a very limited number of states he describes as "phylogenetically ancient" (1997: 16). Paul Ekman (1992a), who (like Tomkins) focuses on these ancient affects and their facial expressions, accepts some cultural variability in the conditions that elicit anger, for example, though he states baldly that "emotions are a product of our evolution, with some biological givens" (Ekman 1992b: 550). Obviously we are on familiar ground here.

Griffiths calls the second group "socially sustained pretense emotions" (1997: 16). These reflect the influence of what Reddy (2001) calls "regimes of emotion," i.e., cultural expectations and norms regarding the appropriateness of particular emotions, which Griffiths argues can even unconsciously factor into their suppression or production. Later in this book I describe a colorful example of this category – what Lempert (2007) describes as the "histrionic wrath" of Tibetan Buddhist disciplinarian-monks – to be distinguished from "vulgar, worldly aggression" insofar as it is unselfishly motivated, aimed at the moral reform of other monks. Griffiths' third category, "higher cognitive emotions," includes "envy, guilt, jealousy, and love" (1997: 9). They vary across cultures, despite having some degree of evolved motivational underpinnings, as the evolutionary psychologists argue. Despite distinguishing among these three phenomena, Griffiths argues that it is wrong-headed to radically separate a putatively hard-wired group of emotions from those that are culturally determined (Griffiths 1997: 159–160). There are heritable differences between human populations in relation to all three sorts of emotional phenomena. These differences may have either a genetic or a cultural basis; either path may determine a kind of micro-evolutionary heredity.

Beatty's and Wilce's questions reflect a kind of relativism, one of anthropologists' most common intellectual commitments. They problematize the tendency to project the global utility of English category terms, including the **hypernym** 'emotion' itself. The issue here, which I dwell on in Chapter 4, is one of linguistic relativity, the axiom that the sign systems we use to relate to the world mediate our relationship to that world in profound ways. For now, suffice it to say that each language offers speakers a unique set of categories, both grammatical and lexical, and that they constitute maps of various features of the world, or semantic domains, including concepts related to our subjectivity.

Speech communities subdivide the semantic field of subjectivity in unique ways, such that 'emotion' is by no means a salient or inclusive category for all such communities. As we move from language to language, not only will we not encounter the English word, 'emotion' – or 'affect' for that matter – but even words that are purportedly translation-equivalents function uniquely within whatever semantic network they are embedded. My fieldwork in Bangladesh has taught me two things: There *are* ways to talk about emotion as a broad category in **Bangla**. But, outside of psychiatry, explicit reference to emotion(s) is uncommon as a practice, and reference to the broad category is even less common. Moreover, the Bangla terms that correspond most closely to 'emotion' have extremely different histories and connotations, certainly not rooted in a medical tradition. Instead, the concepts of *bhāva* and *rasa* – Sanskrit antecedents of phonetically Bangla cognates (in IPA, *bʰab* and *rɔʃ*) – may call to mind 'religious' or 'spiritual experience' rather than a psychologized and medicalized domain of 'emotion.' Historically, the two terms received greatest elaboration in Sanskrit treatises on religious devotion, drama, and aesthetic theory.[13]

The point is that any word in any language is a node in a classification system, but also a tool for doing things in a Wittgensteinian (1958) "language game." People in South Asia, scholars and nonscholars, invoke words like bhāva to perform different sorts of tasks than 'emotion' or 'affect' are appropriate for. Thus, we should answer questions about the fundamental relationship between language and some category like 'emotion' not merely by proving the mere 'existence' of some word(s) we claim are equivalents, but in reference to communicative practices that may or may not make use of a cover term like 'emotion,' or even use emotion labels at all. The performance of emotion (Grima 1992), mediated by various semiotic forms, should be our central focus. Still, we may draw on another of Wittgenstein's (1958) arguments – that, within one language, in observing two uses of the same word, we can assume a family resemblance between them – by way of asking whether, even among speakers of different languages, there is a family resemblance between the language games involving various terms that roughly correspond to 'emotion' (van Brakel 1993). In any case, as we turn in the next chapter toward models of the connection between 'language' and 'emotion,' we use each term, fully aware of its limitations. Invoking these terms in an academic discussion is at the very least a recognizable language game (Wittgenstein 1958 sec. 23).

2

THE RELATIONSHIP OF LANGUAGE
AND EMOTION

Where shall we locate emotion (or affect, used broadly, following Kulick and Schieffelin 2004)[1] vis-à-vis language? Any list of the elements, or layered structures, that make up language or discourse would suffice as a list of places emotion might appear. The loci of emotion in language are as numerous as locusts in a plague: phonology and sound symbolism, morphological processes (including reduplication), lexicon, **syntax**, discourse structure. Affect also emerges in the emergent text-like, even poetic, features of discourse, and in the relation of utterance or **text** to context. Each of these loci explodes into hundreds of possibilities.

The question of the location of affect in language is analogous to the question of the relationship of language to "cultural concepts" (Silverstein 2004). Summing up several decades of linguistic anthropological findings, Silverstein lists the ways in which language-in-use signals cultural conceptualizations. Taken together we can see them as problematizing both **referentialism** – the dominant **language ideology** in the West, defined in Chapter 1– and any sharp distinction between **reference** and the constitution and performance of social identities or acts of identification. A **referentialist** view of language and emotion asks about the truth-value of various emotion-denoting features in the world's languages. In contrast, a pragmatic approach focuses on how emotion talk works in social life (Lutz 1988: 8). We should note, however, that the structural unfolding (emergent **entextualization)** of what becomes recognizable as **denotational text** – simultaneously with **interactional text** – is the richest site for linguistic-anthropological investigation in general (Silverstein 2004: 633), and for an analysis of language-and-emotion in particular. This suggests that we would do well to keep the contextualized deployment of meaningful emotion talk linked, analytically, to the sorts of effects it creates – in whatever way those might be related to the deployment denotative-referential value of words and larger expressions (Silverstein 2004: 622).

Where is emotion in relation to language?

In languages and the speech communities they index, as wholes?

Let us first consider the sort of ideological representation of communities and their codes that portrays some languages, per se, as languages of passion (French? Italian?) and others (say, the Nordic languages, especially Finnish) as inexpressive. (Some would say that inexpressiveness defines the Finnish speech community and not the language.) What are we to make of such statements?

In labeling them **ideological** representations, we call attention to such statements' relation to power. The idea that dispassionate, objective, scientific language ranks higher on some universal scale of value than flowery, emotional, 'rhetoric' has retained some currency at least since the time of Bacon and Locke (Bauman and Briggs 2003). The circulation of stereotypes about the emotional temperature of various languages and their users has long helped to maintain global power relations. A range of historical voices connected with the colonial project have described "the Pacific … as a haven of passion, a romantic alternative to Victorian repression and morality" (Ochs 1986: 251).

In words (the lexicon)?

The lexicon is where many analyses of emotion in language begin and end. Corpus linguists, for example, count "attitude adverbs" like "amazingly" and "regrettably," "attitude verbs" like "hope," and "evaluative adjectives" like "cool" or "terrible" as markers of affective stance (Barbieri 2008). (Unlike cognitive linguists, corpus linguists analyze distribution of larger constructions, such as "be + like" and thus evade my critique of lexicocentrism.) Importantly, folk views of language – i.e., the consciousness of language we have in our capacity as (sometimes unreflecting) social actors – construe language as a matter of 'words.' A critique of a lexicocentric analysis of language and emotion must start by questioning the analytic value of this English **hypernym**. We cannot overlook the particular cultural history out of which 'emotion' emerged as *the* encompassing term for a domain that, even in Western history, was previously regarded as heterogeneous.

All disciplines concerned with the problem tend to focus on 'emotion words,' lexical labels over which realists and nominalists have fought, at times in relative ignorance of the huge scope of other linguistic phenomena that convey emotional meaning. Even within the lexicon, we must consider political labels, for example, to be affect-bearing. Americans sometimes use words like 'liberal' and 'conservative' as weapons; for some, they carry a load of fear and revulsion.

Kin-terms and nicknames are also overlooked affect-laden areas of the lexicon (Besnier 1990: 422). During Sikh-Hindu riots in Delhi, where communal violence often targeted women, "a group of Sikh men was prevented from murdering a group of Hindu women by being told that these women were their 'sisters' " (Trawick 1990a: 152). Trawick describes a Tamil folksong in which changing a form of address from one kin term to another alters the affective atmosphere dramatically. The song depicts a man asking a woman for water. She gives him some, calling him "older brother." He tells her "I don't mean that." The same exchange occurs when she calls him "younger brother." Only when she addresses him as *mama* (mother's brother, who among Tamils could be a preferred husband or lover) does he tell her, "That is the water I want" (Trawick 1990a: 153).

One of the more notable contemporary approaches to language and emotion is that of cognitive linguist Anna Wierzbicka, which focuses on emotion terms per se (Harkins and Wierzbicka 2001). I discuss this model in Chapter 3, along with other major theories of language and emotion.

In metaphor?

Perhaps today's best known cognitive linguist, George Lakoff who, together with his sometime collaborator Zoltán Kövecses, has described emotion metaphors (Lakoff and Kövecses 1987, Kövecses 2000). Metaphor theories of emotion share a common fixation with words, and – unlike Wierzbicka and colleagues – the emotion words on which Lakoff and Kövecses base their universalist claims are English. That is, they attribute some universality to metaphors for "anger," rather than recognizing the potentially deep differences between anger, *rag* (Bangla), and *ärger* (German). Specifically, they claim that all languages tend to speak of 'anger' as HOT FLUID IN [BODY AS] CONTAINER. No doubt this has some truth to it.

Problems, however, attend this approach. When Lakoff and his colleagues say we "live by" certain metaphors, such as metaphors linking body and emotion (Lakoff and Johnson 1980, Lakoff and Kövecses 1987), "they mean that cultural metaphors *reflect* innate biological, embodied experiences" (Wilce and Price 2003: 52–53). Some evidence from the relatively new field of *psychoneuroimmunology*, however, indicates that the metaphors people entertain – e.g., cancer patients using a guided imagery technique – may actually influence immunological processes (Lengacher et al. 2008). Whereas Lakoff and Kövecses presume that human physiology is basically the same the world over, ethnographic studies of embodiment propose the existence of "local biologies" (Lock 1998), an idea consistent with Griffiths' assertion that some local feeling structures may be heritable (1997: 9, 125, 159). Lock's study of Japanese women's *konenki* distinguishes it from its English counterpart, menopause: "Stiff shoulders, headaches, ringing in the ears, tingling sensations, and dizziness are the symptoms that form the core of the konenki experience, an experience that is, in part, contingent upon 'local' biology, inasmuch as hot flashes and other vasomotor symptoms occur rather infrequently." Konenki thus involves a different set of "vitality affects",[2] but clearly, discourse on konenki also differs from discourse on menopause (Lock 1998: 416–417).

There is no doubt that, for those concerned with the discursive expression of emotion, metaphors are a fruitful locus of study. No better example of this can be found than in the **laments** of Ingrians, a Balto-Finnic people. "Central to the language of lament [among Balto-Finnic groups] [wa]s … the metaphorical naming system and other metaphors referring to the object of the lament, to other people and to the lamenter herself" (Nenola 2002: 95). Here, the lamenter avoided directly speaking either the name or kin relation of the departed – and I use 'departed' advisedly, to cover both the dead and brides, whose departure was also ritually lamented. The pervasiveness of metaphoric indirection in referring to the object of grief corresponds with the esoteric-shamanistic nature of Balto-Finnic women's performance as lamenters.

It is time – both for the field and for this chapter – to turn away from lexicocentric views of language and emotion to more sophisticated approaches.

Passion in phonology, sound iconicity?

Human beings *leak* affectivity through their voices – through the intensity, pitch, and quality of voice used in a particular utterance (or scream!). Their capacity to do so reflects eons of evolution linking voice and certain useful affects. We can even say that, at this level (of voice as sound), affect production in human and animal shares a certain *iconicity*. We can define iconicity as a sign relationship in which the sign-vehicle can be said to resemble (in some way, so that for humans, this includes cultural perceptions of resemblance) its object (Peirce 1931–1958: 2.277).

Primate alarm calls index the presence of predators; but, to the extent that call features vary in direct relation to the degree of threat and arousal, they are iconic. Fichtel, Perry, and Gros-Louis (2005) conducted an acoustic analysis of white-faced capuchin monkey calls. They discovered "urgency-based" (or "arousal-based") acoustic differences in two call categories, signaling threats from aerial vs. terrestrial predators. Monkeys producing (and probably receiving) such calls are signaling greater urgency, and thus arousal, in the presence of aerial predators, which "are dangerous from the moment they are detected until they give up the hunt." The "noise," "duration," and "frequency range" of the more urgent calls are all greater, exemplifying call-threat iconicity (2005: 173).

We often take certain sonic features of speaking or singing to be icons of some feeling. Audiences perceive pharyngeal constrictions or *cry-breaks* in the vocal production of a skilled Bosavi lamenter, or a country-western singer, as icons of real crying (Feld and Fox 1994). Note that this iconicity – unlike that of alarm calls – is culturally mediated and subject to layer upon layer of reflection. Statements about 'those who sing like x,' or 'who sound like x,' are construals of first-order indexes or correlations between a social category and certain vocal signs. No such perceptions are ideology-free. Every statement pointing to such a correlation is itself a second-order index, and there is no limit to the layering of indexical reflection on putative icons (Irvine and Gal 2000).

In some languages, regular phonological shifts serve as affect markers. For example, shifting from s to sh (IPA ʃ) in Italian can add intensity to a word (as in ʃtupido; Ochs and Schieffelin 1989: 15). In Bangla, nasalization indexes the speaker's pejoration of someone's talk; thus, it functions like similar transformations in American English that signal sarcasm, or an ironic revoicing of someone else's speech (Sperber and Wilson 1986). In Bangla, nasalizing reported speech iconically represents the reported voice as immature, naughty, irritating, or transgressive. Revoicing others' complaints with nasalization is pejorative (Wilce 1998: 121–122).

In Southern Sotho, *ideophones* – "words, not necessarily onomatopoeic, whose phonological structure itself encodes meanings" – "have been described as 'dramatizations of actions or states'" (Besnier 1990: 424, citing Kunene 1978). Although Kunene presents no recorded, carefully transcribed data, his documenting of ideophones' embeddedness in dramatic reportage, with gestures, is a useful reminder of the inadequacy of focusing on lexemes alone.

In regards to the sounds of language, it is important to remember that people develop specific aesthetic sensibilities, and thus strong feelings. Sapir made that argument in the 1920s (1949a [1927]). New Yorkers (Labov 1972) and the French (Bourdieu 1977a) have strong feelings about class-based habits involving the mouth (i.e., so-called '**sociolect**' features), and in French even distinguish lexically between the refined and the profane 'mouth' – *la bouche* and *la gueule* (Bourdieu 1977a: 661). Inverting the more commonly described relationship between emotion and language in this way – focusing on language as the *object* of feeling – is not new. However, this book weaves the works cited, as well as Friedrich (1986) and Ramaswamy (1997), into one important piece of a coherent general theory of language and emotion.

Is the emotion in the voice?

Clearly the human vocal apparatus carries much of the emotional quality of speech. Analyses of phonatory ('voice') quality, pitch, sound symbolism, and intonation can uncover emotional significance (Ochs and Schieffelin 1989; Goodwin and Goodwin 2001; M. Goodwin 2006). In one of its other senses, 'voice' also carries emotional meaning. In some languages, including Japanese, use of passive voice is "reserved for events perceived as having an adverse effect on the grammatical patient" (Besnier 1990: 425). Bakhtin uses "voice" in a third sense – to denote a particular "socio-linguistic consciousness" (1981: 360) or a "semantic authority" (1984: 188). "The novel can be defined as a diversity of social speech types [i.e., social voices]" (1981: 262). Voices in this sense may carry and also arouse different affects. Anthropologists have applied Bakhtin's theory, originally developed in relation to written literatures in Europe, to the analysis of verbal art, i.e., oral performance. Oral narrators like Don Gabriel (Hill 1995; see Chapter 9) weave together many voices, often representing narrative figures (Goffman 1981); such 'voicing' often involves "intonational shadows" that "break through the narrator's voice." In Hill's perspective, none of these represent "artless emotion"; all serve the "active choice" of a "responsible self," i.e., a narrator responsibly staking out an ideological stance, exercising artistic control over voices to serve that end (1995).

Narrative voices like those of Don Gabriel are often intonationally marked. Voices in Bakhtin's sense, however, may or may not be thus marked. Regardless of intonation and voice quality, any parodic performance involves what Bakhtin (1981) called **heteroglossia**, or double-voicing. Lipset's (2004) ethnographic account of a 2001 mock trial, an improvised comic moment shared by men in a Papua New Guinea community, involved bawdy double-entendre. Parodic discourse in the 'trial' expressed ambivalent feelings toward the Papuan state and especially its legal institutions, and local Murik moral constructions of personhood involving sexual propriety and its violations (Lipset 2004: 74).

In morphology and syntax?

We cannot understand the workings of morphosyntactic structures that convey or stir emotion in audiences in a vacuum. For this function is often a part of a larger phenomenon – the difference between discourse that is *involved* and that which is *informational* (Biber 1988: 128–135), self-indexing or distant and authoritative, emotionally engaged or emotionally cool. Dwight Atkinson (1992) traces the evolution of scientific discourse, specifically that published in The Philosophical Transactions of the Royal Society of London, from the seventeenth through the twentieth century. The distanced (as opposed to involved, engaged, emotionally expressive) authorial self is created in precisely the way the beginning of this very sentence exemplifies. First, the sentence transformed a complex process (verb-centered construction) into a nominalized construction (where the actions of authoring and distancing are transformed into noun and adjective, respectively, Macaulay 1994: 106).

Ochs, together with her colleagues, has long argued that emotion is built into every dimension of language, focusing some of her attention on Samoan children's acquisition of emotionally charged forms. "Most of the grammatical forms for expressing positive and negative affect [in Samoan] are acquired before the age of four. The expression of affect through linguistic structures begins at the single-word stage" (Ochs 1988: 183). To the extent that we may consider intimacy and distance to be affective poles, it is noteworthy here that **ergative** constructions in Samoan, constructions in which agents are made explicit, are negatively correlated with intimacy; men also use these constructions more than women. For these reasons, Samoan children are late in acquiring the ergative. Here we could say that cultural norms governing degrees of affective distance influence the language acquisition process. A second Samoan example involves the expectation that very young children learn highly affective forms of begging – realized in the use of a special "poor I" form of the first person pronoun, which is morphologically productive and thus inflected according to context – along with cursing (Ochs 1986, 1988).

In formal grammar, verb mood may appear to have little to do with emotional mood. Mood or modality is a grammaticalized means of expressing speaker stance toward his or her proposition. Grammarians distinguish epistemic mood (speaker signaling stance toward the actuality of event), deontic mood (the event's obligatoriness or permissability; forms of deontic modality include events that are allowed, imposed, desired, etc.), and conditional mood (Chung and Timberlake 1985). But grammatical mood may not just denote certain real, unreal, or desired states; it can also index affect. Ochs and Schieffelin (1989: 12) list several instances – specifically in Dyirbal, Japanese, and English. The Dyirbal -*bila* suffix denotes a possibility while indexing its undesirability, and the Japanese suffix -*ba* and English *if only* denote conditionality but index desirability. We can at least analytically distinguish the putatively transcontextual denotation of these modal forms from the way they point, in context, to speaker's affective state, e.g., desire.

Is it in discourse-level structure, i.e., poetics? genre?

Silverstein's first of three 'lessons' in how language reveals cultural concepts (2004: 622) invokes the emergent form of discourse as **text**. Such "discursive interaction brings sociocultural concepts into here-and-now contexts of use … via emergent patternings of semiotic forms." Silverstein offers a reinterpretation of an example of such patternings from James Fox's work on parallelism in Rotinese ritual speech. Fox presents a transcript of ritual oratory performed during a succession ritual occasioned by a leader's death. The transcript highlights two examples of renewal from the animal world. A goat whose "yellownecklaced beard" is cut away will regrow the "beard"; a cock whose tailfeathers are plucked will likewise regrow them. The oration's double poetic movement from loss to restoration is the entextualized message, culminating in the lines "still perfect as before, and ordered as at first" (Fox 1974: 74). Silverstein represents that message as metaemotional – a soothing message – "Don't worry …" (2004: 627). "In this way a ritual **text** paints a picture of what it accomplishes in relation to that context and can change our experience of the context to the degree we accept the picture. And we accept it emotionally as well as otherwise" (Silverstein 2003b: 38). We might call this the emotional **performativity** of poetic figuration.

From another perspective, we may view poetry – and particular, highly cultivated, poetic productions – as a cultural means for channeling and hence controlling one's passions. Poets themselves may view their performances thus, and the poetry of Yemeni tribesmen is a classic example. Tribal values to which men conform include piety, honor, hospitality, courage, autonomy, and self-control. The values of emotional equanimity and honor may clash in a particular situation in which that honor is threatened. However, even in terms of facial expression and bodily stance, the response of Yemeni men is stylized. Such an ethos "is perfectly suited to poetry" (Caton 1990: 31), and particularly poetry understood in relation to power as both semiotic and material, personal and political.

> Yemeni tribesmen, however, think that poetry is too precious *not* to use for pressing public issues and that it can have a transformative effect on them as well; hence it possesses considerable power. They believe that it is poetic *form* which gives it this power (1990: 41).

For these Yemenis, *hajis* – the gift of poetic genius or inspiration – carries profoundly mixed value. The gift is said to have structured the speech of highly valued ancestors all the way back to Adam. Yet events that stir passion, and in turn arouse hajis, present some danger to the poet. Just as, in many societies, strong emotion is itself seen as a danger to the experiencer (not to speak of others), the hajis *must* have its way, must – as the inspiration of verbal art – (verbally) play itself out. Yet, unlike in India (McDaniel 1989), the category of divine madness is apparently foreign to Yemeni thought; thus to its poets falls the Herculean task of managing this poetic passion. The ability to harness both passion and inspiration to reason is viewed as natural to men but not women (Caton 1990: 37–39).

If affect is closely bound up with intensity (Massumi 1995), then common Yemeni modes of men's poetic performance – particularly singing – are affective to the core, for the expected singing style requires vocal power and the ability to sustain a high falsetto over long periods of time. In addition to this feature of the poet's individual performance, the call and response of poet and chorus in the *balah* genre (wedding poetry) must add to the excitement of the occasion, which is to emphasize that this genre is oriented to performance rather than potential decontextualization or the memorability of its aesthetics. However, the **textual** features of poems – from their narration of the poet's emotions in response to some event, to their structure *qua* poetry – also play a role in enabling the audience to identify with the **text** and thus find it persuasive. "Alliteration and internal rhyme [are] used to underline certain key ideas of the text, to channel the thoughts and emotions of the audience in certain directions" (Caton 1990: 177).

Does emotion lie in "context of situation," or in genres as structures of expectation?

Certainly we gain a fuller understanding of the emotional impact of speech genres like *balah* poetry if we attend carefully to particular intersections of discourse and "context of situation" (Malinowski 1923: 315). It is worth giving some attention to this relationship before attempting to locate emotion somewhere in it. Malinowski urged ethnographers to pay close attention not only to linguistic context, i.e., the textual surround of a particular word (which Silverstein [2003a] calls "**co-text**") but also to its situation of use. He treated even "aimless gossip" that serves to create "an atmosphere of sociability" as a "context of situation" worth recording. Shared positive affect, Malinowski perceived, arose in the situation. But note that, in Malinowski's view, "the situation in all such cases *is created by the exchange of words.*" Here, a particular use of language constitutes the situation, and its affectivity. Malinowski was reaching for a dialectical model of **co-text** and (situational) context. This view still tends to distinguish linguistic anthropology, which recognizes the contribution of speech to context, from those forms of sociolinguistics that regard contexts as fixed sets of features that determine forms of speech used in them.

Linguistic anthropologist Dell Hymes' (1972) **"ethnography of communication"** offers a more recent argument for interpreting talk in relation to its cultural "scene," "situation," or "setting." With the word "scene" Hymes aimed to capture the local, cultural construal of speech settings. "Speech acts are frequently used to define scenes" (1972: 60). Genre was also central to the ethnography of the communication program. Genres, as I have said, are structures of expectation governing how some sort of discourse is produced and received (Bauman 1999).

Abu-Lughod has demonstrated a tidy distribution of two sorts of affect across three speech genres associated with Awlād 'Ali women. In ordinary conversation, a woman may express anger as well as indifference in talking about a loss, as in a divorce. By contrast, the same woman may sing a poem (*ghinnāwa*, 'little song') that is at least widely understood to address the same loss, but this time evincing feelings of vulnerability – grief, sadness, and hurt. Abu-Lughod denies that these songs, or the ritualized funeral laments (*bkā*, 'crying') that are "structurally equivalent and technically similar" (Abu-Lughod 1985: 254) to *ghinnāwa*, are merely personal expressions of individual sentiment. The paired genres constitute, instead "a highly conventional and formulaic idiom" (1985: 253). They are structures of expectation governing the production of discourse – and affect.

The Yemeni conceptual link between poetry and emotion involves not just the relation of expression, but (like an unruly river forced to flow through a man-made structure) that of canalizing and thus constraining. In tribesmen's poetry, "emotions ... are made governable by their transmutation into aesthetic form or the stylized release of passion" (Caton 1990: 31).

Women who perform laments may speak similarly about the genre's canalizing potential (Wilce 2009). Even the most prototypically emotive expressive forms among Awlād 'Ali Egyptian Bedouin women are structurally "ready-made" and "fixed" (Abu-Lughod 1986: 238). People do perceive the strong emotion expressed in both 'crying' with words (*bkā*, lament) and *ghinnāwa* – both women's performance genres. Still, their structural rigidity and conventionality paradoxically makes it possible for them to index strong, vulnerable feelings while at the same time sending a metamessage indicating that the performers and the performance are honorably self-controlled. "By channeling such powerful sentiments into a rigid and conventional medium and delimited social contexts, individuals demonstrate a measure of self-mastery and control that contributes to honor" (Abu-Lughod 1986: 245).

We find cultural notions – or ideologies – that locate affect not in individuals but in situations (where a particular sort of affect is conventionally expected) distributed around the world; 'our' ideology may not be the most common. "In Japan there seems to be an extensive codification of contexts in which particular feelings are expected; speakers need only indicate, by means of the right formula, that they are experiencing the appropriate reaction, without expressing any more personal, individualized response" (Clancy 1986: 216). Likewise Ishelhin Moroccan Berbers' "language ideology ... holds that individuals need not talk about their emotions, for everyone knows that specific situations bring about anticipated affective states" (Hoffman 2002: 527). Like the Awlād 'Ali, Ishelhin treat everyday conversation (*tjmmḍat*) and various genres of sung poetry very differently, but the difference may not map onto a simple polarity. Two young women who are friends are more able to baldly express regret regarding "unfulfilled aspirations" in conversation than in song (2002: 525). Yet Ishelhin regard song as the appropriate venue for expressing emotion. How are we to understand this apparent contradiction?

This case, it turns out, is not so different from that of the Awlād 'Ali, insofar as the particular kinds of emotion expressed in song – like the technical aspects of the songs themselves – are somewhat predictable. The two major song genres women perform – *tazrrart* and *tinḍḍamin* – differ in terms of the affective relationships celebrated, but for our purposes what is most important is that this too is predictable. *Tizrrarin* (pl. of *tazrrart*) often celebrate bonds between people, particularly those gathered on a ritual occasion like a wedding. By contrast, *tinḍḍamin* glorifies "peer attachment and thus challenges the affective links between kin that are more prevalent in spoken discourse in this moral communicative economy" (Hoffman 2002: 527). Although these genres differ from each other, what sets them apart from conversation is that the latter involves "bald expression" (2002: 526). We may say that these oral genres impose order and predictability, but they themselves have no agency; it is social pressure (since songs are publicly performed) that bleaches them of overt protest.

Written genres are just as culturally embedded, and just as likely to index certain characteristic emotional stances; they may emphatically express affect, or evince a faceless impersonality (Biber and Finegan 1989). As I pointed out in Chapter 1, in introducing Nukulaelae Islanders' personal letters (Besnier 1995), it is advantageous to view such genres as indexing a conventionalized set of "expectations concerning the ... unfolding of the discourse" (Bauman 1999: 84). Islanders have come to associate personal letters with strong affect, the kind associated equally with farewells; writing letters is also emerging as an activity defined by affect in Nepal, where a new genre of love letters has emerged (Ahearn 2003, discussed in Chapter 10). Bauman (1999: 85) argued that understanding a genre's formal/stylistic features is inadequate, without an understanding of the "situated production" and reception of text in relation to cultural expectations embedded in the genre in question. Likewise, Besnier shows that the personal letters' affectivity lies in the conventional way in which they are received – "laboriously read aloud, with tears as it is in their purely textual characteristic[s]" (1995: 109). This ethnographic approach, tying genre to expectations regarding performance/production and reception, is particularly helpful in guiding efforts to locate affect in genres.

In the mind? The body?

Is emotion in the 'mind?' In 'bodies' (conceived of as distinct from minds)? In social relationships? I have already laid out compelling arguments for transcending such dichotomies, based on neuroanatomy and brain function, and on ethnographic evidence of socioculturally mediated emotion, of bodies differently conceived and experienced in various human groups. Yet, in struggling free from our Cartesian prison, it is not enough to posit mindful or intelligent bodies – not if those bodies remain inactive. It is models of mindful moving and acting bodies that offer the promise of escape from dualism (Farnell 1995), and it is moving, mindful bodies – vocalizing words with a particular quality, gesturing, etc. – that perform emotion.

Clearly, we gain much by turning up all these stones in looking for emotion in language.[3]

Interaction and e-motion

In the last chapter I introduced the work of Norwegian psychologist Stein Bråten and his "e-motion" model, his attempt to capture the way emotion and motion merge in the cognitive development of infants interacting with their caregivers. Such early interactions may involve making sounds, even (caregivers) speaking, but always involve bodies, given the embodied ground of talk-in-interaction. **Mirror neurons** might well be the enablers of our earliest forms of empathy and **intersubjectivity** – feeling with another. But in any case, the focus on perceiving (and producing) emotion in complex, multimodal semiotic activities – involving bodies, mouths, eyes, ears, etc. that are both meaningfully positioned in social space, and active – has much to offer.

We find a thoroughly empirical approach to the question of where emotion lies – one that is sympathetic to attempts to locate emotion in the body – in the work of Marjorie and Charles Goodwin. However, their focus is not on bodily states, but on embodied actions "within processes of interaction" (2001: 253). Among those embodied actions we must count the use of the lungs, lips, and voice, e.g., in producing relatively loud or soft speech. How does one measure "outraged indignation," for example, during girls' hopscotch games? The Goodwins (2001: 241) operationalized the extent to which one girl vents at another by analyzing measurable features of voice production, especially pitch leaps. When one girl prefaced her torrent of anger with a single shouted syllable – "N'ai!" – she marked her shout as one of "outrage/ indignation" intonationally, "leaping" from 400 to 600 Hz in the scope of that single syllable. There follows an angry, accusatory pointing gesture, the cry (you stepped) "Out! Out!" and a replay of the offending step, demonstrating where on the hopscotch grid the offense occurred. Bodies acted here within a complex spatial grid given meaning within a particular sociocultural context; and the Goodwins argue that this is typical of displays of emotion (or affect).[4]

Goodwin, Goodwin, and Yaeger-Dror (2002) describe a low-high-low (LHL) intonation contour produced by many Latina girls. What is particularly interesting about this from the perspective of cultural anthropology is that this "contouring" of *Out*!-cries is far more typical of Latina girls than African Americans, occurring in 98 vs. 57 percent of the two groups' *Out*!- cries, respectively. A majority of Latina girls' *Out*!-cries reached a maximum pitch over 500 Hz, but only a minority of African American girls' cries did so. Latina girls crying "Out!" typically used the LHL contour, along with gesture, as part of an embodied affective stance signaling strong displeasure. African-American girls use a "simple level or falling terminal" pitch contour on all "cries" (*Out*! and *No*!). Both groups of girls shared certain practices in common – using "turn prefaces" that made their angry opposition to some other girl's move in the hopscotch game quite explicit, and acting out this angry opposition by taking assertive bodily stances toward their opponents.

The Goodwins describe another, very different, scene involving the display of emotion. In the second scene, most actors are adults. One is flipping the pages of a new calendar with exquisite photographs of birds. "Immediately upon seeing the first bird Pat produces an audible inbreath," which she follows with a "Wow!" – what Goffman (1979) called a "response cry." The Goodwins define this as "an embodied display that the party producing it has been so moved by a triggering event that they temporarily 'flood out' with a brief emotional expression" (2001: 247). Another person in the room, Rob, on hearing Pat's expression, looks for the trigger. He then enters into the groove with Pat and others as the pages are flipped, changing his verbalizations to register appropriate affect at each new beautiful photo, expertly "coparticipating" in the event through the grammar of response cries (2001: 250). I have held back from you the fact that Rob is aphasic and can utter only four words. His response cries included one "Yeah" and one series of enthusiastic vocables. But coparticipation is coparticipation.

The coordinated achievement of emotional meaning can entail angry exchanges, as in the hopscotch challenge, as well as mutual appreciation and tenderness. However, in the context of ontogeny (individual development) and phylogeny (the evolution of species-specific traits), it is likely that experiences of mutuality in expression are enjoyable to infant and caregiver as well as playmates (Trevarthen and Daniel 2005; see this book's cover). A strong motivation to engage in reciprocal emotional play, often involving microlevel synchrony, is part of our evolutionary heritage (Aitken and Trevarthen 1997). Thus, embodied interaction as a vehicle and site of affect and **intersubjectivity** (including the sympathetic connection that led Rob to so closely track the activity of his family) has deep roots. E-motion may well be the ur-form of emotion.

Gesture, stance, and embodied affect

In the previous chapter we saw how work on stance – the speaker's attitude or degree of commitment toward a proposition (affective or epistemic stance) – tends to focus exclusively on linguistic forms that index stance, and how Matoesian breaks new ground in incorporating gesture in the analysis of stance. This move has common roots with efforts by Bråten and the Goodwins to locate emotion in the realm of embodied intersubjective participation. "Stance emerges not just through language or through the body alone, but through both as mutually contextualizing modalities" (Matoesian 2005: 178).

These conclusions reflect Matoesian's close analysis of a focus group interview involving members of a local police department who had recently completed a training session in community policing. An applied social science research institution funded by the US Department of Justice had run the training, and was evaluating its success. One policeman being interviewed made a statement that highlighted the local police force's active attempts to "zero in on" community crime problems. He said, "When we have a problem, we definitely zero right in on it and take care of that problem." This quote represents only the linguistic form of the proposition, and does so as though it were equivalent to a written statement. It indicates nothing about prosody or embodied stance features. However, the policeman conveyed a stance of intense commitment to his proposition "multimodally," for instance through prosody ("marked lengthening and voicing on the alveolar fricative," i.e., the /z/ in "z::::ero").[5] Moreover, that prosody was "delicately synchronized with an affective gestural movement to maximize its visual impact on" the interviewer (2005: 175–176) – an intense thrust of the hands that makes the "'zeroing in' appear to jump out at you." Working together with speech, that intense, muscular hand-arm movement enacted (gesturally, iconically depicting) the zeal with which the police "zero in on" community problems.

Members of the police department were reacting unfavorably to their training, and thus the focus group interview was preordained to be somewhat tense. At one point an interviewee says, "I don't know whether they [the trainers or their institution] just had the money to burn up" (2005: 179). The participant structure had, until that point in the focus group interview, positioned the female interviewer, who had conducted the training, as neutral moderator committed to hearing any response at all to the training. However, upon hearing that remark, she recoils, embodying her reception of and attitude toward the remark.

The trainer "thus abort[ed] the neutral moderator role" as she signaled that she was taking criticism as a personal attack "on her professional integrity" (2005: 184). Even in the position of recipient or hearer, she signaled a new "affective and epistemic stance on the interviewer's representation [that worked] … to shift the form of participation in complex ways" (2005: 169). This embodied stance marked a complex shift in the moderator's pattern of **identification**, a shift that was bound up in the affect signaled by her energetic recoil. She thus shifted from identifying with her institute, and her institutional role as moderator, toward at least a momentary identification with her personal self and her career as a professional.

That shift in the moderator's stance, her pattern of identification, and the overall participant structure, is marked in one more way that deserves mention. When the policeman had partially completed his utterance about the trainers' institution having money to burn, the moderator produced three tentative laughing breaths before she recoiled. The recoil coincided with the speaker's (the policeman's) failure to join in the laughter. The interviewer had at first misconstrued his emerging attack as a kind of joking criticism, and she signaled her new understanding of his interactive turn by recoiling as though "struck by speech."[6] The example underscores the way that emotion is signaled by linguistic means strictly defined, along with bodily posture, movement, and voice modulations.

Deep play

The question this chapter poses – of emotion's 'location' in relation to language – may well presuppose the very sort of cultural framework it intends to question. Other versions of the question – e.g., "Is this spoken emotion 'real'"? – certainly presuppose notions of sincerity or authenticity that are themselves products of a certain Protestant modernity, according to Robbins (2001) and Keane (2002).

The issue of sincerity has recently arisen in relation to **laments** once communally produced in Karelia (see Figure 2.1), a region straddling the current Finnish-Russian border. Ethnomusicologists studying what remains of that tradition worked closely with Martta Kuikka, a recently deceased 'cry-woman.' In the first half of the twentieth century, Martta's mother was called to lament at Karelian funerals – and weddings – and Martta became an accomplished lament singer herself. Both women described lament as extremely dangerous. The danger of laments is tied up with their power, "their overwhelming effects not only on the audience or on the spirits of the dead, but on the performers themselves." Thus, the mother-daughter pair told ethnomusicologist Elizabeth

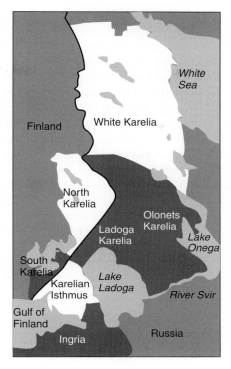

Figure 2.1   *Map of Karelia*

Tolbert, "lamenting is bad for the heart" (Tolbert 1990: 49). "The micro-rhythmic and micro-tonal variations in the lamenting voice manifest *emotional intensity*, which in turn *indexes the presence of spiritual power* and the trance-like state of the lamenter's journey to the other world" (Tolbert 1992: 18; emphasis added).

Cry-women themselves downplayed the emotionally expressive function of their performances. They told Tolbert that "the lamenter projects her own experience of grief through her individual voice as a means to orchestrate the collective experience of sorrow, bringing messages back and forth between the world of the living and the world of the dead" (2001b: 85). The obligation to perform (which, to anthropologists like myself, certainly does *not* imply insincerity) on behalf of neighbors was thus a weighty one.

Were these cry-women expressing a feeling sincerely? Was it their own? Where *was* the feeling? The lamenter herself might feel deeply – indeed so, given the risk to her heart – but, even more significantly, she used the conventions of emotion-signs to create (a) **intersubjectivity** with the grieving relatives who often joined her in lamenting, (b) a bridge for the dead soul to follow to *Tuonela* (the realm of the dead), and/or (c) a magical blessing whose efficacy ensures that a marriage will endure and not end in divorce (Tolbert 1994: 191). The laments Kuikka and her mother performed did not so much *refer* to feeling as were *suffused* with feeling. Karelian lamenters sobbed as they sang, the 'cry-break' in the singing voice serving both as an icon of real crying and an index of power-in-self-risk, the powerful use of emotion-signs. Audience-performer interaction was no doubt central to the production and shared experience of emotion, contributing as much, perhaps, as the lament texts, filled with metaphorical representations of the beloved dead and his or her relationship to those present.

What is the relationship of language to emotion, or where can we locate the emotion? We cannot pin the feelings down. Denotational signs may evoke them. Audiences – particularly when they co-perform parts of a lament – not only feel but help construct the atmosphere of feeling. Bodies together rocking, weeping, wailing, singing, wiping tears away, hugging – these are all productive sites of affect. They are also liable to be objects of feeling and evaluation. An adequate anthropology of language and emotion grapples with all of this complexity.

3

APPROACHES TO LANGUAGE
AND EMOTION

Introduction

This chapter surveys four major theories of language and emotion. It is appropriate to start with (1) *language socialization* approaches, which deal (though not exclusively) with the start of life. In fact, the same scholars who pioneered this approach have also pioneered linguistic anthropological work on emotion. We turn next to *cognitive* theories (2). Although there is often a tension between cognitivist models which tend toward universalism and the more dominant cultural relativist schools of anthropological thought, we will explore attempts to reconcile these two positions. Although cognitive and the (3) *phenomenological* approaches dealt with next in this chapter both concern "human sentience" (Desjarlais 1997: 248), they pursue this concern in very different ways. I focus again, in that section, on a kind of reconciliation – drawing on Desjarlais, who has worked to refigure phenomenological anthropology, to insert in phenomenological studies a materialist concern, i.e., a focus on the political economy that contextualizes subjectivity. The final section presents other materialist approaches to language and emotion (4).

Socialization theories and their relevance to language and emotion

Language socialization and the socialization of emotion[1]

In a remarkable series of studies, Elinor Ochs and Bambi Schieffelin have addressed the important anthropological topic of socialization – the process by which novices (including, but not limited to, children) become competent members of a particular society – using linguistic and ethnographic methods (e.g., Ochs and Schieffelin 1984; Ochs 1986; Schieffelin and Ochs 1986; Ochs 1988; B. Schieffelin 1990; Ochs and Taylor 2001). They discovered that the processes of enculturation and socialization do not occur apart from the process of language acquisition; instead, children acquire language and culture together, in a single, integrated process. Language socialization is socialization both to and through the use of language (Schieffelin and Ochs 1986: 163). That is, it involves both situations in which language is in focus (and cultural lessons are implicit) and situations in which language serves as the medium but remains in the background while cultural lessons are foregrounded.

Ochs and Schieffelin demonstrated that baby talk, i.e., linguistic simplification as an adaptation to children, is not universal. Rather, the question of whether the child is made to adapt to the ongoing situation of speech around it or vice versa is a variable. Direction of adaptation correlates with the direction the child is held vis-à-vis a caregiver's body. In many societies caregivers hold a child facing outward so as to orient it to a network of kin whom it must learn to recognize early in life. The implications for the socialization of emotion as part of the language socialization process are significant. To properly conceptualize language and emotion we must, of course, conceive of them in embodied actional contexts such as holding/ being held with a particular physical orientation.

Ochs and Schieffelin (1989) also pioneered the ethnographic study of language and affect, focusing on how affective expression emerges in children, their linguistic environments, and their own speech production. "From the child's point of view, expressive and referential functions of language are acquired in an integrated fashion, of a piece" (1989: 11). This means that as children acquire the full panoply of linguistic means for making meaning, they are simultaneously learning the tools for signaling feeling. Almost every dimension of language is at least potentially involved in signaling emotion – pronouns; determiners; verb morphosyntax (mood, tense-aspect, voice); morphology of the noun phrase (case and number marking, particles, reduplication); phonology (intonation, voice quality, sound repetition, sound symbolism, lexicon); sentence structure (verb variants, word order); and discourse structure (code-switching, affective speech acts) (Ochs and Schieffelin 1989: 13–14).

Ochs (1988) describes a very wide range of Samoan linguistic structures ("affect specifiers" and "intensifiers"), speech acts, and speech genres that convey affect. She demonstrates the variable distribution of these structures in speech, according to gender, age, and social rank (titled vs. untitled persons). "Most of the [Samoan] grammatical forms for expressing positive and negative affect are acquired before the age of four" (1988: 183), and affect indexing first appears in the single-word phase of language acquisition. For example, Samoan children (like adults) choose between two sorts of first-person pronouns, neutral and affective forms, the latter indicating sympathy toward the speaker and often used to elicit pity. Children acquire the direct, forceful, negative-affect-laden form of 'no' before the affectively neutral negative. Particular speech acts rely on these affective or 'sympathy' forms. Begging is the first speech act context in which the semantic domain of sympathy-love emerges in child speech (Ochs 1986: 266–268). In addition to the neutral vs. affective sets of linguistic forms, alternation involving another paired set – the /t/ register vs. the /k/ register (the phonological shifts indexing 'good speech' and 'bad speech') – achieves rhetorical and affective effects.

Studies of language socialization inevitably bump up against issues of **reflexivity**, by which I mean (here) the layers of semiotic reflection we encounter in any apparently simple speech act. Local actors' ways of *characterizing* linguistic forms and their pragmatic functions influence whether, and how, language is reproduced (Kulick 1992). Many non-anthropological treatments of language and affect focus on semantics; Ochs, however, focuses primarily on "*pragmatic* functions of affect features" (1988: 172; emphasis added), and on speech acts and genres. Samoan speakers have names for many of these, i.e., they are clearly targets of metapragmatic awareness, speakers' awareness of the indexical function of particular speech signs (Silverstein 2001).

Wittgenstein asserted that private experience is inexpressible, and described different forms of speech as "language games," actional building blocks of different "forms of life" (see Chapter 9). In this post-Wittgenstein era, the question for us is not whether there is a one-to-one mapping of isolated emotion words onto 'real' emotions. Instead we want to ask what speakers do with whole '**texts**,' i.e., arrays of signs whose emergent form-in-relation-to-context indexes affect. The absence of a particular word denoting a particular emotion reveals little. More important questions concern the kind of affect that a type of text or utterance evokes, and the extent to which such sign arrays are metapragmatically recognized and regimented. That is, given that a speech fraction can be said (by observation) to co-occur with – or shift the context associated with – some emotion, speakers may or may not recognize, or speak of, the pragmatic relationship between the speech fraction and affect.

In any utterance, the presence of a word that local actors understand to name a feeling probably increases the chances that they will associate that term with the pragmatics of the broader speech. However, this says nothing about the ability of that speech to index affect as a social fact. Beatty (2005: 29) argues that we cannot know what people are actually feeling if they do not name the feeling. This claim reflects the universal tendency to attend to **reference** as language's chief pragmatic function, and particularly the referential significance of neatly packaged semiotic units like words. But linguistic anthropologists also attend to the functions of scatters of semiotic features, and of split structures – e.g., 'is x-ing,' i.e., the auxiliary verb plus /-ing/, appearing discontinuously, straddling the main verb root – in which various parts collaborate to index affect (Silverstein 2001 [1981]). Talk may carry affect without referring to it.

Social referencing

Since the 1980s, psychologists have been demonstrating a fact about normal infant development that became foundational for "developmental pragmatics," or – as the field quickly became known – "language socialization." "A child's understanding of [and emotional reaction to] novel entities develops through and is mediated by the facial expression of others present" (Ochs and Schieffelin 1989: 8). Novices "seek out affective information from one another's language," facial signals, and other signs (1989: 9). This phenomenon is called "social referencing" (Campos and Sternberg 1981). The term means that "infants show the ability to use others' affective cues for guiding their own exploratory behaviors toward novel objects or events" (Flom and Bahrick 2007: 250). The idea is that an infant crawling alone toward the top of a staircase learns to be afraid, or at least cautious, by noticing her parent's facial and vocal expressions of fear on her behalf. Social referencing is a very complex achievement involving the sort of joint attention, affect attunement, interaffectivity, or early intersubjectivity described in Chapter 2. Assuming the child has access to both audible and visible signals from the adult,[2] it also involves perceiving the synchrony of affective facial expressions and audible (speech-related) signs of affect.

Flom and Bahrick experimentally manipulated just this linking of audible and visible signals. They demonstrated a two-month gap in infants' social referencing abilities, depending on whether they were shown "a dynamic, audiovisual object, such as a toy robot ... along with multimodal [audiovisual] *affective expressions*" by the adult gazing at the toy, or a static object that made no sound. Infants as young as 10 months tracked adults' affect in relation to dynamic, sound-producing objects; only at 12 months could they achieve the same degree of social referencing vis-à-vis an object that was "unimodal visual and static" (2007: 250; emphasis added).

Variation in cultural concepts of language and socializing practices

Language socialization studies have demonstrated for many readers the significance of social referencing. However, they have also documented a phenomenon that reverses the relationship between adult and child. If social referencing entails children seeing and hearing adults and inferring an affective stance that they make their own, language socialization around the world, as praxis, reflects and reproduces local understandings of what a child is saying/doing/feeling. Here we have adults listening to children, inferring from (or projecting onto) them a particular affective stance embodied in the sounds (or later, words) the child produces, and thereby confirming what the adult already 'knew' about what children say. Samoans 'know' that any child's first word will be *tae*, 'shit,' and understand this speech act as an assertive affective stance indicative of children's nature.

Several recent studies have uncovered culturally particular forms of affective socialization in which language plays a key role. Mullen and Yi (1995) found that Korean and "Caucasian" mothers – from Seoul and New England, respectively – engaged with their children in linguistic practices that contribute to different outcomes, different forms of the self, though not quite as stereotype would have it. The "Caucasian" mothers engaged in talk about past events with their children, cast the child as a central character in such talk more often than did Korean mothers, and in doing so, spoke more often about the child's thoughts and feelings. Not only this, but – contrary to expectations – the American mothers also spoke more often about others' feelings. "In short, they took a more psychological approach to their discussions. The Korean dyads, on the other hand, took a more normative approach, emphasizing behavioral expectations and social roles with greater frequency than the Caucasian dyads" (Mullen and Yi 1995: 415).

Socialization and the social ontogeny of the self

Socialization is social in origin and outcome. Even if socialization somehow involved just a mother and her child, their interaction (and not either's individual mind) is the socializing matrix. And that matrix produces social beings. The anthropological study of socialization owes much to the early twentieth-century work of the pragmatist thinker, sociologist, and pioneering social psychologist, George Herbert Mead. Mead asserted the interactive emergence of mind and self. In interacting with others we learn to internalize their attitudes toward us, a process crucial to the formation of the *me-self*, that aspect of self seen in the mirror of others' responses to us and our actions. "We must regard mind, then, as arising and developing within the social process, within the empirical matrix of social interactions" (Mead 1995 [1934]: 101).

Later in the developmental trajectory, an *I-self* emergences. According to Mead, the emerging adult quite normally experiences psychodevelopmental crises during which the resources of the internalized, socially conventional self are inadequate to overcome certain problems of existence and identification. In attempting to creatively resolve such personal crises, "the person" (the *I*) emerges in fuller, more defined form. One sort of reflexivity defines the me-self, the experience of self as reflected by others' responses. The *I*, by contrast, learns to *reflect* on her own behavior, and that sort of reflexivity enters the person's own range of competence. Caton (1990: 95) and Mead describe this more mature reflection as a *communicative* act. In a spiraling developmental cycle, successful efforts by the *I* to overcome difficulties are reintegrated into the self's repertoire of conventional behavior – into the *me*. What starts out as a manifestation of personal **agency** of the most creative sort – i.e., a creative identification process – enters into the structure of habit. The evolving sense of oneself results in what we know as identity. Ongoing cycles of internal-and-external interaction – successful (self-)creative efforts, others' responses to them, and the integration of these results – produce an increasingly solid identity.

To better understand how 'mind' and self continually emerge in social interaction, we return to Goodwin and Goodwin's discussion of Rob, described in Chapter 2. Rob has severe aphasia and can use only four words. A kitchen is the shared physical and communicative context in which Rob hears Pat produce a "response cry." He looks around for what triggered the cry of appreciation, which turns out to be a bird photograph on a calendar Pat has just received.

The turning of each page of the calendar provides a groove – a semiotically structured environment – into which Rob can enter. He does so, right on time, producing enthusiastic sounds and thereby coparticipating in a complex semiotic event involving (for some or all actors) seeing, touching and moving the calendar, speaking – and sharing in the experience of thought and feeling. An individualistic model of cognition would be hard pressed to explain how a man with a vocabulary of four words could interact with Rob's expertise. Cognition, as this example shows, is distributed through the social environment – that is, Rob's interlocutors, their gaze, the object, and their speech – and these productions become resources that he is able to take advantage of in order to participate. Rob was thinking, we might say, 'prosthetically' – as in fact we all do, using our environments (including our dialogue partners) as cognitive aids.

During adolescence, young Americans may experience moments when the me-self becomes an obvious mismatch for an I-self identity that bubbles to the surface. Corwin (2007) describes such moments in the retroactively narrated lives of San Francisco Bay area young adults calling themselves "genderqueer," who identify as neither male nor female. One such person, in the process of narrating how *zhe*[3] had come to embrace the term "genderqueer," described for Corwin how *zhe's* mother had warned that *zhe* was giving others no clear indication as to *zhe's* gender. However, this was not a moment to succumb to pressure to conform; instead, hearing such things pushed *zhem* through a kind of emotional crisis into what became, for *zhem*, a more satisfying orbit of identification. The pleasant clarity of the narration, the earlier tension and later satisfaction, and the affiliation this person experienced before and after adopting the label *genderqueer* – signaling a flexible range of identificatory possibilities – all of these exemplify the complex connections between language, affect, and identification in human development.

Cognitive theories of language and emotion

This cursory account of cognitive linguistics serves as a promissory note. In Chapter 4, I revisit in much greater detail the theoretical models of emotion terms put forth by that field, because of their importance to the philosophical questions discussed there. Although it is an injustice, given the breadth of cognitive linguistics and psychological anthropology (e.g., White 2000), I focus almost exclusively on the work of Anna Wierzbicka and her collaborators.

Contributors to Harkins and Wierzbecka's 2001 volume *Emotions in Crosslinguistic Perspective* locate feeling in words, often nouns, denoting particular emotions. Although some contributors address the "grammar" of emotion terms, their descriptions remain lexicocentric, focused on "universal concepts [realized as lexemes] and their universal rules of combination" (Wierzbicka and Harkins 2001: 11). Chapter 2 presented objections to such lexically based models of language and emotion.

Still, Wierzbicka's substantial contributions to the study of language and emotion deserve our attention, and I am in sympathy with much about her approach. Rather than presuming that English emotion terms always find close-enough local counterparts in all languages, Wierzbicka starts with local emotion words in such languages as Polish and Russian as well as English. Like other cognitivists, she uses a 'script' approach to specifying the cognitive content of these local terms. This strategy may indicate a certain kind of cultural or linguistic relativism; however, as with all relativisms, there is a universalist side to hers. In order to adequately compare the semantic differences between labels for ostensibly similar emotions in the world's languages – the different range of phenomena they denote – Wierzbicka (1996) uses what she has dubbed a Natural Semantic Metalanguage (NSM). NSM analysis hinges on a small set of basic semantic building blocks – putatively universal ("natural") "semantic primes" (1996), like "feel." Wierzbicka and her colleagues assemble such primes into statements they call "metalinguistic" to construct the cognitive scripts comprising the putative mental models underlying local emotion terms. Although it is linguists who produce such statements, they ostensively reflect the mental maps of others. I return to questions about "feel," and explore the sense in which Wierzbicka's representations are metalinguistic, in Chapter 4.

Reddy's hybrid approach

William Reddy (2001: 128) defines emotions as "goal-relevant activations of thought material that exceed the translating capacity of attention within a short time horizon." Reddy proposes "activation" and "translation" – terms borrowed from cognitive psychology – as concepts that have good-enough definitional clarity, and lack Cartesian taint enough to support a model of emotion credible to both scientists and poststructuralists. Activation is a state that renders thoughts and other inputs available for processing (2001: 89). Full activation enables sustained attention.

What does Reddy mean by translation? Whatever enters our attention – perceptual inputs of various sorts – requires various sorts of translation, for instance from sensory "codes" into linguistic codes. When engaging in emotion talk, we attend closely not only to inner feelings but to others' reactions. Emotion talk translates subjectivities into words. Likewise, we translate the facial responses of those who hear our talk by accessing various cultural codes; note here the implicit claim that facial expressions are cultural codes. Cross-modal or inter-semiotic translation is always complex and only partially successful at best (Reddy 2001: 322). The stakes are high – because emotions are goal-relevant activations – and translation difficult, in part because goals shift. Our ever-shifting goals require constant "navigation." "We navigate emotional life with extraordinarily odd charts, whose contours change … whenever we make a course correction;" navigation, or responding to feelings and talking about them, alters the navigator.

Reddy's borrowings from cognitive psychology come to life in conjunction with his adaptation of "everyday language" philosopher J. L. Austin's concept of *speech acts*. Reddy extends Austin's insights regarding **performative** *utterances* to shed light on statements about emotion (Reddy 2001: 96–111). At least for argument's sake, Austin (1962) distinguished "constatives" – merely descriptive statements – from "performatives." Explicit performatives are first-person, present-tense utterances that name the speech act they perform, as in "I assert that [X]" (Reddy 2001: 97) and in that sense are "self-referential" (2001: 105). They "do things" in the world if they are happily or "felicitously" performed, as when authorized persons say "We do hereby enact ..." (2001: 98). Statements about the speaker's current emotions, on the surface, *seem* descriptive (i.e., constative) but in fact share with performatives structural (first-person, present tense) and functional features (changing some world or universe). To signal their similarity with performatives, Reddy calls these first-person present-tense feeling statements *emotives*. What do they change? Reddy argues that they change the speaker and his or her feelings. Along with other inputs from within and without, the emotives themselves become involved in cognitive-emotional activation and translation. Uttering an emotive may cause an increase in activation of the emotions named; in others the emotive back-fires, causing increased awareness of "translation" and navigation problems, highlighting the never-quite-manageable flow of emotion in relation to social demands. For example, one might thus feel "insincere," even like a hypocrite, immediately after saying "I love you."

Reddy focuses his analytic attention on the French Revolution. He highlights its demands for sincere expressions of generosity toward "the people" and loyalty toward the people's revolution – demands that were coupled, during The Terror (1793–4), with the threat of death for insincere statements of loyalty. In interpreting such situations, in which "emotional regimes" allow more or less "emotional liberty" – including the freedom to be insincere, and particularly to change goals or undergo "conversion experiences" in response to shifting awareness of translation problems – Reddy demonstrates the political implications of his model. His claim, that some regimes cause comparatively more "emotional suffering" than others, is unique in the literature on language and emotion. He defines this suffering as acute goal conflict brought on, for example, by political torture to extract information – conflict between loyalty to compatriots and desire to live. An emotional regime is a "set of normative emotions and the official rituals, practices, and emotives that express and inculcate them" (2001: 129). Although Reddy's representation of (emotional) freedom as the highest good seems to me a more American than universal political and ethical vision, his blending of cognitive, historical, anthropological, and linguistic-philosophical forms of evidence and modes of argumentation is a powerful brew.

Phenomenological approaches to feeling, embodiment, and discourse

Phenomenology in the tradition of Husserl attempts to study consciousness or subjectivity as experience, reaching to describe tacit, prereflective, and preobjective perception. It describes the world as felt and lived by actors. Intentionality from a phenomenological perspective refers to the "directedness" or "aboutness" of human action (Duranti 2008: 492), its orientation rather than rational goals; to the extent that such orientations are readable, they may enable prediction of what someone might be about to do, or how she interprets what she *is* doing. Such acts include speaking and otherwise enacting emotion.

Phenomenological theories of emotion focus on embodied experience. Desjarlais is an anthropologist whose evolving phenomenological arguments have dealt with embodied experience and expressive forms. His 1992 analysis of funeral songs – *tsher glu*, 'songs of pain' – focused on the experience they convey, on "what poetic discourses ... seem to speak about," and "the experiential force of plaintive poetry" (1992: 100). He attends to these and other songs' "style, tone, textual, and overall mood or spirit" (1992: 88).

Since any reference to emotions implies, by definition, something 'felt,' and since any rhetorician must convince her audience that she is, in fact, feeling the pain or anger to which she refers, we need to take into account the play, however hypothetical, between language and feeling (1992: 101).

Desjarlais' 1992 work challenged interpretivist, Geertzian anthropology, rejecting its focus on the *public* meaning of symbolic action the observer could interpret as a kind of text. Yet *embodied* meanings – Desjarlais prefers to speak of embodied aesthetic values (e.g., "balance," "integrity," "control" [1992 :83]) – are discernable, he says, to the phenomenological anthropologist. "It becomes less important to map the semiotic lineage or intellectual heritage of specific imageries than it is to evoke their presence in concrete manifestations" (1992: 89). Despite his expressed skepticism toward Geertzian (1992: 89, 247) semiotics, we can interpret Desjarlais' approach as an implicit call to go beyond the symbolic and referential, a search for a more adequate semiotics of culture and expression.

Desjarlais later (1997) explored a Peircean semiotic approach, combined with a trenchant political analysis, as complementary with a phenomenological agenda, i.e., describing experience. However, his *Shelter Blues* (1997: 24) asserted that the very "idea and assumed nature of 'experience' must be placed in brackets." Desjarlais applied his new "critical phenomenology" (1997: 24) to the Boston shelter for the homeless mentally ill where he conducted post-doctoral fieldwork (sandwiched between earlier and later periods of fieldwork in Nepal). Of particular interest here is his critical phenomenology of emotion talk. Citing Besnier (1990: 428), who observed that "overt avowals [of feelings] in the first person are likely to be associated with rather marked situations,"

Desjarlais scrutinized one such marked situation – therapy (if that is a proper label for the work of the shelter). The shelter staff adopted what I have been calling a **referentialist language ideology** (1997: 180). Their commitment to reforming residents' use of language, pushing them in the direction of "truth, sincerity, and responsibility" (1997: 211), indicates their political power. More generally, Desjarlais asserts that "acts of feeling are, from the start, immersed in rhetorical stances, pragmatic situations, and political relationships"; "acts of reasoning, narration, and feeling are political through and through" (1997: 245, 248). Thus, while Desjarlais continued to signal his theoretical concern with experience, emotion, and embodiment, his phenomenological perspective now situated "human sentience" alongside the political – a perspective fully consistent with my argument in this book.

Language, emotion, and the political economy

I start this section with an example that will appear, at first, to be unrelated to the political economy or ideology. In the United States today, neither parents, teachers, nor "assertiveness trainers" typically consider themselves ideologues. But the American assertiveness movement, and its embrace of "I-language," and psychological investigators' corresponding interest in "locus of control," is strongly ideological, and significant for comparative cultural analysis. Assertiveness courses resocialize adult students by teaching them a new communicative style. Learners come to accept constructions like "*I feel* hurt [or angry, etc.] when you do that" as models of assertiveness. The training requires at least two features – the explicit referentiality modeled in that construction (in contrast with a scream, *No!* that does not refer to, but performs feeling) – and its agent-like first-person singular subject. (In Bangla emotion talk, by contrast, the experiencer *cannot be* the grammatical subject, in the nominative case, and is often unexpressed, as discussed in Chapter 4). The training thus reproduces the **referentialist ideology**.

Some American elementary schools equip 'peer mediators' or counselors with skills in conflict-resolution and violence-avoidance. They teach children, when they or their untrained peers feel hurt or angry, to "use their words" (not their fists). Encouraging children or adults to "use" I-language ideologically construes the self as the proper locus of control over "privately owned" words and affects.

Rotter (1966) proposed that individuals vary in their ascription of responsibility for the occurrence of "reinforcement," some ascribing that responsibility internally to themselves, while others locate it externally, to powerful others or some forces beyond their control. Extending Rotter's work, scholars began to ask whether locus of control varied across "cultures," and – not surprisingly – much of that more recent literature is in the field of business (e.g., Thorne and Saunders 2002). From the viewpoint of anthropology such studies are problematic. They tend to equate "culture" and "nation" ("national cultures," e.g., Hayton, George, and Zahra 2002) and treat cultures as things rather than as signs and metasigns that social actors deploy strategically across various contexts, thereby constituting and reconstituting culture in an always-reflexive process (Kroskrity 1993, Agha 2007). Still, the locus of control notion might be heuristic in exploring variability in socialization and thus the production of various ways of being a person in society. The cross-cultural locus of control literature alerts us to the possibility that postindustrial Western societies produce persons defined by ambition, assertiveness, and internal locus of control.

Exhortations to speak in such a way as to "own your feelings" reflect and enact an ideology of self, feelings, and language that is quite at home in capitalist social formations. Such an ideology reflects, more or less accurately, relations of production involving private ownership. The metalanguage of "ownership" assertiveness trainers use – the notion that using I-language represents a proper "owning of one's feelings" – betrays the fact that adopting such a communicative style is required if one is to properly perform a specifically capitalist self.

Previous work has not examined affect as a factor mediating language and political economy (Gal 1989). Gal does note that the sort of sanctions that social networks may use to control speakers are both "material and emotional" (1989: 354). Judith Irvine (1989) at least implicitly situates affectivity in a more directly mediating position between language and power. Central to her model of the relationship between language and political economy is the ethnographic case of Wolof, to which I devote more space in a later chapter. There are two important points of relevance here. First, the fundamental Wolof social division sets "nobles" against low status "griots" whose traditional role involves very intense "emotion work" (Hochschild 1979) on behalf of nobles (performing *their* emotions). It is the very thing griots do (or traditionally did) in order to live, and to please their employers – viz., "perform emotion" (Grima 1992) – that signals and reproduces their subordinate status. But secondly, and even more importantly for my argument that any theory of language and affect must consider affect that targets linguistic forms, Irvine speculates that all Wolofs must feel something about performing the griot register. Nobles must speak like griots if they find themselves needing to praise or thank someone. For a noble in that situation, "Whether or not you 'really feel' the particular emotion you display, your subjective experience presumably includes knowing that you sound like a griot (about whose emotionality you have certain beliefs)" (Irvine 1990: 156). Thus, the political economy may be organized to *reflect* an invidious distribution of emotion-performing roles (Lutz 1990), and also be grounds for a conventionalized set of feelings *toward* speech registers or styles.

Developing a full-blown materialist or Marxist approach to language and emotion, centrally concerned with the political economies in which language and emotion participate, would require renewed interest in the affective under-pinnings of community. For Marx the "feeling of community" was essential for effective action in relation to the interests of a class (Roseberry 1997: 42). Kenneth Burke (1969) developed a theory of **identification** not merely as a psychological process, but as the fundamental *social* process. For Burke, invoking identification neither ended discussions of social structure nor represented a eufunctionalist invocation of social harmony. Rhetoric – Burke's primary field of investigation – is defined by the tensions and fissures criss-crossing communities; "identification is affirmed with earnestness precisely because there is division. Identification is compensatory to division" (1969: 22).

Burke's early work focused on how capitalist rhetoric manipulates identification through propagandistic misrepresentations of corporate business and our relationship to it. Burke later came to distinguish rhetoric from persuasion, "foregrounding the possibility of the unconscious, the dreamlike, the nonspecific yearning in speaking **subjects** seeking to compensate for 'real differences or divisions' that, in turn, prompt further identifications" (Burke 1967: 62–63, as cited by Jordan 2005: 269). Hence, identification is for Burke a process deeply implicated in social inequality, and vice versa.

I seek to ground my model of language as emotional object in a theory of the political economy whose workings are in part feeling based. I explore this topic more fully in Chapter 7.

4

THE PANHUMAN AND THE PARTICULAR

Introduction

In languages around the world, the relation of emotion to linguistic structure and practice varies in meaningful ways. This fact becomes a first-order index. As I have been arguing, first-order indexes – apparent social facts – come to us already reflected on through second-order indexes, **language ideologies**. And these ideologies are never innocent of power.

This chapter treats several heatedly debated topics relevant to our study. The first is: what does affirming that language and other semiotic capacities *evolved* with our species imply in relation to the expression of emotion? The second topic – that of the universality of particular emotions – is closely related. Discussion of this is often linked to the issue of the universality of metaphors (Kövecses 2000) by which we "gloss emotions" (Crapanzano 1992). Such discussions echo older arguments about linguistic relativity. Although typically figured in terms of "thought," linguistic relativity has important implications for language and emotion. Here I explore Friedrich's (1986) notion of "the master trope." Metaphors represent only a small portion of the range of tropes. Friedrich argues that there arises in every speech community (universally) a tendency to naturalize a (very particular) connection between the aesthetics of the sounds the society produces (especially in ritual moments), and the shared "mythic content" figured in its rituals. This naturalized model he calls the master trope because it influences lesser tropes speakers use. Friedrich (1986) thus offers a feeling-based or aesthetic form of linguistic relativity.

The third and fourth debates are closely related to each other. The third is whether or not the emotions form a natural class, kind, or category as Ekman, Kövecses, and Jonathan Turner (2000) assert. Philosophers disagree over whether the notion of a "natural class" has validity beyond the merely intuitive (Van Brakel 1992, 1993). **Bangla** grammar provides an illustration of how problematic is the assumption that emotions represents the natural class of the things human beings universally feel. Emotion nouns in a particular syntactic slot in Bangla sentences fall into a Whorfian (1956a) "covert category" that we might label 'things that can touch, contact, or *strike* people' (see Ali et al. 1994: 202); thus 'emotions' (keeping in mind the label is ours) take their place alongside snakes, crowds, tight clothing, and coughs and colds (other common noun-types in that slot).

The same Bangla example has particular relevance to the fourth debate, which is over the nature of the self. This is a question that has long attracted religious and philosophical attention; the function of language vis-à-vis subjectivity, and the degree to which emotion is attached to the self, has also been of great interest in anthropology. This chapter closes with a review of cross-linguistic variation in the extent to which emotion is related to the self and – to the extent that it is – how that relationship is grammaticalized.

Implications of the co-evolution of Homo sapiens, language, and music

At least since the time of Darwin various investigations have tested his understanding that the title of his book *The Expression of Emotion in Man and Animals* (1998 [1872]) suggests a matter of semiotic forms and functions with strong similarities across species. Darwin described the "use of the voice" by all mammals – i.e., varying pitch, loudness, and voice quality (i.e., "resonance and timbre") – as a crucial communicative resource among conspecifics. We can add 'patternment,' or structure of voiced elements, to Darwin's list, as with capuchin alarm calls, whose intensity varies with the urgency of the threat. We find examples of such iconicities in human vocal productions, linguistic (yelling angry words) or non-linguistic (a long, loud scream) – the more the words or the louder the scream, the greater the affect signaled. Little is gained by making an overly sharp distinction between linguistic and nonlinguistic uses of the voice, or between 'language' and 'gesture.' Indeed we can speak of verbal gestures (Merleau-Ponty 1964: 89).

For the most part, those who approach language and emotion from an evolutionary perspective, and those who study them ethnographically, talk not with but past each other. Jonathan Turner's *On the Origins of Human Emotions* (2000), or Lieberman's most recent (2007) statement on the evolution of language, for example, make little attempt to interface with ethnographic evidence. Conversely, contributors to Lutz and Abu-Lughod (1990) – ethnographers – do not engage evolutionary theory. The former works stress innate human universals, the latter sociocultural variation; more precisely, the former explore biological substrates, while the latter uncovers connections among semiotic processes, intersubjectivity, and culture.

Such dueling monologues invite challenge and reconsideration. Note, first, that studies of the evolution of language (e.g., Lieberman 2007) concern themselves with emotional expression, not just language's semanticoreferential capacity (particularly as envisioned in relation to the truth conditions of utterances). Certain contributors to that field, such as Tomasello (e.g., 2003), are in dialogue with linguistic anthropologists.

Ethnomusicologist Elizabeth Tolbert (2001a) demonstrates the potential to supersede dualities like expression vs. denotation, or language vs. pure expressivity, offering a model of the evolution of emotion, language, and music that draws on theoretical rubrics familiar to linguistic and sociocultural anthropologists. 'Music' around the world encompasses movement, dance. Tolbert argues that the capacity for music and language has arisen, jointly, out of the capacity for **mimesis**. Thus, music is also related to mirror neurons, which, in primates from monkeys to humans, link the observation of others' movements to one's own movements (i.e., the neurons fire during observation and imitation). In Tolbert's model of hominin evolution, embodied expressions were once involuntary, and hence purely indexical of inner states; but at some point in hominid evolution these were freed up to be *either* indexical *or* symbolic, involuntary or voluntary-and-thus-manipulable. What had previously been an unchallengeable truth-value – the indexing of emotion – became referential and challengeable. However, musical and linguistic mimesis has never lost its connection to "intercorporeal iconicity" or mimesis, which always involves some "corporeal [or 'tactilekinesthetic'] invariants" such as upright posture, gait, and binocular vision (Tolbert 2001b: 88). Granted, at some point as *Homo sapiens* was emerging, a quantum leap into the realm of the symbolic, in which signs represent by arbitrary convention, occurred. Yet, where some argue this entailed largely abandoning the indexical and iconic (sign relations built, respectively – as Tolbert says – on contiguity and similarity), language has never abandoned these roots.

Discussions of human evolution, if they mention music at all, have tended to link it with the feminine, the bodily, the animal, the irrational, and the affective; they construe language, by contrast, as rational, abstract, and relatively cut off from emotion. For this to make sense requires viewing the function of language as **reference**-and-predication, period. However, such a view has little to do with language as it lives and breathes, in talk-in-interaction, which always has a melody to it, or even with writing, an act always embodied and often passionate (Besnier 1992, 1995).

Selective pressure at work on our ancestors apparently created prosody, a key linguistic site of affect, on the basis of "innate primate calls" (Tolbert 2001b: 90). But these calls were also the foundation for the evolution of human musicality. As Tolbert points out, evidence for this commonality lies in the partial overlap in the neural processing of speech prosody and melodic pitch contours (2001b: 90). If indeed music and language originated in the mimetic capacity common to primates, phonatory quality (including speech timbre) and intensity, as well as intonation contours – all central to affectivity – must have been the focus of imitation.

Language, emotion, and linguistic relativity

Many anthropologists argue that our interaction with the world is "semiotically mediated" (Mertz and Parmentier 1985), i.e., that our use of sign systems (particularly language) shapes not only our perception of, but the style of our engagement with, the world – especially the social world. Early versions of such arguments come from Herder and Humboldt, but famously from Franz Boas (often regarded as the founder of American anthropology), his student Edward Sapir, and Sapir's student Benjamin Lee Whorf (1956b). More recent versions of the argument are less likely to naively compare 'English' with 'Hopi,' for example – in part because we now recognize the tremendous diversity within 'languages'[1] – than to ask about the effects of signs used in various contexts (see the discussion of Kiksht [also known as Wasco-Wishram] in Chapter 8).

We encounter far more *folk Whorfianism*, popular evocations of a kind of linguistic determinism (a distortion of Whorf's writings), than we do serious Whorf-inspired attempts to interpret linguistic features related to emotion. We thus hear claims that this or that language 'has a word for x' – e.g., for a certain feeling putatively *unique* to that speech community – while another lacks such a word. As Silverstein observes of folk views of language in general, these discourses on the referential 'capacities' of various languages, in focusing on *lexis*, take "linguistic structure as a 'background' phenomenon and [focus] on how well a particular language's lexical expressions correspond to the 'reality' they denote" (2000: 94). Leaving such notions behind, let us consider serious contributions to debates over relativism, starting with anti-relativist arguments.

Metaphor

We first encountered Kövecses's metaphor-centric approach, and Wierzbicka's Natural Semantic Metalanguage (a modified universalism), in previous chapters. In what follows, I consider the claims that metaphor theory offers the best interpretation of emotion in language, expanding on my criticisms of this approach.

George Lakoff has been a dominant force in cognitive linguistics. His sometime collaborator, Zoltán Kövecses (Lakoff and Kövecses 1987) has long argued that emotion metaphors around the world are amazingly consistent, and that this consistency points to universals of embodied experience, driven by our purportedly invariant physiology. Metaphors are iconic signs, semiotic relations built on similarity. But cognitive linguists' approach to language largely overlooks the complex interactions of iconicity and indexicality in emergent, entextualized discourse. The approach has, at best, a positivist view of "cultures" and their "contents" (Kövecses 2000: 168). It neglects the layering of reflexive signs that so pervade social life. The popularity of the metaphor approach, however, warrants attention.

Kövecses claims that people around the world speak of emotions as though their bodies were CONTAINERS,[2] enclosed spaces for feelings. Anger is commonly depicted as a boiling up that threatens to explode the container. Another "master metaphor" is EMOTION IS FORCE (Kövecses 2000: 71–72,

83–85). It is difficult to assess Kövecses' universalist claims based on his examples from languages around the world, in part because they do not seem to derive from naturally occurring discourse. Levy, whose respected work on Tahitian emotion Kövecses cites, reports that Tavana, Chief of Piri, told him, "The Tahitians say that an angry man is like a bottle. When he gets filled up he will begin to spill over" (Levy 1973: 285). This leaves linguistic anthropologists with at least two important questions: First, is this a paraphrase? Paraphrasing Others' talk may be acceptable to many sociocultural anthropologists, but prevents us from analyzing the linguistic forms people actually use. In any case, even if Tavana's English words represent a close translation, we lack the original language. The second question the Levy passage raises is whether Tavana's words might reflect a widely shared ideology of emotion. How do his words relate to common, everyday, discursive practices, including use of metaphor?

The container metaphor might *not* be universal. Balinese consider themselves capable of truly forgetting (not 'repressing') harmful feelings that might hinder them in their efforts to maintain a "bright face" (Wikan 1989). As we shall see below, Michelle Rosaldo cites evidence that "bridewealth" societies generate metaphors indicating that emotion held inside is dangerous, but the metaphor might not make sense to people in face-to-face, foraging, "brideservice" societies (1984: 150).

What of the arguments that linguistic diversity correlates with real diversity of experience, in emotion and other domains?

Aesthetics and linguistic relativity

From Aristotle to Croce and Sapir, Western aesthetic theories have been a major influence on theories of language. For Aristotle, to conceive of "poetics"[3] in aesthetic terms involved emotion; aesthetics and emotion were intertwined. Twentieth-century Italian philosopher Benedetto Croce (1992 [1902]), by contrast, distrusted an aesthetics linked with affect. As one influenced by Croce, Sapir is positioned in a long line of Western scholars who distrust passions altogether, decoupling emotions from his theory of aesthetics. The closest Sapir comes to acknowledging a link between aesthetics and feeling is in discussing the particular form of practical consciousness the linguistically untrained native speaker of a language has of rules she cannot state: "This knowledge is not capable of conscious manipulation in terms of word symbols. It is, rather, a very delicately nuanced *feeling of subtle relations* …" (1949a[1927]: 123). This sort of feeling plays a role in modern human language, but emotion for Sapir is primarily an anti-modern signifier. It gave rise to a primitive protolanguage good for releasing tension (Sapir 1949b[1934]: 565). Once language evolved emotion took a back seat to cognition. Moreover, emotion is a private rather than a fully social matter (as he conceived language to be, at least in early writings [Sapir 1921: 39]).

Yet any theory of aesthetics, Sapir's included, must deal with feelings and sensibilities. For Sapir, anyone with linguistic competence experiences linguistic patternment aesthetically; a notion of aesthetics allows Sapir to capture speakers' relatively unconscious judgments about the rightness of certain linguistic forms. As a representative of American **structuralism** (Murray 1983), Sapir describes the "single sound" or phoneme as but "a point in a pattern, precisely as a tone in a given musical tradition is a point in a pattern which includes the whole range of aesthetically possible tones" (1949a [1927]: 554). It is not that I cannot hear the sounds of a language foreign to me, or those produced by speakers of some foreign-sounding form of my own language; but to *make* them offends my aesthetic sense of the proper patternment of sound(s). As an untrained language user, one is "impelled by strict loyalty to forms of behavior that one can feel with the utmost nicety and can state only in the vaguest and most approximate fashion" (1949a [1927]: 261).

Friedrich's version of linguistic relativity builds on Sapir's aesthetic model of language and sound. What makes translation, particularly of a sacred text-in-performance, difficult is not the particular tropes in any given utterance, but the "master trope," in which the very musicality of a sacred utterance expresses its mythic content. "To create felt consubstantiality between language music and myth *is* the master trope of poetry – 'master' because it is superordinate to and in control over such lesser figures as image, metaphor and paradox" (1986: 39). For Friedrich, what makes particular languages potent, allowing them to conjure up a particular world, is not that language's particular set of obligatory grammatical categories as "cold" structures, but – taking each language as a graveyard of dead metaphors (and a maternity ward for new ones) – the fact that these may at any moment come to life again and "shape the imagination" (1986: 43). The unique feel of a Sanskritic verse chanted by a Brahmin, or even the mere repetition of the sacred syllable *Om*; or the wonder of the Qur'an, recited in its untranslatable Arabic original: in both of these a local instance of the master trope is at work. The reason the Qur'an cannot be 'translated' (what we might call translations are referred to as interpretations in other languages) is that the sound of the Arabic text itself contains the resonances of the divine message. The devout *feel* this – even if they do not understand Arabic. It would be more accurate to say they cannot parse the denotative-referential meaning of the Arabic verses; what they *do* understand, viscerally, is the sacredness of the text, its numinous quality. Again, that feeling attaches to the sound. Friedrich's vision of tropes sharply differs from that of the cognitive linguists. "All tropes … interact constantly with social situation, cultural values … and so forth" (Friedrich 1991: 23–24).

Semantic categories and emotion: are emotions natural kinds?

The term 'basic emotions' in the cross-cultural literature (Ekman 1992b) is modeled on 'basic colors' – a focus of research for another set of scholars arguing for innate universals, against cultural relativism. The concept is closely linked with the philosophers' notion of 'natural kinds.' A natural kind is a category that exists in nature, and is indifferent to what it is called (Hacking 1999: 105). What Hacking calls "interactive kinds" *do* "interact with their classifications." For example, "Classification as schizophrenic affects the sensibilities of those classified in many ways. One of the reasons for the changing symptom profile of schizophrenia is, I suspect, that it is a ... target" that moves as people's way of describing their symptoms changes over time (1999: 113). Which kind are emotion terms?

Van Brakel argues that "all proposed criteria fail to identify what 'intuitively' are considered natural kinds" (1993: 39, n. 75), which throws the question about emotion or emotions up in the air. Van Brakel states the relativist position clearly: "emotions disclose forms of life, both in a manifest and a deep sense" (1993: 48). Thus he invokes Wittgenstein's famous dictum that "to imagine a language is to imagine a form of life" – *Lebensform* in German (van Brakel 1993: 41, n. 79) – which, in regard to humans, is commonly called 'a culture.'

Two weaknesses beset relativist approaches to emotion in anthropology. The first is their failure to offer an experience-near description of emotion itself. Abu-Lughod and Lutz, for example, have proposed removing emotion from the realm of psychobiology in order to "argue for a view of emotion as [social-] discursive practice," (1990: 10). Although this book concerns emotion's relation to discourse, I do not *equate* the two. Desjarlais disputed Foucault-influenced representations of emotions *as* discourse (including Lutz and Abu-Lughod's), presenting ethnographic evidence of the way the *Yolmo wa* of Nepal spoke of emotion – as bodily experience (Desjarlais 1992).

Similarly, Wikan rejected Geertz's famous claim that the Balinese only appeared to have emotions – other than "stage fright" (Geertz 1973a) – and should be described as having an aesthetic rather than an emotional style of being-in-the-world. Wikan ironically borrowed Geertz's own term (1984: 124) for the sort of ethnographic description he himself advocated – "experience-near" – in order to assert the urgent reality of emotion for Balinese people. People feel because their actions have stakes. Wikan's experience-near description of emotional experience in Bali, concerned as it is with sorcery, centered on people's fears that others would see their emotions, making them vulnerable to others, even to sorcery attacks. This leads Balinese, Wikan argued, to "manage the heart to brighten the face" and thus maintain an outward appearance of strength, whatever they might be feeling. This is not simply a "suppression" strategy, however; Balinese say that feelings are actually transformed through this management.[4]

The second weakness of relativist depictions of emotion is that they provide little ground for a comparison, for example, of what Reddy (2001) calls "emotional regimes," discussed in Chapter 3. The utility of Reddy's model – which transcends false dichotomies such as nature vs. nurture, body vs. mind, psyche vs. culture, and power vs. felt experience – motivates marshaling evidence needed to compare emotional regimes. More on that below.

A universal Natural Semantic Metalanguage?

In Chapter 3, I touched briefly on Wierzbicka's Natural Semantic Metalanguage (NSM), her attempt at script-centered, formalist, cognitive-semantic representations of local emotion terms. NSM representations rely on the "semantic primes" or "primitives" that Wierzbicka identifies as cross-cultural universals, like 'feel,' 'good,' 'something,' or 'want.' Asserting the existence of these primes and their utility in representing cognitive scripts underlying local emotion terms is one approach to balancing particularist and universalist perspectives. Wierzbicka's group occupies a tense sort of middle ground in relation to universalist claims. They claim to reject using English emotion terms to represent ostensibly universal emotions, while insisting that, by uncovering certain cross-linguistic universals (both the "primes" and rules for their co-occurrence), they have uncovered universal concepts. Emotional experiences may or may not be universal; Wierzbicka's colleagues take no final position on that argument. They do, however, challenge the attitude prevalent in psychology – that issues of language (differing ways of structuring the semantic domain of 'emotion') are dismissible as unimportant, on a priori grounds, vis-à-vis emotion 'itself.' They advocate case studies in the lexical semantics of emotion labels.

The English emotion label, "pleased," is analyzed by the following NSM script:

Pleased (X was pleased)

(a) X felt something because X thought something
(b) sometimes a person thinks:
(c) "something good happened
(d) I wanted this to happen"
(e) when this person thinks this, this person feels something good
(f) X felt something like this
(g) because X thought something like this (Wierzbicka and Harkins 2001: 15).

In what sense are such representations "metalanguage," as claimed? For the most part, linguistic anthropologists concern themselves with metalinguistic forms that occur naturally in human discourse – everyday reflections on language, using language. An NSM script is metalinguistic in a different sense, and Wierzbicka's notion of 'naturalness' also differs from that in the phrase 'naturally occurring human discourse.' Her metalanguage reflects upon (i.e., is 'meta-' in relation to) all natural human languages, and to the lexical dimension of their semantic systems concerned with the category 'emotions.' Wierzbicka uses NSM as though it were a (meta)language of a totally different sort than its "object languages" (all of the thousands of human languages); in this respect it is like sentence diagrams that abstractly represent syntactic structure. NSM representations of particular emotion labels are putatively 'natural' because they putatively reflect "lexical universals" (Wierzbicka 1996). The idea that NSM is of a different sort than natural languages, while simultaneously being natural, is paradoxical at best.

Durst's (2001) chapter in Harkins and Wierzbicka compares three German words (or two other nodes in a cognitive-lexicosemantic structure) that are related to English *anger*, either semantically or (in the case of *Ärger*) as a cognate. I appreciate Durst's concern for cultural-historical factors in the particular semantics and metaphors of emotion labels. At their origin, these three German "anger"-like words reflected a humoral theory of the body. Durst's NSM analysis of *Ärger* follows:

Ärger/ X ärgert sich (über Y)

(a) X feels something bad
(b) sometimes a person thinks
(c) "something bad is happening (Y)
(d) I don't want this to be happening"
(e) this person thinks about this for some time
(f) when this person thinks about this, this person feels something bad because of this
(g) X feels something like this
(h) because X thinks something like this

Durst highlights similarities and differences between *Ärger*, *Wut*, and *Zorn*. All three share the sense of "something bad happening" which the experiencer "doesn't want." "The stem *Wut-/wüt-* is related more closely to spontaneous and immediate action than the stem *Zorn-/zürn-*, which rather focuses on a ... state including the ... experiencer's ... attitude towards something, so that an action which is done out of *Zorn* seems to be more deliberate rather than uncontrolled" (Durst 2001: 136). Thus, in Luther's German Bible, God experiences *Zorn*, not *Wut*. Historically, a distinguishing feature of *Ärger* is its long simmering nature. In contemporary German, however, it has come to serve as the *inclusive* anger-like word, of which *Wut* and *Zorn* are subtypes or hyponyms. Wishing someone harm is part of the 'script' of *Wut* and *Zorn*, but not *Ärger*.

Despite my appreciation for some aspects of the cognitivist program – especially contributions like Durst's – several features are problematic, as I have already noted. Contributors to Harkins and Wierzbicka (2001) present their NSM scripts as universally accessible, not dependent on English, and in fact "language independent" (Wierzbicka 1996: 22). The logic behind this claim is that, although particular emotion terms are not universal, other English terms can be recruited to stand as "semantic primes" (Wierzbicka 1996), and in that capacity transcend their Englishness. Having collected evidence that certain concepts are lexicalized, or otherwise expressible, in every language – from 'something' to 'think' and 'feel' – and that certain universals also obtain in the "grammar" of their co-occurrence, Wierzbicka concludes that these universals can be accurately represented using English words, expressions, and grammar. I question, however, whether the NSM actually *is* an analytic (as opposed to an everyday) metalanguage, whether the NSM differs enough from "English," for example, to count as the *sort* of metalanguage Wierzbicka thinks it is (a formal language such as the language of logic or mathematics).

The model of cognition Wierzbicka's group appears to hold is also problematic. Cognitive linguists see 'cognition' as strictly individual mentation, rather than as an activity or process that is distributed across interlocutors, objects, and cultural tools like (for example) the Munsell Color Chart (C. Goodwin 1994: 609).[5] Cognition is viewed as separate from bodies and embodied action; bodies in this model passively experience affects that are generated elsewhere. Wierzbicka's group links emotions with scripted thoughts or cognitive schemata; it is those schemata (as well as the feelings they generate) to which emotion terms refer. But surely there is at least a residue of feeling that defies schematization. As Massumi and Damasio point out, a residue of affect slips past the loop we call 'cognition;' "emotional contagion" (Hatfield, Cacioppo, and Rapson (1994) is an example. Lyon (2003) documents how, in face-to-face interaction, interlocutors fall into respiratory co-rhythms. Breathing together is associated with feeling (something) together (see Chapter 1), and involves the same mechanisms used in speaking.

For Wierzbicka and her collaborators words 'label' emotions, and such labels have an exclusively *referential* function. In fact, this referentialist bias appears to be built in to the notion of labeling. What we call 'labels' appear to presuppose the reality-in-the-world of their semiotic objects. Wierzbicka's concern in the work reviewed here (not elsewhere in her oeuvre) is with semantics, to the neglect of pragmatics. Words are labels; labels only refer; emotion talk, from such a perspective, must be primarily "about something". Any consideration of what such talk does is deferred.[6] Anthropologists will find little of interest in any approach to language that focuses exclusively on decontextualized words and ignores the dynamic interaction of speech, body, and environment. We find value in examining emerging patterns of discourse-in-context, and take it as axiomatic that emotion (for example) is constituted in such relations, rather than isolated words (Rosenberg 1990).

Wierzbicka and Harkins assert "the availability of a universal *tertium comparationis*, provided by universal concepts" (2001: 9), i.e., semantic primes deployed in NSM scripts. In addition to questioning whether the NSM is really *not* just English, we must ask about the meaning of "availability." Actually, the authors clearly mean "available to analysts" involved in comparing data from many languages; but permit me to take the word in another sense. Phenomenologists and cognitive neuroscientists speak of "cognitive availability" (i.e., transparency to awareness), and in such usage the notion of "availability" is democratic; "availability" goes far beyond analysts. Although Wierzbicka and Harkins meant that the primes that are the building blocks of the NSM are available to them as analysts, their case actually rests on those terms being *universally* "available" to human experience. In that context, we must ask whether the data analyzed in their edited collection can demonstrate that the scripts are more than analysts' playthings. To do so, wouldn't the data need to reflect naturally occurring everyday speech? And doesn't that question in turn lead us to ask *whose* everyday speech, since in any given speech community, we presume that relatively more or less emotional talk is unequally distributed (who has the right to speak angrily? who is stereotyped as speaking emotionally?)? And if our concern is with local cognitive habits and linguistic forms that might point us to those habits, wouldn't "fashions of speaking" be a 'natural' place to look for them (Whorf 1956b)?[7]

Let us look at one putative 'prime' in particular. Is 'to feel' [an emotion] truly universal? In order to argue that it is, Wierzbicka must to some extent do what she criticizes psychologists for doing – deny the importance of language (in this case, culturally, and socially, variable fashions of speaking that frame something like we call feeling in very different ways). **Bangla**, for example, may 'have' a verb phrase corresponding to "feel" (*anubhab kar-*, 'to do feeling'); such a VP (verb phrase) is 'available.' However, by far the most common way **Bengalis** speak of feelings involves a completely different structure and lexicon than Wierzbicka paints as "natural." Rather than making emotion a sort of direct object of a verb like *feel*, Bangla makes "feelings," rather than experiencers, the grammatical subjects of impersonal constructions, using the verb *lāg-*, 'strike.' In this construction, experiencers (if encoded at all), take what South Asian linguists call a dative case (see the large literature on "dative subject" constructions in South Asian languages, e.g., Klaiman 1980, Pappuswamy 2005). Is the sentence 'Terror strikes me' (in which the 'me' need not even be expressed) really the *equivalent* of 'I feel terror/ terrified'? Doesn't a claim of equivalence render the crosslinguistic differences in grammatical framing of such things insignificant? To treat Bangla and English framings as insignificant undermines Wierzbicka's relativism and restricts "semantics" to words.

Emotion, language, and the self

In anthropology, relativists such as Michelle Rosaldo have argued that subjectivity is culturally shaped in relation to polities, and that different polities or cultural milieux give rise to different expectations for the self, emotion, their relations, and their relation to speech. Many in the contemporary West share a model of emotion with "more complex, tribal – in my terms, 'bridewealth'

– groups," as Rosaldo claimed. That is, they (or we, depending on your perspective) share part of "the notion … that 'anger' can and should be publicly revealed (in words) and, correspondingly, that 'anger' held within may work to other people's harm in hidden, witchlike ways" (Rosaldo 1984: 150). Western individuals may be concerned, as Freud was, about lasting harm caused by 'repressed' emotion; the primary concern, however, is with harm to the self that is 'storing' it up, not necessarily to other individuals or to the polity. Thus, what Bertha Pappenheim dubbed the "**talking cure**" (Showalter 1985) aimed to relieve modern individuals of their inner emotional burdens.

Such an understanding of the importance of emotional release may originate in Aristotle's *Poetics*, in which he imagines performances of tragedy exercising a purifying effect on the audience – in Greek, *katharsis* (catharsis). Scheff (1979) links Aristotle's reflections on drama with psychotherapeutic theories of "emotion work." The historiography of more recent Western cultural theories of emotional imagery, and the meta-image of therapeutic re-experience or expression, must acknowledge Shakespeare. Whereas some regard him as a source of insight into "universal" human nature and emotions, his work more likely resonates with us because he reproduced or re-presented fundamental Western cultural themes. Consider these lines from Macbeth, in which Macduff is finally told the truth about the murder of his wife and children. Malcolm, standing by, says

> Merciful heaven! –
> What, man! ne'er pull your hat upon your brows;
> *Give sorrow words*: the grief that does not speak
> Whispers the o'er -fraught heart, and bids it break.
>   (1938b: 879, emphasis added)

Shakespeare's poems and dramatic characters counsel verbal disclosure – giving sorrow words, a phrase frequently echoed in various forms today (e.g., "Putting stress into words," Pennebaker 1993). It is precisely because Aristotle and Shakespeare located emotions in the individual **subject** that they 'knew' these feelings 'need' expressing.

Shakespeare inherited and passed on a cultural image of cathartic disclosure of images and feelings too awful to bear within. Images of interiority (one's insides as the seat of feeling); of hearts that can break unless relieved of emotion-stuff; of emotions-as-fluids, over-filling and overflowing hearts; and of narrative as catharsis or therapy, come down to us as powerful cultural affirmations. As much as these metasentiments stir us, we must recognize that they are not universal. That is made clear by contrasting them with metasentiments from other traditions.

Some Pacific island peoples, for example, doubt any direct connection between any concept of an interior, private self, and language – although globalizing religious transformations may undermine that traditional skepticism.

Writing of the recently Christianized Urapmin of Papua New Guinea, for example, Robbins explains:

While they recognize that, as modern, Christian subjects they are supposed to speak truthfully at all times by accurately and openly representing their inner states in speech, their traditional linguistic ideology does not constitute them as subjects capable of performing in this way. Try as they might, they find it hard to believe that language will ever be able to express adequately what it is people think, feel, or desire (2001: 906).

Explicit metapragmatic norms in such societies – i.e., normative ideas about what speech does or should do – strongly discourage speaking about others' internal states; such talk is not only speculation but morally offensive (B. Schieffelin 2007).

Reporting from Tuvalu (Nukulaelae atoll), Besnier writes of a similar preference for self-reporting and avoidance of others' inner states. Moreover, "when thoughts are self-reported, they are constructed like reported speech" (1992: 166), as though only when experiencers speak of inner states do those states become legitimate topics. One limit on reporting affect, at least when such reports might depend on a conscious analysis of affective features in others' speech, is that such speech features are not always transparent to speakers' consciousness. In everyday talk on the atoll, "the more affectively charged features are also the least transparent" (1992: 178), and here Besnier refers to features that are nonreferential, including prosody and the "rhetorical style of the quote" (indirect vs. direct). In Nukulaelae quoted speech, therefore, affective signals are distributed over a whole utterance. Citing Silverstein on the limits of awareness of pragmatic function (2001 [1981]), Besnier indicates that certain uses of quotation allow speakers to deny their role in manipulating the affect of the reported speech. It is the distribution of pragmatic markers across larger units – in contrast with packing those signs into a single word – that places them beyond the limits of metapragmatic awareness. Affect, in this Nukulaelae case, is *not* associated with the ("reporting") speaker.

Comparing how 'emotives' in different languages frame experience and **agency** is somewhat simpler. English 'to feel' constructions seem to portray experiencers as agents, and what is 'felt' as a real object, 'out there,' whether 'feel' means 'touch' or 'experience' (setting aside contexts in which 'feel' means 'believe'). By contrast, Bangla and other North Indian languages frame what we call feelings as things acting on somewhat passive experiencer-subjects. Japanese emotives work like those in Bangla. Japanese grammar does not require that speakers specify who is experiencing a particular feeling.

At least in Clancy's (1999) study of the socialization of emotion and language, Japanese mothers and children commonly left experiencers unmentioned. Encoding whether an emotion is linked to experiencers or stimuli is optional. Although context may make the identity of relevant experiencers and emotion-stimuli clear, the flexibility of Japanese grammar in regards to the encoding of emotion is a resource used in the socialization of affect and social values related to affect.

Thus *kowai* ["be scary, be afraid (of)"] can mean "Experiencer is afraid (of Stimulus)" and/or "Stimulus is scary (to Experiencer)." ... [T]ypically first and second person experiencers are left implicit. ... The expression of affect using predicates without explicit mention of experiencers is a pervasive feature of early affect talk in Japanese; this lack of differentiation among potential experiencers of affect – the child, the caregiver, people in general – *may be important in socializing language learners into a community of shared affect in which people can be assumed to have similar feelings...* (Clancy 1999: 1418; emphasis added).

Particularly because context may strongly suggest what grammar leaves unspecified, any argument about the cultural significance of 'ambiguous' affect statements must be qualified. Nonetheless, Japanese and Bangla discursive practices raise important questions about purportedly universal schemas associated with purported semantic 'primes.' The cognitivist claim that concepts like 'feel' are universal runs into the same problems common to most universalist arguments about language, emotion, cognition, or culture – the model has difficulty accounting for crosslinguistic variation, e.g., in the grammatical framing of experience.

Different languages, different feelings? The question of salience

Beyond the diverse grammatical framings of emotion, discursive practices surrounding emotion differ in various speech communities. Language socialization routines are an important example; they reflect diverse ideologies, and help form emerging subjectivities, as children develop into social actors whose competence extends to the realms of experience and expression. If Levy (1973) is right that various emotions that may indeed be universal are nonetheless "hypocognized" or "hypercognized" in various communities, we would still need to ask about discursive practices that accomplish such backgrounding and foregrounding.

Clancy sheds light not only on the Japanese "affect lexicon," but the pragmatic effects of deploying such labels. *Kowai,* 'be scary, be afraid (of),' which was mentioned above, is "the most frequent affect word denoting a particular emotion in [Clancy's language socialization] data" (1999: 1399). But it is not only the high frequency of *kowai*, but mothers' particular use of it in dialogues with their young children – along with *okashii*, 'strange' – that is most significant for an anthropological theory of language and emotion. Clancy's mothers use *kowai* and *okashii* to give voice to a generalized social other. They tell their children they are *kowai* 'scary' or *okashii* 'strange,' or that their behavior was. (The kind of utterance Clancy describes could also mean 'I'm afraid of [child's name].') These mothers appeared quite concerned to shape their children's actions and emotions in relation to generalized social norms rather than 'because I said so!' They worked hard to help their child sense others' gaze (even the gaze of generalized or imagined others), and thus to intuit a feeling subject who is never referred to but is very significant nonetheless. The ambiguity as to whether, or how, an affect word used in a Japanese utterance is attached to an experiencer or stimulus may iconically conjure up this generalized feeling **subject**. Japanese mothers' ways of referring to emotion could not be further from the 'I-language' of assertiveness training in the United States, described in Chapter 3.

"Phatic communion" and affect

In this section I review theories of discursive interaction that locate affect in situations that may, in turn, elicit feelings in individual selves. In 1923, anthropological pioneer Bronislaw Malinowski broke new ground in the study of conventional expressions of emotion, and more broadly in the anthropology of language, by focusing attention on speech as action. Malinowski coined a new term for the function performed by the verbal exchanges of niceties: "*phatic communion* I am tempted to call it ... – a type of speech in which ties of union are created by a mere exchange of words" (1923: 315). This coinage is relevant here in that it indicates yet another relationship between talk and affect, one in which talk itself gives pleasure. Inserting another phrase that the fields of discourse-pragmatics and anthropology have found useful – "context of *situation*" (to contrast with the *textual* surround studied by philologists of his day, i.e., "**co-text**" [Silverstein 2004]) – Malinowski asks,

[W]hat can be considered as situation when a number of people aimlessly gossip together? It consists in just this atmosphere of sociability and in the fact of the personal communion of these people. But this is in fact achieved by speech ... The whole situation consists in what happens linguistically ... Once more language appears to us in this function not as an instrument of reflection [**reference**, or representation] but as a mode of action (1923: 315).

In phatic communion – a pervasive phenomenon around the world – a particular kind of speech activity constitutes 'the situation' and its affectivity. Is this an example of a language variety attracting feeling (emotional attachment) to itself (the theme of Chapter 6)? One the one hand, yes, speakers may associate the pleasure the activity generates with the form of talk; but speakers may just as well attribute the warmth to the gathering and its constituent members (even one other speaker).

The capacity of talk itself to generate enjoyment is no secret. Some **Bengalis**, however, consider themselves to have perfected this art, which they call *āḍḍā,* "careless talk with boon companions,"[8] or "the chats of intimate friends" (Chakrabarty 1999: 110, citing Chattopadhyay 1979[1913]: 210) (Figure 4.1). Chakrabarty argues that this practice, at least in its

Figure 4.1   *āḍḍā by Protick*

twentieth-century middle-class Kolkata form, enabled some Bengali men to
"sing to the ever-changing tunes of capitalist modernization and at the same
time retain a comfortable sense of being at home in it" (1999: 113). Thus the
comfort that conversation appears to generate may have a darker "context-
of-situation" underside.[9]

A broad comparison of phatic communion as a practice that varies across
speech communities must examine the discursive topics involved. Greeting
routines, studied by anthropologists like Duranti (1992), have a phatic function. The salience of phatic questions in greeting exchanges may even be a
universal. However, various cultural traditions of relational lubrication may
not probe addressees' inner states with questions like "How are you?" or may
get at such assessments indirectly. Polynesian greeting routines traditionally
focused on movement in space; the routine phatic question was, "Where are
you going?" In Bangladesh as well, rural people often called out as I was passing, "Where are you going?" Although for some time I treated the question
as informational, I finally understood the question as quite conventional, the
answer optional, and the function phatic. Such question-answer exchanges
may generate good feeling, without directly broaching the subject of feeling.

Conclusion

Linguistic diversity, and variation in the means and even salience of 'doing emotion' in words, is a basic indexical fact. This fact, however, as the remainder of this book points out in relation to numerous case studies, is always filtered through higher order indexes. Our reflections on language, emotion, and the nexus of the two – particularly on others' emotion and language – draw on the aesthetic sensibilities cultivated in our own acts of speaking and evaluating. They draw on the aesthetic judgments of our own speech communities. 'Aesthetics' may appear to be apolitical, even asocial. In fact, however, the judgments people produce about others' emotionality or apparent linguistic and cultural difference, referring explicitly or implicitly to their own practices as a standard, are always socially grounded and politically pointed. This chapter has explored linguistic diversity, and diverse ways of linking language and emotion. The challenge for this book is to do this without exoticizing, to do it while keeping in mind the political consequences of our representations.

PART II

LANGUAGE, POWER, AND HONOR

5

LANGUAGE, EMOTION, POWER, AND POLITICS

Introduction

In Part II (Chapters 5 and 6) I explore the relationship of language and emotion with power. Dominant Western discourses have historically associated emotion with femininity, vulnerability, and weakness (Lutz 1986). Martin (2000), however, points to evidence that these associations may have flipped. She argues that "loss of control" – once associated with weakness, and with women – may now be the prerogative of alpha males in the guise of wild bulls. Martin's indirect allusion, here, to stock markets (bullish ones) is intentional. The stock market, Martin (2000: 578, citing Pocock 1985: 112–113) writes, is "a pathologically unstable force [that has] placed 'politics at the mercy of a self-generated hysteria (in the full sexist sense).'" The market (surely a central locus of power in late capitalism) *must* be driven by "male passions that might need to be out of control to be powerful in the market – to manifest themselves in the form of the male manic as a potent, risk-taking entrepreneur" (Martin 2000: 581).

What about the politics of emotion in American presidential elections? Ed Muskie (a Democratic Party candidate in 1972) self-destructed when, "trying to express anger" as his wife was being rhetorically attacked during the campaign, he cried on television (Reddy 1999: 271). But in the January 2008 New Hampshire Democratic Presidential primary, pundits widely attributed Senator Hillary Clinton's victory to her becoming tearful when a voter asked how she was holding up. Such incidents have not received much anthropological attention. But one wonders whether, today, other anthropologists would describe it in quite the way Lutz did ("Tears … are expected at funerals but not in political contexts," Lutz 1986: 306).

Perhaps it *is* still politically problematic when emotive language gives way to "screams" – as in Howard Dean's speech the night he lost the 2004 Iowa Caucuses and gave a sore-loser speech that came to be known as the "I Have a Scream" speech. The speech spread over the internet like a metastasizing cancer (from his perspective). Some claim the scream was intended as a "rebel yell" reminiscent of those produced by soldiers for the South in the American

Civil War (Gilleland 2004, Shiflett 2004). No matter; for candidate Dean, it was downhill from there. The press and others treated the incident as a serious loss of emotional control (Crowley and Potter 2005: 234).

Repeated showings of Senator Clinton's tears on television, and their 'viral' distribution on sites like YouTube, are indicative of a sort of **agency** arising in and from these media. Mediation has helped create scandal – i.e., a sense that someone's communicative acts are shameful. The semiotic complexity of visual media making embodied action available for evaluation helps constitute new shared forms of affectivity, and creates particular links between signs and feelings. The press coverage surrounding Clinton's and Dean's emotions, and its attention to some of the very details of vocal production anthropologists attend to in analyzing emotional talk, reminds us that academic discourse has no monopoly on reflection and analysis.

Probably politicians have always manipulated emotions in addressing their constituencies; rhetoric takes its place in what is often described as a game. "Strategies, tactics, moves and countermoves are played with [in] political rhetoric and ritual in an attempt to reach emotionally charged idealities ... and unrecognized assumptions ... of the voting public" (McLeod 1991: 40). While such an analytic tack misses the mark when viewed in the light of some neuroscientific research on emotions' importance to rational decision-making (Damasio 1995, 2003), it certainly reflects dominant cultural perspectives.

More recent work by linguistic anthropologist Duranti (2006) describes emotion's place in American political rhetoric in different terms. In 1995 and 1996, Duranti followed a Congressional candidate, recording his speeches at campaign stops. At least for this candidate – and, I wager, for most – it was urgent to position himself discursively as one who had shared emotional experiences with his constituents, creating a sense of identification. Duranti's findings, I believe, point to a recent shift in American culture toward a "culture of therapy" (Desjarlais 1996). Conservative commentators (Sommers and Satel 2005) loudly decry this "**therapization** of America" (Dimien 1994: 74). The critical analysis of "therapeutic governance" – epitomized in Bill Clinton's famous statement, "I feel your pain" – is not an active area of anthropological research. With some exceptions (Graham 2002, describing Sweden's "emotional bureaucracy"), it has been left to others (Scott 2001: 41).

What does it mean to live in an age when a political claim may well be staked out in terms of feeling? "You just *feel* that it's so right, so natural to be here," said Aviva Winter, a resident of Migron, which (according to court papers in the case) is an illegal Israeli settlement on the West Bank, built on land owned by Palestinians (National Public Radio and Westervelt 2007). A local Arizona radio station covering a controversy over making snow from treated wastewater – strongly opposed by Native American groups for whom the alpine area in question is sacred – interviewed a Euro-American woman demonstrating with her son on behalf of his hobby, skiing. She said, "I *believe with all my heart* that snowmaking will not harm Native American religion." How do we understand such invocations of heart in relation to power and politics? What does it mean to live in a country like the United States, where – days after September 11, 2001 – President G. W. Bush's upbeat emotional address to "first responders" (to a disaster, in this case mainly New York City firefighters) elicited the sort of animal-like affective response (a sort of 'cheer' that sounds like grunting or hooting) heard at sports events?

For the most part, this chapter's perspective is synchronic; diachronic views follow in later chapters. Offering a snapshot in time, this chapter describes the multifaceted relations between language, power, and emotion.

Language, power, and the politics of emotion

The field of language and emotion is an ongoing site for the clash of values; a systematic treatment of the field must acknowledge that. To attribute emotion to a person or group is at least potentially an act of power, and such indexical acts have important histories, explored further in Chapter 9. Yet questions surround some of the literature in the late 1980s and early 1990s that speak of the relation of "emotion discourses" to power. The work of Lutz and Abu-Lughod (1990) exemplifies the controversy. (Our discussion here prefigures the focus on gender in Chapter 8.)

Lutz underscores the role of emotionality in representations of women, and how closely linked those are with representations of the colonial Other (1990: 77). She argues that women and colonial Others become "mirrors" in which powerful white males see their own fears and weaknesses as well as their aggressiveness or dangerousness. She examines the stereotype that (American) women's speech is "more emotional" than men's speech using several measures of the degree to which emotion statements "'personalize' the emotion experience" (1990: 83). Stereotypes of women's emotionality might lead us to expect that women would personalize emotional expression by emphatically locating themselves as its experiencers, using the present tense, attributing personal causes to emotions, and not denying having feelings as frequently as men might. In fact, Lutz finds no significant differences between men and women on these measures. Still, there is some reality to "mythic construction ... of the emotional female"; it is "an outcome of the fact that women occupy an objectively more problematic position than does the white, upper-class, Northern European, older man" (1990: 88). Those who occupy problematic positions may engage in *problem talk*, which is at least perceived as emotional talk. Whatever women may say, or however they speak, Lutz argues that men may hear women's speech as "dangerously close to erupting into emotionality/ pointing to a problem/moving toward a social critique" (1990: 88).

Mueggler's (1998) analysis of Chinese mortuary poetry led him to "a view of mourning as an ethical activity which ... 'acknowledges the creative involvement of action in the configuration of power and law'" (G. Rose 1996: 12, as cited by Mueggler 1998: 983). Mueggler could not ignore the grief, sadness, and pain in mortuary poetry, insisting that we not view emotion only as a discourse related to power, as Abu-Lughod and Lutz (1990) asked us to do. Instead, we should see emotions themselves as caught up, together with speech, in practice-bundles related to law, ethics, and yes, power. Walking this fine line between recognizing feeling in experience-near terms (and losing the political edge of the analysis), and recognizing the power of representations (and ignoring phenomenological considerations), will be difficult.

Lament and its representation: a case study in power

One genre universally associated with emotion – and perhaps endangered because of that – is ritual **lament**. Feld's prize-winning book on Bosavi sung-texted weeping (*sa-yelab*) is called *Sound and Sentiment*; the title makes the association clear. The emotional force of Bosavi funeral weeping scandalized the Australian fundamentalist missionaries who were working there. In the process of becoming Christians, Bosavi people gave up many things, including this.

But Bosavi lament (or Karelian lament, for that matter) was never purely a matter of passion, to be judged on some pseudo-quantitative scale. What is it that makes ritual lament *ritual?* And what practices of power are inscribed in labeling lament an 'emotional genre' rather than 'a ritual practice'? The single feature that best distinguishes ritual practices from others is probably their transformative efficacy (as locally conceived). Lament in Karelia (described in Chapter 2) and elsewhere was dangerous for the same reason it was ritually efficacious – though it was a woman's practice, it involved shamanistic feats, soul travel (and travail) on behalf of the dead whose safe journey to the beyond was at stake. It is in large part because of the pre-Christian nature of such work, and the efficacy attributed to it, that churches, theologians, and Islamic scholars have fought against lament since at least the third century CE.

Although Australian-missionary condemnations of lament as inappropriately passionate were indeed discursive assertions of power, such condemnation was not foreordained to succeed. Bosavi women's crying songs had power of their own – to move men to tears (Feld 1990), to aid the safe journeys of the non-Christian dead, or to accomplish other ritual goals (Wilce 2009). The relationship of this particular discursive genre to emotion is thus complex; like other speech practices, it becomes the object of ideological evaluation.

Passion, parallelism, and the force of political rhetoric

There is an ancient tradition in philosophy, warning of the dangers of passion and its connection to rhetoric, setting both in opposition to rational discourse. Plato (1969) warned of the power of the poets to upset the political order:

> We shall request Homer and the other poets not to portray Achilles, the son of a goddess, as … weeping and lamenting in the measure and manner attributed to him by the poet; nor yet Priam, near kinsman of the gods, making supplication and rolling in the dung,

> *"Calling aloud unto each,*
> *by name to each man appealing."* [Iliad 22: 414–415]

Elsewhere Plato wrote, "we beg of [Homer and other poets] at least not to describe *the gods* as lamenting and crying" (1969: Book III, section 388b; emphasis added). This is one of many passages in which Plato represented poets – the orators, those entrusted with speaking to the polity – as a corrupting influence on the young men of Athens.

The **textuality** of the most effective examples of political rhetoric, i.e., its structures of coherence, inevitably involves various forms and levels of **parallelism**, complete and partial repetitions. According to Jakobson (1987a, 1987b, 1987c), parallelism is the "primary 'device' of poetry" (Caton 1987: 239). Homer's line, cited above, manifests a particular *chiastic* form of parallelism.[1] President George Herbert Walker Bush announced the initiation of hostilities with Iraq on January 16, 1991, with lines such as these:

While the world waited,	*Saddam*
	sought to add to the chemical
	weapons arsenal he now possesses
While the world waited,	*Saddam*
	stalled.
While the world waited,	*Saddam Hussein*
	met every overture of peace with open
	contempt.[2]

Such parallelistic structure – repetitions of "while" clauses, Saddam's name, and past tense verb phrases – has its own emotional effect, whether through sheer force of repetition or through complex patterns of emergent textual *movement* (Wilce 2008, 2009). A great example of political rhetoric such as Lincoln's Gettysburg Address – a ritual text of and for the collective life of a nation – changes our experience in part by presenting a picture (an *icon*), creating "chain-complexes of ideas" (Silverstein 2003b: 38). Plato was right to acknowledge and even fear the effects (emotional and otherwise) of finely crafted ritual texts. Today as before, even those politicians who ostensibly eschew rhetoric rely on the affective force of finely crafted **text** – typically written by speechwriters, specialists in the art of rhetoric. Increasingly, we know how to study such apparently timeless – i.e., memorable, decontextualizable – denotative textual arrays, *together with the* **interactional texts** *of those same discursive events that very much unfold in particular times and places* (Silverstein 2004).

Claptrap: oratory and the manipulation of displays of affiliative affect

The word *claptrap*, first defined in the 1727 edition of Bailey's *Dictionarium Britannicum*, denoted "a trap to catch a clap by way of applause from the spectators at a play." Since then, it has come to refer to "language designed to catch applause; cheap showy sentiment," with the "modern use passing into sense 'nonsense, rubbish'" (Oxford English Dictionary, second edition, "claptrap"). Speakers and orators of all sorts, but perhaps especially political orators, make excellent use of such traps. By various means, they display a certain affect, and a certain degree of affectivity or intensity, in the interest of affiliating themselves (affectively or evaluatively) with an audience. Such displays invite audiences to clap in a return "display of affiliation" with the speaker (J. Atkinson 1984: 405). (Getting an audience to laugh is another type of affiliation-eliciting, and much of what I say about the organization of applause also applies to the organization of laughter in interaction [Glenn 2003].)

Atkinson's perspective is that of ethnomethodology/conversation analysis. In the conversation analyst's view, a speaker's affective-cum-evaluative display, and the corresponding affective-affiliative response (clapping), are social-interactional achievements orchestrated by metasigns from both sides. Like face-to-face conversation, the coordination of applause in relation to 'invitations' involves a form of **intersubjectivity**. In such communication, timing and reciprocal awareness are everything. At least in the English speaking world, Atkinson finds that audience applause normally ends after eight seconds; those who applaud and those who are speaking ensure this, jointly. Word stress and pauses are framing devices that reveal to audiences something of the structure of the speaker's utterance, lending it some predictability. The orator must signal not only that she is coming to the end of a 'turn,' but fairly clear information about when the audience can expect that end. Audience members demonstrate their attunement to these signals with applause, the duration of which is exquisitely timed to coincide with what conversation analysts call a transition-relevant moment (Sacks, Schegloff, and Jefferson 1974).

Thus, the **denotational text** constituting a speaker's applause line indexes an orientation to the stance and feelings of the audience; its rhythm, intonational contour, and unfolding structure signal to them when to add their emotive 'second' to the speaker's (e)motion. And what sorts of affective-evaluative comments in political speech elicit applause? "Assertions which convey positive or boastful evaluations of *our* hopes, *our* activities or *our* achievements" (J. Atkinson 1984: 37) are most likely to do so. Essentially, Atkinson's study of hundreds of examples of applause in response to oratory reveals that affirming the crowd's feelings elicits the sign of their pleasure. Putting the matter a bit more crassly, political messages "where the speaker in effect says either 'Hooray for *us*' or 'boo to *them*'" (1984: 44) constitute the overwhelming percentage of applause lines.

Optimistically, we might choose to believe that a politician who clearly identifies with his audience in a common 'we' might somehow draw the crowd toward their better instincts. Was that the result of this applause line from President Kennedy?

We shall pay any price,
bear any burden,
meet any hardship,
support any friend,
oppose any foe,
to assure the survival and success of liberty
(as cited by J. Atkinson 1984: 37).[3]

A more critical perspective sees in this the political system's need to create common sentiment, loyalty, and – arising out of this – commitment to national causes that are seldom if ever completely innocent.

President G. W. Bush in the days following September 11, 2001

In a culture where emotional "sharing" is widely valued, perhaps it is not surprising that President G. W. Bush's affective communication may underlie his electoral success. Like President Reagan before him, Mr. Bush was able to "produce ideological effects by non-ideological means … His means were affective" (Massumi 1995: 104). Despite being born with a silver spoon in his mouth, this scion of American nobility was, at his best, a favorable object of identification for many Americans. This phenomenon arises from his apparent ability to identify with them, and nowhere better than in New York City on September 14, 2001 in his interaction with "first responders," particularly the members of the NYC Fire Department who had survived 9/11, but lost many of their comrades.

Saurette is one of a growing number of scholars from across the humanities and social sciences who point to the role *humiliation* and *shame* play on the global political stage.[4] Saurette's (2006) article, "Humiliation and Post 9/11 Global Politics," includes an analysis of the September 14 Presidential visit to the site of the World Trade Towers and of so many first responders' heroic work. Video from the event is still available at WhiteHouse.gov (as of early 2009). Rather than trusting Saurette's transcript of the crucial minutes in the encounter, I analyzed the video myself. Bloggers explain that the firefighters who had gathered for this encounter with the President at the World Trade Towers site could not hear him; so someone handed him a bullhorn – and a small American flag. Here is my transcript of the videotaped interaction:

Transcription guide
AM = audience member (a clear individual voice)
Aud = collective audience
(comments) = my comments, not words spoken at the original event; descriptions of visible actions or speech quality
[x?] uncertain hearing
(.5), (1) = length of pause in tenths or whole seconds

CAPS = speech that is louder than surrounding transcribed lines
BOLD CAPS = *very* loud speech, shouted speech

Transcript 1: President Bush and first responders, September 14, 2001
  1 GWB: Thank you all! (with arm around older firefighter from the outset)
  2 AM: Go get'm George!
  3 GWB: (Very calmly): I uh (.5) I want you all to know
  4 AM: Louder
  5 GWB: It can't go any louder.
  6 GWB: (Leans back – away from the bullhorn – playfully, smiles to someone in
  7 audience – almost the only affective facial display in the speech)
  8 Aud: (Laughter)
  9 GWB: (Louder, into megaphone) I want you all to know
10 GWB: that America today
11 GWB: America today (1) is on bended knee
12 GWB: in prayer for the people
13 GWB: whose lives were lost here
14 GWB: for the workers who work here
15 GWB: for the families who mourn.
16 GWB: This nation stands with the good people of New York City
17 GWB: and New Jersey and Connecticut
18 GWB: as we mourn the loss of thousands of our citizens.
19 (The camera backs up just then, to show GWB leaning back as if to prepare to lean
20 into the mike, providing bodily momentum to amplify what he would say next.)
21 GWB: I CAN HEAR YOU!
22 Aud: (Roars, applauds, whistles)
23 GWB: I CAN HEAR YOU, THE REST OF THE WORLD HEARS YOU
24 GWB: AND THE PEOPLE
25 Aud: (Interrupts with whistling, applause, responding to "rest of the world hears you")
26 GWB: AND THE PEOPLE WHO KNOCKED THESE BUILDINGS DOWN
27 GWB: WILL HEAR **ALL** OF US SOON.
28 Aud: (Roars)
29 Aud: (Hoots, "ai, ai, ai, ai," then just clapping …)
30 Aud: USA, USA, USA, USA, USA, USA, USA, USA, USA, USA
31 GWB: THE NATION (1) The nation sheds its love
32 GWB: and compassion
33 AM: (angrily) GOD BLESS AMERICA!
34 GWB: [on?] everybody that's here.
35 GWB: THANK YOU FOR YOUR HARD WORK.
36 GWB: THANK YOU FOR MAKIN' THE NATION PROUD! (raises eyebrows)
37 GWB: AND MAY GOD BLESS AMERICA.
38 Aud: (Roars, whistles – stimulated in part by GWB grabbing and holding up the little
39 flag he had been given, and waving it)
40 USA, USA, USA, USA, USA, USA, USA, USA…

Clearly *hearing*, which was originally a practical issue at this event, became
an organizing trope for much of what was said, particularly by the President.

Saurette's discussion, focused on just what it was that Bush thanked the fire-fighters for, sheds little light on the dynamics of national sentiment involved in the event. The President said the first responders were "making the nation proud" (line 36) – which is relevant because the nation's humiliation was palpable.

Several features of this interaction, particularly audience speech and sound, mimic the highly emotional behavior of crowds at sports events (which can also be sites of production for specifically nationalist sentiment, Bendix 1992). Aggressive emotional phrases like "go get'm" and chants of the 'home team's' name (*USA, USA, USA* …) combine with sounds of raw feeling (such as the chanted, shouted, or hooted vocable *ai ai ai* …) to constitute the audience's intense emotional involvement in this aggression-oriented **speech event** that foreshadowed military action. Again, cheers and hoots from audiences at sports events may also foreshadow, or may aim at producing, a more energetic performance by the team cheered on to such heights.

The President utters his first recorded lines (starting line 1) in a *subdued* voice, befitting the state of a nation that had been, as we say, 'brought down' by a horrifically effective terrorist attack. To say that America is "on bended knee" (line 11) is of course ambiguous, suggesting the nation not only at prayer (12) as the President said, but bent, if not broken. The President recognized the nation's mourning, and spoke on its behalf, transmitting its love and com-passion (31–32). Those two emotionally positive expressions framed his short speech, catching up individuals (those addressed and those represented) in a collective **identification**. But between the two references to positive emotions, Mr. Bush turned the theme of being heard into a figure for threatened action that indeed was imminent. If his anger was somewhat apparent in the prosodic peak reached as he utters his threat (line 27, his loudest), anger was also audi-ble in the audience member's shout, "God Bless America!" (33).

Generating national sentiment through national memorials: the central place of narrative

The event analyzed above foreshadowed a sharp rise of nationalistic sentiments in American public discourse. As with Pearl Harbor, various *memorializations* of the 9/11 terrorist attacks – official and unofficial – have nurtured and sus-tained national sentiments.

Terrifying *images* of the attacks on American ships in Pearl Harbor and the Trade Towers are now all the more available for public viewing, with the internet now playing an important role in shaping political sentiment. Anthropologist Geoff White argues, however, that images are "'empty signifiers' that require some form of narrative to fill in their human drama" (2004: 296). "Narrative productions in popular media, news reporting, film, and the internet now create a vast electronic archive of and for national sentiment" (2004: 294). Of par-ticular interest for our purposes is the incorporation of personal narratives into 'sites' of memorialization, literal and figurative.

Visitors to the USS Arizona Memorial (memorializing the Pearl Harbor attacks) can hear not just 'the voice from nowhere,' i.e., 'objective' historiography that appears to be written or spoken from no particular point of view. They can also hear personal stories of loss and survival from volunteers who work at the site. Speaking with White, one such volunteer mentioned the eliciting of emotion in his audiences as an explicit goal. On some level, the man's story connects hearers "with the 'real experience' of death and loss represented by the sunken ship" (White 2004: 304). Narrative helps to concretize the more nebulous affect elicited by images alone.

The American media, ostensibly not official government mouthpieces, nonetheless became semi-official 'sites' for public mourning. *Story Corps* – an ongoing project of the Corporation for Public Broadcasting, AT&T, the National Folklife Center, and National Public Radio (NPR) – records "extraordinary stories from everyday people" at its mobile recording booth currently crisscrossing the United States. Among the many different sorts of stories recorded and selectively broadcast on NPR are stories told by survivors of 9/11. The *New York Times* ran a series of personal stories of 9/11 called "Portraits of Grief." Television broadcasts for some days and weeks immediately after 9/11 similarly featured "A Nation in Mourning." The City of New York recently made available to the public tapes and transcripts of the frantic phone calls placed to its emergency operators on September 11, recordings that in many cases captured the very last words of those trapped in the World Trade Center.

All of these personal stories move even the most emotionally distant scholar, although many scholars share a concern "that emotion is easily recruited to the service of militant nationalism" (White 2004: 296). Still, it is quite clear that some mass-mediated revisitings of history evoke something other than nationalistic sentiment in contemporary American audiences. Americans flocked to see the (mostly fictional) personal stories of the Japanese soldiers who fought and died at Iwo Jima in the film *Letters from Iwo Jima* (Eastwood 2006).

The national narrative about Operation Iraqi Freedom, the second Gulf War, has become a story of tragedy or farce for many in the United States, long after this happened in the rest of the world. The national(ist) hold on language and emotion surrounding the war is tenuous at best. Bits and pieces of language, like the names of Americans killed in Iraq, have become the ground on which competing actors wage a new battle in the American 'culture wars.' (No such concern is apparent in regards to the Iraqi dead, who are almost never named.) In Flagstaff, Arizona – my home – an entrepreneur has been selling T-shirts bearing the names of the American war dead, and the slogan "Bush lied, they died." The Republican-dominated Arizona legislature passed, and Arizona's Democratic governor signed, a law banning the commercial use of the names, targeted at the T-shirt entrepreneur. The argument over the ban turned on who had the right to invoke those names, and for what purposes. The families of some of Arizona's dead claimed that the particular emotions stirred by such discursive products had nothing to do with, or offended, the patriotic feelings of the dead or their families.

Challenging the dominance of the sorts of national(istic) sentiments at work in the United States since 9/11 is still tantamount to treason in the eyes of many. Stories of war ('national' and 'personal,' the personal always being caught up in the national) will continue to reflect and stir passion.

Language ideologies, power, and hate speech

Speaking is always a historically, culturally situated form of social action, and the apparent indexical 'facts' that give meaning to speech acts are constituted to a large extent by higher-order indexes, particularly ideologies of language. **Language ideologies** are inherently political. They are "representations of social relationships through politically charged images of language and linguistic difference" (Eisenlohr 2006: 8).

Hill (2008) describes two "implicit language ideologies" that inform public discourse in the USA, undergird white racism, and shield discursive expressions of racism from challenge – "**personalism**" and "**referentialism**." By personalism Hill means the notion that the meanings speakers produce emanate from a core, inner self. Furthermore, insofar as those meanings are recoverable in the semanticoreferential structure of their utterances, they are held to reflect that core, including its 'beliefs,' intentions, and affects. However, discourse analysts treat beliefs not as "resources" for, but as topics of, discourse. Beliefs are discursive products; we cannot presume that discourse is a product or reflection of beliefs (Bilmes 1986: 104–105; Good 1994: Chapter 1). Ironically, personalism and referentialism make it possible to distance the speaking self from charges of racism, as long as one can claim such 'feelings' or 'beliefs' are not part of the affects, beliefs, or intentions of a core self. By contrast, a language ideology that renders statements like "I didn't mean that" nonsensical results in speakers being held accountable in a way that personalist-and-referentialist imaginings of discourse prevent. (Samoans, for example, locate meaning in the words one utters, i.e., in their socially received standard meaning, indefinitely deferring questions of the intent behind them, Duranti 1988, 1997). Personalism and referentialism sustain power relations to the extent that they naturalize them.

For example, they can coat speakers like former Senate Majority Leader Trent Lott with Teflon as they did after public comments in 2002 that the United States could have avoided "all these problems" if a friend of Lott's, running on a racist platform, had been elected President. Whatever inflammatory racial statements he might have made are dismissed as "slips." Personalism and referentialism, which informed press accounts of Lott's gaffe, permitted him to declare and thus retrospectively manage the meanings of his utterance, and the sincerity of his protestations of innocence. His 'heart,' we hear, is clean.

Although Senator Lott's so-called gaffe occurred in face-to-face communication, the story was of course mass-mediated. The media play a crucial role in reproducing personalism and referentialism. Websites with messages of hate and violence, including White supremacist sites, are now fixtures in the electronic world. As a final example of (new) media, Kenyans were shocked, in February 2008, to learn that text messages on cell phones were being used to stir interethnic hatred (Quist-Arcton and National Public Radio 2008).

What Hill calls "Mock Spanish" is found in face-to-face communication and online. When non-Latino Americans use mispronounced and decontextualized Spanish words like *mañana* or *cojones*, or incorrect forms like *problemo*, they may be reproducing negative images of Latinos (Hill 2008). To assert that such speech straightforwardly reflects a speaker's personal intention (one reading of illocutionary force), that its meaning is determined by that intention, makes almost any conventional meaning that speech entails, 'performs,' or contextually brings into play plausibly deniable. The importance of that ideological work becomes clear in relation to those particular instances of hate speech, or speech that incites violence, whose pragmatic meaning becomes deniable when overwhelmed by invocations of private intentions.

A common reaction to Hill's argument runs like this: "Unless it's meant with disrespect, it really is *no problemo*," which reproduces precisely the Mock Spanish Hill problematizes. Confining such problems to personal intention places Mock Spanish, or racial epithets, beyond criticism; who can know, after all, the intent behind them? If they arouse passions, that's not the speaker's problem. We are reminded of the byword of assertiveness training: "Own your own feelings." Don't blame the one who uses a racial epithet, for example, if you get angry. The fault, as the argument goes, is not in the words but in the hearts of either speaker or hearer.

Conclusion

Language has a politics, in the broadest construal of the term. So does emotion. The constant attention to histories of language and emotion that characterizes this book reflects a commitment to uncovering the discursive strategies for subordinating certain classes of persons, strategies that are often so old or deeply rooted as to pass unnoticed. Taking language, emotion, and power seriously means refusing to reduce any one of these to a mere shadow (epiphenomenon) of any other.

A particular political speech may or may not possess the features necessary for it to embed itself in the national memory; apparently President Bush's September 14, 2001 speech has not done so. Particular utterances and whole **speech events** reflect, contribute to, and reproduce (or challenge) **language ideologies**, those broadly circulating ideas about language and society that form an analytic bridge between speech and the political economy. Ideologies like personalism and referentialism enable certain speech to pass as acceptable in civil society, while its contribution to everyday white racism remains hidden. 'Hate speech' thus remains a category invoked on relatively rare occasions, tightly sealed off from ideological construals that render innocent any speech that, to its apparent targets, at the very least inflicts pain. Although 'ideology' is often conceived of as ideas, and 'power' is represented in terms of a kind of physics (of force) or economics (of monopolization), recognizing the infusion of both with affect, and noting their affective consequences, enriches our understanding. We have gained ground in this chapter by uncovering the mutually implicating nature of ideas and powerful, socially circulating emotions about language, as well as emotions constituted through arrays of linguistic signs (particularly forms of parallelism). The next chapter carries forward the analysis of language, emotion, and the political economy.

6

STATUS, HONORIFICATION, AND
EMOTION FOR HIRE

Several centuries ago, the English language lost one of its functions – the ability to mark status distinctions grammatically. The loss of T-forms of the second person pronoun – thou, etc. (like French *tu* and associated verb marking) – left English with only the V-form, you (originally comparable to French *vous*, requiring analogous forms of verb agreement). English now lacks a grammatical status/intimacy marking system. Such pronouns and agreement forms are analogous to more elaborate systems of honorification in non-Indo-European languages, which occupy us in this chapter. We call such systems *honorific registers*. Registers are "linguistic repertoire[s]… associated… with particular social practices and with persons who engage in such practices" (Agha 2004: 24). Honorific registers encompass whole sets of lexical alternants that may index respect for one's addressee, bystanders, and/or referents.

I focus here on two sorts of registers as described by Irvine (1990, 1998). Registers such as these are associated with practices (and indirectly with groups), whereas **sociolects** or social dialects are associated more stably with demographic fractions. Irvine's ethnographic work in Senegal on the emotional and honorific speech of Wolof griots – praise-singers and storytellers descended from slaves, and contrasted in the Senegalese caste system with the nobles who often hire them to speak emotionally on their behalf – shows that affect-laden speech is not a sociolect restricted to griots. Rather, such speech constitutes a register available to nobles, too (Irvine 1990), i.e., anyone who engages in praise or thanks (practices).

Irvine's cross-linguistic generalization that "grammatical honorifics … are embedded in an ideology in which a low-affect style can be other-elevating" (Irvine 1998: 62) is what interests us here. Why should this be? Why should a style that suppresses emotion be taken as deferential? Linguistic anthropologist Joseph Errington provides one of the case studies that inform Irvine's generalization. Errington's long-term fieldwork on the Javanese language, known for its honorific registers, has led him to understand why a low-affect style *is* respectful.

Javanese honorifics and a semiotic theory of language

At least 75,000,000 people speak Javanese. Its system of linguistic etiquette reflects a cultural history in which magico-religious power emanated from exemplary centers – royal courts. The elite known as *priyayi* – contemporary descendants of kings and servants of kings – embody the exemplary behavior associated with Java's royal past. The priyayi are regarded as exemplary speakers of Javanese and the keepers of its high honorific register, *krama*. Krama distinguishes itself from *ngoko*, the relaxed register of the everyday conversation of commoners, and *madya*, a middle register devolved from krama.

Readers are by now quite well aware that individual lexemes, such as interjections, are certainly not the only means by which languages signal emotion. It is noteworthy, however, that when Errington asked his priyayi consultants to produce examples of ideal speech, their krama utterances lacked interjections and what he calls "psycho-ostensives," "elements of speech that index subjective and occasional attitudes of a speaker" (Errington 1988: 196). These would include response cries (discussed in Chapters 2 and 3) like "ouch," but also interjections "like 'gee' 'hey' and 'the hell' (as in 'What/who/when …')" (Errington 1988: 219), which tend to occur in relaxed speech in both English and Javanese. These particles "were quite prominent in … negative examples of [utterances] that were not sufficiently 'polished' (*besut*), these occasionally being lampoons of country bumpkins or foreigners who fail miserably to achieve true refinedness" (1988: 220).

It is no accident that Errington discusses interjections in a chapter on "the muting of gesture." Interjections are verbal gestures. "Much of the relative refinedness of krama use resides in the avoidance or muting of … gestural aspects of speech." Among such aspects he lists deictics – terms like 'here,' 'there,' and 'now,' whose use is a form of context-bound pointing, and whose understanding relies on sharing that context. These are Peircean **indexes**.

Peirce delighted in groups of three. I discussed the first triad – icons, indexes, and symbols – in the Introduction. Peirce related these loosely to another, more abstract, triad, which he simply called First, Second, and Third, or Firstness, Secondness and Thirdness. Peirce described Secondness – related essentially to indexicality – as "*brute* actions of one subject or substance on another" (Peirce 1931–1958: 5.469; emphasis added).

In seeking to explain how interjections, and affect in general, could offend a sense of honor in Javanese etiquette, Errington indirectly reminds his readers of the brute dimension of Secondness and, thus, of the 'force' entailed in signaling one's feelings through interjections but also intonation and other indexes. In effect, his priyayi consultants told him indexes were rude; for priyayi, there was a certain (negative, because excessive) emotional quality to all indexes! This makes sense from Peirce's perspective: "The index asserts nothing; it only says 'There!' It takes hold of our eyes, as it were, and forcibly directs them to a particular object, and there it stops'" (Peirce 1931–1958: 3.362, as cited by Errington 1988: 249). Secondness appears quite far from any notion of refinement, politeness, or respect; thus *alus* ('refined') Javanese tamp down all indexicality, including emotion, in speech and conduct (1988: 250).

Note that, despite the persuasiveness of claims that a certain kind of connection between high status and low affect may reflect specifically modern **language ideologies** that are inherently distrustful of emotion, the Javanese case demonstrates that such connections are not necessarily modern, or European, in origin. The Wolof case, explored below, is another such demonstration.

Wolof griots and nobles

In order to understand griot and noble speech – called *waxu gewel* and *waxu géér*, respectively – we need to know a bit about the Senegalese Wolof social system. Nobles and griots are often referred to as castes; griots occupy the lower end of the caste ladder, and nobles the upper end. Griots are bards, known for praise-singing and other forms of highly emotional expression (though it is not simple "self-expression," since griots are understood to be performing *someone else*'s feelings).

Irvine's generalization about the pragmatics of a low-affect semiotic style applies only to language situations like Javanese, Zulu, Ponapean, Zuñi, Japanese, Thai, and Lhasa-Tibetan that have been described has having grammatical honorifics or honorific registers. The generalization does not apply to Wolof, which lacks *grammaticalized* honorific registers. What sets griot speech apart as other-elevating and yet demeaning to themselves is precisely its affectivity. Just as Peirce's semiotic categories helped explain Javanese speech etiquette, they help explain Wolof perceptions of status, emotion, and speech. Whereas Secondness was most relevant to Errington's explanation of honorific registers in Javanese, Irvine turns to Peirce's First category, iconicity, to explain why griots' highly emotional speech style contributes to ranking them below nobles.

Language is not just a tool for thinking or talking about economic exchanges; Irvine (1989) argues that linguistic signs, and acts of speaking, actually enter into local economies. Crucial to this argument is her construal of griot and noble speech as two very different forms of verbal labor. Besides praise speech (a form of emotion work, Hochschild 1979), griots do other forms of hard physical labor. And though you might not think of bardic labor as demanding, the physical energy with which griots perform emotion is an icon of their status as laborers. Their patrons, those who pay to have them perform their feelings, sit quietly, impassively, and listen.

Stillness is an icon or index not only of nobles' status as those who do not need to do physical labor – those for whom others work hard. It is iconic of nobles' essence. "Wolof nobles rationalize their claim to superiority over lower ranks in terms of sangfroid and restraint" (Irvine 1990: 153); perhaps more surprisingly, nobles and griots actually agree that nobles' restraint and griots' energy reflects what they are made of, so to speak. Nobles are stable because they are of the earth. They lack the dangerous, passionate dynamism of griots, for of the four constitutive elements – earth, air, fire, and water – the stable earth predominates in them (Irvine 1990: 133). Here is a local model of iconicity, a metasemiotic model: Wolof villagers understood each other's speech, embodied performance, and habitual levels of emotionality to be the very image (sonic and visual) of constitutional differences.

Lamenters for hire

Irvine (1990: 146) tells of a group of Wolof village women, five nobles and two griots, who were at the village well drawing water one afternoon when another walked up to the well and threw herself in. Whereas presumably all were shocked in equal measure, it fell to the griot women to scream "on behalf of all."

Screams or "paroxysmic utterances" are not laments (Danforth and Tsiaras 1982: 73), or not its discursive face (Lloyd 1980: 407). But just as the low status of griots is justified in part by their emotion work, certain people understood to occupy a low status have historically been hired as professional lamenters, universally women. Plato (*Laws* 800e Plato 1903) considered laments only fitting for the lips of such women, not for women of high birth (Book III, 387e, Plato 1969). St. John Chrysostom (1886) one of the fathers of the early Christian Church, wrote scathingly of women who serve as hired lamenters.

The feeling expressed in the earliest traditions of Islam toward these women was no warmer. According to several *hadith* (traditions ascribed to the Prophet and his closest followers), the Prophet once declared, "Three pre-Islamic customs ... are not to be retained by the Muslims. They are: invoking the planets in order to receive rain ... attacking genealogies,... and lamenting the dead (*al-niyāḥa 'alā 'l-mayyit*)."[1] The Prophet had to clarify this ban when he wept at the death of his son Ibrāhim. "Someone said to him, O Messenger of God, did you not forbid weeping? He replied, 'I forbade raising one's voice (*nawḥ*) in two instances, both equally stupid and impious: a voice raised in a state of happiness (which shows itself) in celebrations, disporting and diabolical chantings (*mazāmīr shayṭān*) and a voice in times of misfortune (which shows itself) in mutilating one's face, tearing of clothes and a diabolical mourning cry'" (*rannat shayṭān*, i.e., the *nēnia*, i.e., funeral laments, of the Romans).[2]

Emotional language: a sign of the subordinate?

These case studies have pointed to the tendency for affective language to be associated with social weakness or subordination. Irvine makes clear that this is not raw fact but ideology. Lutz (1990) points to the similarity, at least in her data, in levels of emotional expression in men's and women's speech. The image of the emotional female and the dispassionate male, for example, may not bear scrutiny. What appears to be an absence of emotion in men may in fact be its creation in women through and as a kind of work (1990: 85). However, this work – insofar as emotional expression can represent pointing to problems – renders the pointer problematic or troublesome (1990: 88).

American courtroom speech may well be passionate in actuality, yet rationality reigns supreme at least in the elite law school classrooms Mertz describes. And in this case what is for hire is the profession ostensibly associated with a low-affect style. Professors at elite law schools model for their students appropriate legal speech and reasoning (Mertz 1998: 157–158) and convey the need to translate people "into their roles … and actions into their legal categories." "A key presupposition of the legitimacy of those results in our society is the untying of the drama as legally translated from its usual social moorings, the putative objectivity of the story once told in the apparently dispassionate language of the law" (1998: 158). Thus law schools become sites for the reproduction of language ideologies descending from Bacon and Locke (Bauman and Briggs 2003), which assert the possibility and desirability of 'purifying' language of its social and emotional indexicality. Lawyers – whose power in Western societies is almost unrivaled – exemplify the (ideological) association of affect suppression with high status.

Yet hegemonic ideologies do not go unchallenged. Yes, among the caste groups of Tamil Nadu (India), it is the Paraiyar women – so-called untouchables – whom Trawick (1988, 1990b) finds performing highly emotional genres. Paraiyar women sing scandalous love songs, lullabies, and *oppāri* 'laments,' or crying songs. Yet pronoun use in all three genres tends to blur the line between 'you' and 'I,' and Trawick argues that the boundary-blurring style is not accidental. Paraiyar women's discursive style represents their resistant ideology, broadcasting their opposition to caste/hierarchy, declaring (as Trawick puts it) that "Feelings of love come through only where walls between voices dissolve, and the fundamental pair, 'I' and 'you,' face each other as kindred spirits, needing no mediation" (1988: 212). What emerges in and from Paraiyar women's song performances is unpredictable; high-caste male targets of such songs appear to fear them.

Conclusion

Anthropologists have long been experts on local, face-to-face communities. More recently (e.g., Fischer 1999), as the discipline grapples with globalization, many practitioners advocate multi-sited ethnography. The challenge is to preserve ethnographic "thick description" (Geertz 1973b) while expanding its reach to encompass global horizons, or at least particular connections between, say, India and West Africa.[3]

The historical approach I embrace poses certain risks, including losing ethnographic particularity. It would be tempting to attribute to some global connective process, for example, the fact that we find widely disbursed instances in which high linguistic affectivity indexes social, political, and economic marginality or subordination. However, Irvine (1998) demonstrates in relation to precisely those cases that language ideologies play a crucial mediating role, that simple economic or political determinism cannot account for the distribution of grammaticalized honorifics, or of honorific registers like that of Wolof griots. Irvine exemplifies the balance needed, taking political economies very seriously, recognizing their local peculiarities, and weighing their global entanglements.

Where does this leave claims about the globalization of (ideologies of) affect and language? In order to truly assess such claims, we need more ethnographic work at particular intersections of the local and global. In the next chapter we explore the historic emergence of passion for the Tamil language, a product of just that sort of intersection.

PART III

IDENTIFICATION AND IDENTITY

7

LANGUAGE AS EMOTIONAL OBJECT: FEELING, LANGUAGE, AND PROCESSES OF IDENTIFICATION

The place of this chapter in the overall argument

This chapter explores a variety of ways in which feelings about language become much more central to sociolinguistic processes than past reviews of language-and-affect have made clear. Here I most fully develop one of the book's central arguments, inverting the common vision in which language 'expresses,' refers to, or indexes emotion. This chapter analyzes cases in which feelings make language their object. First, I review previous sociolinguistic work to foreground what that work reveals about feelings toward language while leaving that dimension undertheorized. I then explore a set of three cases, starting with two from India. The first is the case of *āḍḍā*, a particular gendered imagination of conversation in twentieth-century Kolkata. I then review Ramaswamy's discussion of *tamilparru* – passion or devotion toward Tamil, a major language of south India. The last case study concerns contemporary Apache expressivity and identity. Finally, in order to more adequately theorize affective attachments to, or disidentification with, speech varieties, I explore the divergent literatures on language attitudes and language ideologies.

Affective relations to language constitute metasemiotic relationships of attachment. All such attachments, be they positive (pride, passion) or negative (shame), are mental **interpretants** (Peirce 1991) of other signs. That is, they are metasigns whose function is to interpret other (object-) signs. For Peirce "all thought is in signs that have no immediate content but require a subsequent thought, an *interpretant*, to give them meaning by interpreting them as representations" (Hoopes 1991: 34; emphasis added).

This model of cognition, always involving two levels of dialectic engagement – between two times, and between one thought and another in which an interpretant-thought fills in the meaning of an object-thought – is useful in modeling identification and identity. Affective attachments to language involve both. We think of linguistic variants ('languages,' **dialects**, registers, etc.) dynamically indexing, indeed helping to constitute identity – and difference. Although Others may well assign speakers of some form of language a certain 'identity' label, all such labels and identities involve objectification.

The dynamic processes of identification resist objectification. By **identification** I mean not only altercentric labeling processes (in this context, the self's labeling by or in relation to others), but processes by which some person or group actively senses, claims, or voices a certain relationship – in this case, with some linguistic variety – through which the personal or social self is constituted. To investigate identification processes is to ask about social, semiotic, and psychodynamic complexity, rather than the apparent fixity of 'identities.'

From a post-Freudian feminist perspective (Fuss 1995: 3), "Identification is, from the beginning, a question of *relation*, of self to other, subject to object, inside to outside." Fuss (1996) describes identification as the engine that produces identities, though not stable, centered, autonomous, 'authentic' selves. Identification is "the detour through the other that defines a self ..." (Fuss 1996: 387). Acts of identification are – paraphrasing Fuss – internalizations of others (1996: 388), and thus do not add up to a unitary self-identity. Freudian thought has stimulated work on identification in **cultural studies** (Fuss) and anthropology (Kulick 2003: 148–9), including Biddle's (2002) exploration of "melancholic identification" in ethnographic fieldwork. Humanistic scholars have described mourning in terms of the bereaved's identification with the dead (Wickett 1993, Schubel 1993, Lloyd 1996). In the larger scheme of things, identification is an "ongoing social and political" phenomenon accomplished by the semiotic processes of practice, indexicality, ideology, and performance (Bucholtz and Hall 2004: 377). There is growing interest in research at the interface of depth psychology and conversation analysis (see discursive psychology's reinterpretation of psychoanalytic concepts like repression as a function of *talk-in-interaction*, Billig 1997).

An anthropology in which Freud is neither taboo nor totem offers the possibility to examine various feelings toward language with a richness other approaches lack. Adding identification and desire (Fuss 1993: 1) to the mix of language and emotions adds yet another layer of richness. Freudian object relations theory describes object loss (what happens when we lose a love object) as a process in which we identify with the object, and internalize a likeness of the object, somehow compensating for the loss. Identification and identity, its more objectified counterpart, are in a dialectic relationship: "At the very same time that identification sets into motion the complicated dynamic of recognition and misrecognition that brings a sense of identity into being, it also immediately calls that identity into question" (Fuss 1995: 2).

We need not posit universal biological tendencies, or deep unconscious drives, as the cause of processes such as identification or repression. If we wish to pursue Billig's agenda, and try uncovering the sorts of processes Freud described as being enacted in conversation (rather than in autonomous and mysterious minds), we may find a road of various difficulty ahead of us. It is perhaps easier to imagine "conversational moments of repression" (Billig 1997) than to put our finger on conversational symptoms of "melancholic identification" (Biddle 2002). It is not hard to imagine interactions – even a lifetime of interactions – leading to disidentification with, or even shame in regards to, the culture and language with which others identify us (Hoffman 2008: 44). But where can we find an empirical description of particular forms of personal and sociocultural loss contributing to a collective melancholy or identification with death? How might expressions of such loss, and destructive forms of identification, actually emerge in frequent and widely distributed instances of talk-in-interaction?

To the extent that strong sociocultural identifications may generally coincide not only with a foreclosing of other ethnic identifications, but even some hostility or distrust toward those Others, the challenge seems urgent. And we need not look only at the discourse of 'folks' in constructing such potentially destructive identifications; it may be that the very collecting of folklore that we label 'Ours' conjures up an identity, i.e., reflects and contributes to processes of identification that are inherently exclusive if not xenophobic (Anttonen 2005, Hill 2005: 346). Thus it may well be at the metadiscursive level – e.g., discourse about culturally 'authentic' discursive springs of 'identity' – that identification is most active.

Language as emotional object in early Western modernity

A strong current in the history of Western humanistic accounts of passion in relation to language – from Herder, Croce, and Sapir to contemporary figures – tries to envision how people project all sorts of feelings on to language itself and the constituent phenomena of language. I introduced this theme – the aesthetic interpretation of linguistic relativity – in Chapter 4.

Johann Gottfried Herder, writing in the second half of the eighteenth century, tended (like the previous generations of philologists and antiquarians discussed in Chapter 9) to project passion onto a relatively backward spatiotemporal Other. Yet Herderian "romantic nationalism" marked an important departure in two respects. First, this Other for Herder was the Volk (Folk) living shoulder to shoulder, practically, with bourgeois Germans (Italians, etc.) even as he wrote. It was the Volk who retained the passionate discursive genres – folklore, including folk poetry and folk song in performance – that were, Herder argued, the only possible sources of modern European nations' revitalization. But more importantly, Herder's romantic nationalism itself evinced an obvious passion toward (a certain vision of) language. In a departure from Bacon's and Locke's modernist ideologies, which deeply distrusted emotion, romantic nationalism celebrated it (Bauman and Briggs 2003: 190). And it celebrated Europe's vernacular languages, with all their signs of folk influence, as so many particular signs of each particular emerging nation-state.

As the following case studies show, feelings about language are by no means confined to modern Western movements.

Adda: a Bengali-modern ideological construction
at the nexus of talk and feeling

Chapter 4 briefly noted a Bengali-modern phenomenon, the *āḍḍā* (hereafter, *adda*) – a sort of interstitial space of comfort created by Bengalis actively coping with capitalist modernity (Chakrabarty 1999). According to Chakrabarty, *adda* as comforting/comfortable talk emerged as a key sign of Kolkata/ Bengali modernity linked with the twentieth-century emergence of a reading public (1999: 119).

Adda became respectable in the twentieth century, as its core meaning shifted from a place (of rest) only, to the quality of the talk occurring there (Chakrabarty 1999: 119). *Adda*'s fit with capitalism involves its tone – not simply one of intimacy, but of "the intense spirit of competition that such friendship generates" (Bandyopadhyay 1988: 148, as cited by Chakrabarty 1999: 142). Yet, in order for *adda* to become a key sign and a valued practice, its competitive qualities had to be downplayed. Despite the fact that *adda* discourse was literary, the emotional import of this largely male gathering of boon companions is equally clear, and centered on its "homosocial and sometimes … homoerotic" nature. Yet, for both (some, relatively privileged) men and some women, *adda* as space and practice not only produced affect: It also became the object of affect, and specifically nostalgia. This nostalgia increased with the perception that "with the slow death of *adda*, the identity of being a Bengali will also die" (1999: 111).

Chakrabarty's story is one of a profound f – not with language in the abstract (or the Bangla language in particular), but with a certain speaking practice or, perhaps more accurately, a practice ideologically conceived. The Bengali *adda* is roughly analogous with conversation or "coffeetalk" in the contemporary United States, as it is commonly conceived – i.e., as a sign of freedom, leisure, and equality. Conversation is conceived, that is, as unconstrained, a pure reflection of participants' selves. Although Gaudio (2003) does not describe this ideological vision of conversation in primarily affective terms, Americans' identification with conversation – as a sign of much that they hold dear – involves some affection for the practice. Gaudio also recognizes the importance, for capitalism, of commodifying experiences (e.g., "the Starbucks experience") and assigning them "positive aesthetic and emotional qualities" (2003: 674). For Starbucks, it doesn't hurt if such positive affect is associated with its brand and its stores, ostensibly places for free and equal conversation. In both Kolkata and the US at the dawn of the twenty-first century, ideological representations of particular registers or genres of speech have constituted them as valued emotional objects.

Whereas the just concluded section concerned affective attachment to particular forms of talk, the next case – also from India – concerns identification with a language (again, ideologically conceived).

Tamilparru: passion for Tamil

Sumathi Ramaswamy's *Passions of the Tongue* (1997) walks a fine line. Ramaswamy would distinguish *tamilparru* – Tamil language devotion – from the many other European-inspired stories of "linguistic nationalism." Yet she also points out that the framework within which devotees have asserted the uniqueness of Tamil – claims that Tamil is divine (like Sanskrit), or "just as 'classical' as Greek and Latin" (1997: 243) – undermine assertions of its uniqueness. Ramaswamy's work thus unveils a profound paradox. On the one hand the argument of Tamil devotees seems to stand or fall on the basis of claims of its antiquity and the implication that their campaign represents a fusion of Tamil language and Tamil subjectivity that is somehow ancient. Yet clearly the movement is recent. The Tamil language – and Tamil people – in the hands of the activists have become something quite new. The understanding of 'a language' itself underwent modernization as this particular language was reinvented as the object of devotion. Tamil came to be 'ours,' the possession of Tamil-speaking people.

Over the course of the movement, 'Tamilians' were newly defined as those whose very being was shaped by being Tamil speakers. Tamil had to be discursively represented in a certain way to convince speakers that Tamil deserved their devotion. What sort of object of devotion is a language? Tamil attracted devotees through the rhetoric that made it out to be their Mother, even a mother goddess, *Tamilttay,* while "affective figures of speech" (Ramaswamy 1997: 8–9) of devotional rhetoric swayed listeners. The strategic, poetic uses of Tamil in devotional talk evoke praise for the language itself as "soft" or "sweet." Thus particular performances somehow come to stand for the language's essence.

Having considered what sort of devotional object a language might be, we must consider what sort of emotion this 'devotion to Tamil' (tamilparru) is. "The lexical meanings of *parru* include adherence, attachment, affection, support, love, and devotion" (Ramaswamy 1997: 5). Parru clearly entails identification. But beyond a term's denotation, we can also describe the action it produces. One spectacular pragmatic meaning or effect of tamilparru is self-immolation for the sake of Tamil. In 1964 a young language devotee named Chinnasami burned himself alive. In 1954, the poet Kannadasan wrote these words that, as Ramaswamy says, "eerily anticipate Chinasami's immolation a decade later": "Even in death, Tamil should be on our lips. Our ashes should burn with the fragrance of Tamil. This is our undying desire" (1997: 66).

Chinnasami was educated up to the fifth grade and worked as a day laborer. He read in his free time, immersing himself in the literature of the Dravidianist

movement that sought to restore the place of the Dravidian languages and
remove Hindi from South India. A few days before his death he confronted
a high official, begging him to do something "to save Tamil." As he doused
himself with kerosene on January 25 and set himself ablaze, he cried out, "Let
Hindi die! May Tamil flourish!" (Karunanidhi 1989[1975]: 498–501, as cited
by Ramaswamy 1997: 231).

For the moment I defer comment on the gendering of Tamil in linguistic
devotionalism. What are we to make of this modernist movement that stakes
its authority on an unproblematic link with the non-modernity of a language
and its speakers? It turns out that contemporary Apache musicians, to whom
we now turn, loosen such ties.

'Apache' music

An equally hybrid form of affective attachment to semiotic forms is found half
way around the world, in Arizona. In his evocative ethnography of music and
forms of identification on the San Carlos Apache Reservation, David Samuels
claims, "If 'being Apache' is a feeling [which he says it is], then the exploration of Apache identity must be an exploration of that feeling" (2004: 257).
Performing 'being Apache,' at least in music, seldom involves traditional songs.
More commonly, if ironically, rock and roll and country songs provide an outlet
for Apache identity. These performative acts of identification entail "engagement with, and revoicing of, 'dominant cultural expressions'" (Samuels 1999:
464). This revoicing entails feeling the music in a particularly Apache way. To
express oneself as a contemporary Apache person, Samuels argues, is always
to dialogically engage the Other. The revoicing of traditions associated with
Euro-Americans thus involves "an ironic and layered rereading of that which
is 'not Apache'" (2004: 233) in a manner that refashions such traditions as
Apache. Singing or hearing rock and roll or country songs in a particular (feelingful) way achieves a kind of appropriation of the cultural material.

"Apache culture," in this sense, is not a collection of indexically marked ideologies,
values, texts, and practices. Rather, it is a deeply and feelingfully sensed *identification*
with a shared history that flows through the present reservation communities (2004:
261, emphasis added).

The legacy of romantic nationalism has led moderns to expect one-to-one map-
pings of '**traditions**' onto 'cultures,' and 'cultures' onto territories. Telling traditional stories associated with ritually significant places in the Apache world
(Basso 1996) constitutes Apache identity, or so we believe. But this "essential-
izes the indexical relations between knowable groups of people and expressive
practices" (Samuels 1999: 467). Ramaswamy and Samuels have uncovered the
hybridity of recent performances and identification processes. We could sche-
matize Samuels' argument, and the common one, as follows, with the arrow
representing the function "indexes x:"

Apache feeling + 'non-Apache' vocal performance → new/old Apache identification
Vs.
Traditional Apache performance genres → Apache identity

Language attitudes and linguistic ideologies

Scholarly models like the schemata above claim to capture local representations; such models constitute **ideologies**. When conceived of as models,
ideologies appear cognitive in the narrow sense, i.e., as thought, not feeling
(recent work indicating the close integration of cognition and emotion notwithstanding). Is there another approach to ideology that would enable us to relate
affect – as embodied, and representationally nebulous (a la Massumi) – with
ideology, typically defined as ideational? Could 'ideology' encompass attitudes and sensibilities (Kulick and Schieffelin 2004: 352)? Before we can
explore possible convergences between research on ideologies and attitudes,
we should consider what is at stake in making an analytic distinction between
them, vs. synthesizing them.

Decades before **language ideologies** emerged as a central focus of linguistic
anthropology, social psychologist Wallace Lambert and his colleagues developed the "matched guise" (Lambert et al. 1960: 44) method for discerning
language attitudes. Lambert's first matched guise experiment involved asking
a group of Canadians "to evaluate the personality characteristics" of Canadians
speaking either English or French (1960: 50). Subjects understood they would
be hearing ten male voices reading the same passage, but did *not* know that
some of those voices would be reading the same passage twice, in English and
French. That is the "matched guise." Wallace "predicted that the differences in
the favorableness of any S's evaluations of the French and English guises of
speakers would reflect his attitude toward" the two languages and speech communities, as well as "the influence of community-wide stereotypes of English
and French speaking Canadians" (1960: 44, 50). Later work by linguistic
anthropologists like Kathryn Woolard (1985) distinguishes language attitudes
along two dimensions, status and solidarity. Describing subjects' reactions to
a tape-recorded speaker as favorability ratings (i.e., "solidarity") makes salient
their affective nature. One could explore the affective dimensions of "status,"
although Woolard (1985) does not.

Linguistic anthropologists have mostly abandoned the language attitudes
rubric in favor of language ideologies (for an exception, see Bilaniuk 2003). If
there were any tendency for anthropologists of late to want to see a bit of themselves in the communities and individuals they study (which, if it were true,
would represent a shift from previous generations), they might well see those
Others as intellectuals, generators of models. Such projection could come with
a cost, leading us to deemphasize feelings or attitudes. A more likely explanation for anthropologists' talk of ideologies, however, is that it focuses our

attention on social relations, and even more, power relations; talk of attitudes (which is more at home in psychology) does not.

It is not that psychology is necessarily reductionist and anthropology enlightened. Anthropologists may expect ideologies to find expression in discourse (or even to *concern* discourse), rather than in bodies, feelings, or embodied/ emotional acts. Yet, we should resist linking ideologies simplistically with 'notions' rather than feelings. Linguistic anthropologists like Ochs, Schieffelin, and Kulick have recognized the value in Louis Althusser's inversion of "the notional schema of ideology:" "Pascal says more or less: 'Kneel down, move your lips in prayer, and you will believe.' He thus scandalously inverts the order of things ..." (Althusser 1971: 168). Ideology, in other words, is often embodied. Althusser's vision is completely compatible with our understanding of language and emotion as social action or practice. Ideologies are not just 'ideas;' they appear materially in the embodied, the vocal, the experiential, and in the concreteness of being a certain kind of "**subject**" (Althusser 1971: 169). If affective states like desire (Cameron and Kulick 2003) or identification (Kulick 2003) attach themselves to forms of speech, this signals the presence of ideology. Ideology then consists of attitudes and aesthetic sensibilities along with notions or models.

Linguistic insecurity and/as language shame

I have hinted above at the possibility that anthropologists and others interested in language have tended to undertheorize such phenomena as affect that targets languages or particular linguistic varieties. Sociolinguists have used the relatively sanitized phrase, "linguistic insecurity" (Labov 1972) for what seems to me to be a kind of shame surrounding certain linguistic varieties. Dorian has described the "negative social prestige" or "stigma" attaching to East Sutherland Scottish Gaelic, a contracting language, and its speakers; both are charged with "backwardness" (Dorian 1980: 88). Prestige and stigma describe social facts with apparent objectivity. Scholars may prefer such terms over others like 'shame' that more overtly denote feeling. The experience of the Breton community in France is similar, but Kuter *does* speak of shame: "Bretons have learned that their culture, and language especially, are considered inferior and backward, and ridicule has served to reinforce feelings of shame in being Breton" (Kuter 1989: 80). For Bretons and speakers of Scottish Gaelic, language may be simply the most obvious index of their socially damaged 'identity,' leading both to *dis*identify with the offending language.

Labov discovered in the 1960s that New York City was a single speech community, sharing a common post-war attitude toward phonological variables like postvocalic *r* in words like 'floor' – *r*-dropping was "bad" speech. He found that New Yorkers shared with outsiders some disdain for their own speech; among them, the lower middle class was most likely to regard its own speech patterns as incorrect, and to *hypercorrect*. Labov's (1972) description of this pattern as "linguistic insecurity" is experience-distant. It is useful, I argue, to refer to such experiences as Kuter (1989) and Bonner (2001) do, as a form of shame attaching to one's speech as a sign of oneself. If, as Labov wrote, some New Yorkers accept and internalize outsiders' disdain for their speech, if indeed they internalize others' judgment of speech variables such as dropping postvocalic *r*, (1972: 133), this matches many a definition of shame. Psychoanalyst Helen Lewis's classic work traces shame to an **identification** with a subjective image of an admired Other; "failure to live up to this internalized ... imago stirs shame" (Lewis 1971: 23). "In shame we are reduced to being an object only for the other's jurisdiction," writes anthropologist Jennifer Biddle (1997: 227).

To speak an r-less dialect of New York English ranks the speaker on a vertical scale as possessing an inferior amount of social capital (Bourdieu 1991). The stakes are high, involving power/prestige (which we can describe objectively) and shame – not as a private feeling but as an experience of "the loss of a social bond" (yet another definition of shame [Scheff 2000]). Speech behavior is a matter of taste, civilization, or Kultur – one of many domains across which the expanding shadow of shame has fallen in what Norbert Elias called "the civilizing process" (Elias 2000: 5–6, 414–415).

Language and modernity, shame and impurity

From a psychodynamic perspective, 'purity,' 'linguistic purism,' or 'purification' – certainly important terms, if not obsessions in social studies of language – are powerfully linked with shame. Cameron's book, *Verbal Hygiene*, explores how and why people express concern over others' language use. Sometimes popular concern over some lamentable facts of contemporary language use verges on *disgust* (Cameron 1995: 1). In psychoanalytic theory, disgust is a visceral response associated with things children are taught to feel ashamed of playing with – bodily excretions. Children learn that such excreta are refuse, i.e., refused by civilization. Using a similar figure, Orwell called the sort of language he did not like "verbal *refuse*" (Orwell 1946: 139, emphasis added). One purist, concerned at ongoing changes in English usage, fulminated at "the *linguistic perversions* that nowadays characterize the debate about British broadcasting"! (Naughton 1993, as cited by Cameron 1995: 70, emphasis added). Such phrases reflect and play on shame reactions.

Shame hides. Shame is contagious (Lewis 1971: 15–16); "to discuss it is likely to invoke it" – a powerful disincentive for academics (Biddle 1997: 227). Hence the near total absence of a theory of purity and impurity, or shame, in Cameron's book, despite its title. What Cameron does offer is a compelling narrative – the story of an upper class British woman who ends up in prison surrounded by the more typical prison population, "poor people." Amazingly, what galled her was having to hear the 'bad' speech all around her. Prison was for her "the ultimate humiliation" (1995: 217). "The woman's concern about glottal stops and split infinitives need not be read solely as a matter of class. It is also a concern about preserving the orderliness of the world and the integrity of the self against the forces of disorder and fragmentation" (1995: 218).

Julia Kristeva's argument about "abjection" – the self-alienation that results from confrontation with what one can neither reject nor take into oneself – offers an interpretive key for that last statement by Cameron. "[I]t is thus not lack of cleanliness or health that causes abjection but what disturbs identity, system, order" (Kristeva 1982: 4). Such **structuralist** insights are most useful in conjunction with an analysis of the power-laden origins of categories like 'pure' and 'impure,' of class itself, of how language has come to stand in for social inequalities – and of how paradoxes arise in these processes (Bauman and Briggs 2003). An adequate anthropological understanding of shame must then confront it as affect, recognize its social production and its relation to (dis)order, and follow its many histories.

Conclusion

In one way or another, many scholars have at least hinted at relationships in which affect attaches to a language or a speech form. What has been missing, at least from the most systematic treatments of language and emotion within linguistic anthropology, has been a theory that encompasses language passions, and language shame, in a larger model of language, culture, and emotion. The number of well-known past investigations that can be fruitfully reinterpreted to elucidate their implications for this larger model is impressive. If you have read these previous studies, and now agree that they offer more than has met the eye, then this chapter has succeeded.

Reinterpreting the field of language-and-emotion in relation to processes of identification and disidentification has made possible several steps forward. First, it has helped us derive from previous work a maximum of insight into the social life of language and affect. Second, it has shifted our attention from reifications ('identities') whose thing-like existence is empirically dubious to dynamic processes requiring close ethnographic study. And finally, it has provided a bridge between newer work on language passions and language shame on the one hand, and older work on language as an indexical system, and speaking as an indexical act. The levels of reflexivity, subjecting pragmatic signs (for example) to metapragmatic comment, that have occupied us in this book can now be acknowledged as not only ideational but emotional. Particular linguistic acts signaling emotion, and mass social movements encouraging and evincing passion toward linguistic codes, are both historical, and identificatory moments.

8

LANGUAGE, AFFECT, GENDER, AND SEXUALITY

Introduction

The triple relationship of language, emotion, and gender is a minefield. Representations of that relationship, no doubt including my own, scarcely avoid reflecting biases old and new. Indeed the very mention of emotion, for some, evokes gender. This chapter, however, seeks to shed new light on this intersection rather than simply recirculate old ideas. In doing so, I continue to draw on models arising out of research on **language ideologies**. Studying language ideologies can bridge linguistic and social theory, providing "a mediating link between social forms and forms of talk" (Woolard 1998: 3). Thus, for example, they link power-based, always partial visions of gender relations, with equally power-related visions of language use and practice. These visions are crucial to processes of **social reproduction** insofar as they undergird socialization (or enculturation) and rituals central to the social order. The interplay of ideology and practice involves relative degrees of awareness; various forms of (potentially distorting) awareness can provide powerful insights into "language as a social tool" and "cultural resource" (Duranti 1997: 1, 2). Duranti's description points, among other things, to the ideological uses of language, i.e., cultural models of language. (Concepts of) language(s) are tools for doing important ideological work.

We can also theorize language ideologies in terms of **orders of indexicality**. From this perspective, language ideologies are second-order indexes, i.e., social acts of pointing to (or imagining, constituting) lower-order indexes. The latter include, e.g., popularly perceived co-occurrence patterns involving 'gender identity' – the reality of shifting moments of identification being perhaps less stable than 'identity' would indicate. But higher-order indexes – here, language ideologies – influence lower-order instances, by increasing or otherwise shaping consciousness.

Relationships of indexicality, at least in the realm of discourse and culture, are historical products. In asserting this, I do not mean simply that correlations between some linguistic variable and some sociological variable are historically unstable. I mean that the very relationship between the two, defined as one of indexicality (with or without the term), and even the sociolinguistic variable itself, are historical products *qua* social imaginaries. This is the process of *indexicalization* (Inoue 2006), a kind of invention of relatedness or correlation, often an invention of the very linguistic 'facts' said to index some social group. The invented index, however, may well become truth, acting as a kind of magnet that pulls reality in its direction. This process exemplifies the play of sign and metasign, language and metalanguage, pragmatic effect and metapragmatic characterization – such interplay being *the* true and fundamental social fact (Agha 2007), which is quite essential to the following argument. I return to Inoue's concept of indexicalization in Chapter 10 for its great relevance to social histories of language and emotion.

If you keep in mind that I am using 'ideologies' as a convenient shorthand for politically grounded reflections, and that some of these reflections may be feelings or aesthetic sensibilities, you will find it easier to remember the link between ideology and affect. Like Volosinov's "behavioral ideology" – "that atmosphere of unsystematized and unfixed inner and outer speech which endows our every instance of behavior and action and our every 'conscious' state with meaning" (1973: 91) – what I am treating as the aesthetic face of ideology is evaluative, always socially grounded, but unsystematized. The point of distinguishing this aesthetic dimension of the always politically grounded reflection on emotion, language, or both, is to stress its affinity with affect.

Ground well trodden

Studies of language and gender have often addressed the putative role affect plays in gendered linguistic performance. Chapter 5 reviewed Lutz's problematizing of claims about gendered speech, claims that point to the power of those who make them. Eckert and McConnell-Ginet (1992) exemplify the recent tendency to eschew any generalizations about 'men's' or 'women's' language.

By contrast, linguist Robin Lakoff's pioneering work argued that 'women' and 'men' may feel with equal intensity, but differ "in how forcefully one says how one feels," using "oh dear" vs. "shit" (1975: 10). "Only a man can bellow in rage" (1975 :11). Susan Speer (2005: 47) criticizes Lakoff for taking a realist approach (in the philosophical sense) to emotion talk. That is, Lakoff interpreted discourse as a reflection of mind, feeling, etc., construing language as a resource for signaling inner states somehow constituted apart from speech, rather than a form of social action. We find the same realism in Lakoff's analysis of intonation patterns; for Lakoff, women's putative tendency to make declarative statements using the rising intonation pattern proper to questions indexes a real, independently existing, inner hesitation or uncertainty (1975:17), perhaps an anxiety to please.

In work on language and gender produced well into the 1990s, Speer sees a tendency to take interview-elicited metadiscourse at face value. In response to an interviewer's question, a woman might characterize her own speech, or some difference she perceives in men's and women's speech patterns. Taking such metadiscursive statements as indicators of the way gendered speech actually works is problematic, and linguistic anthropologists advocate a very different approach. Although we cannot dismiss the sort of language ideologies we hear in interviews, neither do they straightforwardly reveal sociolinguistic realities. Thus, Norah Vincent's (2006: 14) reflections on gender differences – particularly the sort of affectivity indexed by the breathless rapid pace at which (she claims) women speak – is a representation that deserves its own scrutiny.

Men, language, and emotion

Until recently 'women's' discourse has attracted far more scholarly attention than 'men's.' Fortunately, scholars are increasingly investigating masculinities, and men's speech and emotion. Yet too little of this new work concerns non-referential features that might index some sort of masculinity, and at the same time constitute the emotional quality of men's embodied speech-in-interaction.

Charteris-Black (in submission), drawing on Galasinski (2004), questions the degree to which a dominant form of masculinity is "hegemonic," at least in the discourse of British men experiencing illness. Such men resort to the language of feelings, and particularly soft, vulnerable feelings. Charteris-Black's **corpus analysis** study focused exclusively on words – particularly "emotion adjectives" referring to positive or negative feeling states. Some men in the study did resort to emotional forms conventionally associated with male speech, including swear words. However, some of that swearing occurred in surprising contexts, such as one man's wish that his wife would share more of her most personal emotions with him. Other men seemed to be groping toward a new "construction of masculinity." In discussing illness experiences, they were *more* likely than women to use the adjectives 'emotional,' 'frustrating', and 'embarrassing.'

Marsden (2007) describes "all male sonic gatherings" among Chitrali Muslim men in Pakistan that involve at least two contrasting kinds of performance, aesthetics, judgments, and masculinities. Despite the differences between the musical and emotional aesthetics of the contrasting performance genres, men attending both often spoke openly of vulnerable feelings, particularly their unfulfilled love for female sweethearts of long ago. In fact, such talk is "central to the proper affective constitution of Chitrali men" (2007: 483).

Marsden actually downplays the role of discourse and symbolic meaning in these performances. His sharp contrasting of the discursive and musical realms (2007: 474) is a common stance, but one convincingly critiqued (as noted in Chapter 4) by ethnomusicologists like Tolbert (2001a) and Feld et al. (2004). Not only is there a "music of language," but a "language of music" observable most markedly in lyrics (though the expression has obvious metaphorical meanings as well).

In their own ways, these authors limit the possibilities of discourse and its analysis. Charteris-Black relies exclusively on interview data. Although interviews can offer rich insights, particularly to the analyst who is prepared to mine them for indications of language ideologies, it is essential to record naturally occurring discourse as well. Galasinski (2004:2) claims to uncover "how men talk about their emotions," as does Charteris-Black. In reality, they discovered how men talk within one context – narratives elicited during interviews. Rather than discussing all the many ways in which speakers might perform or index emotion, these two authors limit their analysis to the talked-about, i.e., **referential**, dimension of that speech. Marsden indeed explores performance, but treats speech and language – including men's explicit reflections on performance, aesthetics, and emotions, as well as the discursive structure of their songs – as something separate, rather than one dimension among others that constitutes performance. We need studies that recognize this broader range of linguistic or **semiotic** functions.

Language, desire, and sexuality

As real as the **social construction** of affect is, there will always be a portion of subjectivity that resists ideologies as well as any attempt at self-control. As I indicated in Chapter 7, the Freudian unconscious is making something of a comeback in some circles of linguistics and linguistic anthropology. Paradoxically, the recent focus on "desire" – a Freudian theme – has enabled Kulick (2003, Kulick and Schieffelin 2004) to uncover the workings of power in relation to **language socialization**. Adult authority vis-à-vis children often works through linking actions and outcomes desirable to them, with actions they frame as desirable for the child (Kulick and Schieffelin 2004: 361). Instances of language socialization involving an authority manipulating discursive images of desirability may also involve adults such as audience members in a congregation listening to a fundamentalist Protestant sermon (2004: 362).

Desire falls under the scope of "affect" as defined in recent linguistic anthropology (Kulick and Schieffelin 2004: 352); but it seldom appears in lists of 'universal emotions,' perhaps being conceived as more primitive than emotion. Kulick's work on language and desire, which draws on and modifies psychoanalytic notions like 'the unconscious' and 'repression,' breaks new ground in several ways. First, in relation to previous work apparently relevant to language and sexuality (i.e., analyses of "gay and lesbian language"), Kulick finds a striking undertheorization of sexuality as desire, and a much clearer focus on **identity**. This approach, he says, takes key terms like 'gay' as givens, obscuring the dynamic workings of desire. Kulick thus advocates

vis-à-vis an important kin relationship comes from the Southern Highlands province of Papua New Guinea (mentioned in the Introduction). For decades, Bambi Schieffelin (1990, 2000, 2007) has studied Kaluli, a Papuan language spoken on Mt. Bosavi. She has focused on language socialization, and the linguistic dimensions of transformations brought about through missionization.

Two "modalities of action" are central to Kaluli speech acts – assertion and appeal. Kaluli models of childhood and the developmental process treat appeal as something children are born knowing. Despite the fact that this renders socialization to appeal apparently unnecessary, the telling of the *muni* bird myth has a clear socializing function. Children must learn when to accede to others' requests. Girls in particular learn, in part through this myth, of their obligation to respond to their younger brothers. Older sisters and younger brothers call each other *ade*, which is "one of the profound social and sentimental relationships; outside of marriage, it is the most important bond between men and women" (B. Schieffelin 1990: 112–113).

The myth tells of a boy whose verbal appeal to his older sister failed to sway her, resulting in his transformation into the form of a *muni* bird whose plaintive cry becomes an eternal reminder of the *ade* relationship (in the breech, as it were). It reminds older sisters of their obligation to share with their ade (B. Schieffelin 1990: 113). In addition to the myth, maternal appeals "to the older child to 'feel sorry for'" the younger reproduce the all-important ade relationship. A number of linguistic features mark mothers' utterances as 'appeal' – a) a unique "voice quality" that receives its own metapragmatic label, *geseab*, b) the "sympathy-eliciting expressive [discourse marker] /heyo/," and c) "negative directives, such as 'Don't disturb [younger] /ade/ (who is asleep)'" (1990: 120).[3]

We can view Kaluli language socialization practices as the outworkings of ideologies of language, personhood, gender, and emotion. As "rationalization[s] … of perceived language structure and use" that influence what is passed down, and how (Silverstein 1979: 193), such ideologies contribute to **social reproduction**.

The gendering of lament

The *muni* bird story bears a relationship to a set of richly described Kaluli expressive genres we can gloss as **laments**, especially *saya:lab*.

In many societies – especially stratified societies – lament has suffered from its association with women, whose sexuality and emotion are regarded as somewhat dangerous generally, and not just in relation to death. In other cases – Egypt, throughout much of its known history, and pre-twentieth-century Karelia – lament's gendered power was honored. Until recently Egyptian women regarded their role in lamenting the dead as one of great magical-ritual

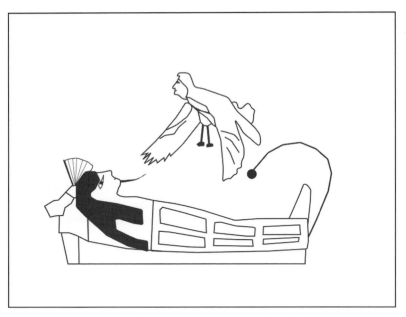

Figure 8.1   *Nefertari as bird hovering over husband, à la Isis and Osiris.*
Drawing by Laureen Coveney-Thom, based on a photo by Jacques Livet

power (Wickett 1993: 335). The Pyramid Texts, dating from around 2300 BCE (during the Old Kingdom), describe the magician-goddess Isis, in the form of a bird of prey, hovering over the dead body of her brother-husband Osiris, lamenting (Figure 8.1). Her magically empowered lament brought him – or at least his phallus – back to life, so that she was able to conceive Horus by him. Even into the Late Period (lasting from 664 BCE until 323 BCE), texts like *The Lamentations of Isis and Nephthys* that reproduced this origin myth of Egyptian lament continued to serve as models for noble women who were to sing their laments in "the temple of Osiris" (Budge 1972: 521).

Strong assertions about **laments**, about the propriety of certain classes of women singing them, and about the ritual power of those who do – these linguistic ideologies function as examples of **metaculture** (Urban 2001), i.e., as cultural products that comment on and evaluate other (lower-order) cultural products. Statements that appear descriptive, e.g., "Lament is primitive and irrational!" (Wilce 2009) – may function prescriptively. The circulation and replication of these ideologies serves at the very least as a guide or template for the reproduction of a certain cultural order entailing certain gender relations, regimenting discourse and other semiotic forms and managing their social distribution.

Table 8.1: *The dichotomizing language ideology of Gapun village, schematized*[4]

Hed	Save
Taiap	Tok Pisin (TP)
Paganism	Christianity (the Catholic Church)
Backward	Modernity
Women	Men
Passion	Reason
Kros	*Men's house oratory*

Gender, emotion, and language shift

Emotion may play a role in empowering Karelian lament-women (Chapter 2), but – mediated by ideologies of language and gender – it has played a very different role in Gapun village, Papua New Guinea (Kulick 1992). There, the gendering of **ideal-types** (Weber 1999: 248) of language set *Taiap mɛr* ('Taiap language,' a Sepik-Ramu Papuan language) on the path to extinction. These ideal-types gained influence through the dominance of language ideologies that figure men as calm speakers of the modern Tok Pisin (TP, New Guinea's national language) – and women as wild and dangerous speakers of the village tongue, Taiap.

Such ideologies hinged on the binary contrast between two ideal-types of personhood, intimately associated with communicative style – *hed* and *save*. Gapuners associate these, in turn, with two speech genres – *kros*es, and oratory. To succeed in life, Gapuners need both *hed* (or *bikhed*) – personal autonomy – and *save*, "the sociable, cooperative side of the person" (1992: 19). Indeed elements of each are found in expressions of the other; "overt displays of *save* can sometimes be interpreted as containing dimensions of *hed*" (Kulick 1992: 253). Gapuner ideologies, however, *construe* the two as far apart. Gapun became a Roman Catholic village after WWII. By the 1980s, Gapuners increasingly valued *save* (over hed), linking it with modernity, the outside world, and Catholicism. They associated the two languages – Taiap and TP – with the two sets of opposing values. The associations proliferate.

Gapuners hold women responsible for those outbursts of vituperative obscenity known as *kros*es, a TP word meaning "crosses, fits of anger" (1992: 35). A *kros* is a loud, angry, vituperative, often vulgar monologue aimed from a woman's home at some offender the former perceives as bikhed (full of hed). Kroses always occur in Taiap. Gapuner men and women alike associate them with women, even though men may benefit, or even stir up their wives to lash out in this way. Villagers perceive kroses as inflammatory and socially damaging and associate them exclusively with hed, even though a kros displays some *save* insofar as it often results in the apparent resolution of the matter that prompted it (1992: 253).

Gapuners perceive *men's house oratory* as a genre that iconically represents men's nature. This is precisely the sort of "iconization" Irvine and Gal (2000) describe, a process by which an indexical 'fact' is construed as an icon, a revelation of some group's essence. 'Women' and 'women's speech' in Gapun village were also undergoing iconization. The name *men's house oratory* denotes the setting in which the genre is performed – in the men's cult house. Although such performances once occurred in Taiap, the genre is now performed in TP, which Gapuners believe to be the language of white people (outsiders), and associate with Christianity. Whereas the kros stirs dissension and passion, oratory soothes tensions and brings about consensus and peace. Women find themselves excluded, structurally, from the performance of oratory. And, whereas topics of kroses are, like the women who deliver them, quite limited to the village, men's oratory spans a broader range of concerns, often invoking ties between the village and translocal institutions like the Catholic Church.

However, just as men may provoke a kros, they may also slip into Taiap during oratorical speech. Significantly, they do so at the most critical, emotional moments of a harangue, e.g., to make a statement like, "I'm sick of this!" (1992: 147). This fact, and the possibility that men sometimes provoke women to engage in kroses, complicate the dichotomies constructed in the dominant **language ideology**, and are not discussed locally. Nor is the degree of *save* apparent in "successful" kroses discussed.

The shift from Taiap to TP was not inevitable, even with the array of negative associations Taiap built up in the 1980s. A proximate cause for the failure of linguistic reproduction is necessary, and Kulick uncovered it. Without any conscious intent, but clearly influenced by new ideological and emotional associations with the two codes spoken in Gapun, caregivers began using more and more TP in addressing their children. Although mothers certainly continued speaking Taiap in their children's presence, they came to use only TP in any utterances, e.g., commands, to which children were expected to respond. As a result, by the late 1980s, children were growing up unable to speak Taiap fluently. Adults blamed language shift on the children's hed; in fact, they themselves had precipitated it.

How did such associations come to dominate Gapuner consciousness, so that Taiaip almost disappeared? And further, what generalities, e.g., about linguistic ideologies, might this case illustrate? Macrosociological variables such as urbanization have driven other cases of language shift. However, the ideological imaginings in Table 8.1 – of practices and speech genres associated with women vs. men, of *hed* vs. *save*, of intense vs. controlled affect, and of Taiap vs. TP – drove this shift.

Scholars praise Kulick's study for its contribution to our understanding of language shift, i.e., for revealing the role of language ideologies in such change.

We have seen that men's house oratory is not performed purely in TP, and that women's *kroses* are not just women's. The language ideologies, however – like all ideologies – are selective, partial representations of reality reflecting current power relations (Woolard 1998). Gapuner language ideology is no exception; to the extent that it offers a very partial representation of the complex relationships between codes, genres, settings, emotions, and genders, it distorts. Boas treated language ideologies as "secondary rationalizations" irrelevant to anthropological study (1995[1911]: 23–24). But Kulick (1992, following Silverstein 1979, 1985) demonstrates, to the contrary, that language ideologies actually influence the evolution of linguistic forms and practices. Gapuner-modern ideology changed practice – villagers stopped speaking to children in Taiap, and the language appeared to be doomed.[5] "Gapun might be held up as a case in which the macrosociological changes that are occurring can be said not to have caused language shift, but rather, to have been *caused by* shift: in attitudes, perceptions of self, and ideas about language" (Kulick 1992: 260; emphasis in original). And in this shift emotion, and ideologies linking it with women and the traditional vernacular, played a central role.

Lurking in the background of this discussion are complex layers of indexicality, and a powerful construal of iconicity. Even if we take it as a simple (lower-order) indexical fact that women *were* associated with the *kros* and men with oratory, the second-order index proved to be both more distorting and more influential. That index (language ideology, pointing to practices, actors, etc.) generalized from the women=kros (in Taiap) and men=oratory (in Tok Pisin) 'facts,' making Taiap a sign of irrationality and Tok Pisin of rational, Christian modernity. Taiap – and women – became iconically, essentially, linked with anger, and Tok Pisin (and men) with constructive sociality (Silverstein 1998).

Imaginings of modern nationhood played a part in Gapuner language shift. They are at the center of tamilparru.

Revisiting tamilparru and tamilttay

Chapter 7 explored a significant case study: the constitution of Tamil as a particular sort of emotional object, the object of devotion, *parru*. In part, that devotion reflects the gendering of the object. In the Dravidianist movement, from "the late nineteenth century on," the Tamil language is not an 'it' but a 'she,' a mother, a mother-goddess (Ramaswamy 1997: 121). The feminization of Tamil was part of a rhetoric of grievance or outrage. Tamil linguistic nationalism casts first the foreign colonizers, then Hindi-speaking north Indians, as linguistic imperialists bent on the destruction of Tamil (1997: 124). Such rhetoric, and especially talk of the "selfless love" of "Mother Tamil," is bound to stir passion. The Tamil language became both the loving, naturalized, emotional matrix of origin of its speakers, and also the proper object of the same love.

Tamilparru, devotion to the Tamil tongue, is a language ideology/attachment that reflects India's colonial and postcolonial history. It also reminds us that any encompassing theory of language and emotion must grapple not only with emotion as a referential or indexical object of language, but with language – a particular language – as an object of passion. The apparently local, nativist, nationalist Tamil movement, and even the imagining of Tamil as woman/mother, are somewhat predictable successors to colonial imaginaries. That the Tamil movement has helped make some of those colonial imaginaries a reality (1997: 255) exemplifies the ironies of modernity.

Conclusion

As our understanding of speaking and "languaging" (Becker 1991) has evolved, linguistic anthropologists have problematized the comparison of 'languages' at the heart of the linguistic-relativist vision (Whorf 1956b). Current understandings of sociolinguistic diversity among speakers of 'a language' offer both an obstacle to and an opening for further theorizing of linguistic relativity. For instance, describing language as a tool, used (of course) differently in different situations (Duranti 1997: 1–2, and Chapter 3), cuts both ways in relation to arguments for linguistic relativity. Then too, whereas the very power of language in constituting cultural perception relies – in the Boasian (1995 [1911]) vision – on the false consciousness (and irrelevance) of the untrained (non-anthropologist) subject's understanding of his or her own language, work on language ideologies has revealed how such ideologies affect the unfolding histories of linguistic forms and practices. In this regard, the examples this chapter has discussed invite further consideration.

Indexing affect toward female referents is such an example. "In ordinary interaction one cannot speak Mohawk, Oneida, or Onondaga for very long without having occasion to refer to a woman, and when one does one has to make a choice. ... of a kind that English speakers do not have to make" (Chafe 1997: 21). When speakers of these languages need to refer to a woman, the unique resources – and perhaps constraints – those languages offer differ from those offered by English. The discursive-cognitive habits of the two sets of speakers differ; Chafe's argument is consciously Whorfian.

We have also explored **lament**. Wilce (1998) argued that the representation of Bangladeshi lament as an exclusively female performance genre reflects an ideology of language and gender; that is, it reflects the iconization (essentialization) of what is but a probabilistic (indexical) relationship. Some lament genres aim to magically bring about transformations – some local genres effecting primarily a social transformation, as when Warao women challenge the authority of shamans by implicating them in the death they lament (Briggs 1998), other genres effecting a cosmic transformation (as when the laments of early twentieth-century Karelian 'cry-women' safely carried the dead to *Tuonela*, the beyond).

But what of the affective stance and gendering of ethnography, especially ethnographies of lament? Anthropological writing about death, mourning, loss, and lament can mimetically reflect laments (Wilce 2009), in theme (traditional laments mourn someone's death; ethnographies of lament may thematize *its* death) and structure (a lament's unfolding organization iconically captures its ritual 'goal'; the rhetorical themes of an ethnographic essay may unfold in similar patterns). Anthropology's refusal to study the real-world effects, not of fieldwork (alone), but of its primary product – writing (whether about lament or anything else) – reflects a clinging to objectivist presumptions about the real-world neutrality of our descriptions.

This, too, constitutes an ideology of language, an ideological vision of our own discourse and its function. Our somewhat distanced approach to lament in fieldwork (why does no one admit to engaging in our most definitive method in its case – participant-observation?) correlates with the distant style of much ethnographic writing (see Introduction). The irony is not only that this, too, constitutes an affective stance (cool), but that the self-distancing strategy appears to fail when we look carefully at thematic and structural parallels between our writing and the laments of 'folks' we study. In the same way that some feminist anthropologists have embraced a dual, academic-activist, role (Mascia-Lees, Sharpe, and Cohen 1989; Scheper-Hughes 1995), a demasculinization of academic writing (about emotion, for example) might well begin with intentionally blurring the line between observation and participation, description and action, reporting and performing.

HISTORIES OF LANGUAGE
AND EMOTION

9

A HISTORY OF THEORIES

Part IV, and this chapter, situate contemporary approaches to language and emotion historically. Chapter 10 outlines macrolevel shifts in emotion-and-language regimes in the world at large, whereas here we more narrowly examine shifts in scholarly theories.

Such reflections on academic discourse are still not widespread in anthropology, its postmodern turn notwithstanding. Broad ethnologies of emotion, and ethnographic studies of models of emotion and selfhood (or subjecthood), have tended to be synchronic. A smaller group of anthropologists have admirably historicized emotion; a few (Reddy 2001) even offer a general model of emotion (for example, Stewart 2007). However, anthropologists working on emotion have not always put their own theories under the historical microscope, tracking the extent to which they parallel developments in the broader world of scholarship and the arts not for the purpose of justifying them, but to subject them to critique.

We cannot separate our work from our own social, cultural, political histories. We are shaped by various histories of modernism and its tendency to lament a lost past (Lévi-Strauss 1974[1955] and sources cited by Bauman and Briggs 2003), one of simplicity and directness of experience and expression; and by inherited polarities, especially that of a "rational male versus emotional female" (e.g., Martin 2001). We also shape those histories. Linguistic anthropologists and **conversation analysts** often express skepticism about reading emotion 'itself' from language. This stance deserves more attention and reflection than it has received thus far, and this chapter addresses that absence.

Although much of what I have written in previous chapters has strong anti-essentializing implications, I have not raised the category problem: what makes us trust the universal validity of the inclusive term, 'emotions'? I will not attempt an adequate history of theory, but only an overview of historic transformations in select theories of emotion and discourse of most relevance for our purposes.

Indian aesthetic philosophy and the rasa theory

Before following the well worn path of tracing the history of Western philosophical musings on emotion and language – certainly an important source of contemporary thought – I briefly describe strands of Indian thought that concern the relationship of various sign-modalities, including language, to what might be translated 'emotion.' One reason for doing so is that this particular ancient discourse on emotion (actually on *rasa* and *bhāva*) has influenced recent anthropological work on emotion (especially in South Asian communities, both in the homeland and in various diasporas). I return to that current relevance at the end of the chapter.

Scholarship on medieval Sanskrit theories of *poetics* (often referred to as "rasa theory," Gerow 1981, 2002; Larson 1976) – notes the centrality of two Sanskrit terms, rasa and bhāvā (Bangla *bʰab*), and their close cousins in the Indic languages (e.g., Bangla rɔʃ). Rasa denotes

emotions evoked in a listener or spectator that are aesthetically distanced and more pristine and rarefied than any feeling derived from direct sensual perception or experience (Toomey 1990: 161, citing Masson and Patwardhan 1969).

Speakers of today's Indic languages, like Bangla, use *bʰab* to refer to basic human moods, but also bodily sensations and thoughts. Rasa is not used in everyday Bangla emotion-talk.

The common meaning of rasa in contemporary Indic languages reflects the semantic core of the Sanskrit term. In the philosophical literature, rasa is literally the 'flavor' or 'taste' (Higgins 2003: 681), 'juice' or 'essence' (Timm 1991), 'extract' or 'quintessence' (Lynch 1990a) evoked by discursive events, particularly dramatic performances. Thus, rasa's denotation is grounded in embodied, gustatory experience. Still, despite the currency of that material sense (denoting 'juice,' the object) even in the tenth century, philosophical writings of the time clearly treat rasa as a spiritual state. They describe the *rasika* as the spiritual initiate, whose discipline and spiritual achievements become clear in his ability to experience ecstatic rasa states while he focuses his attention during a religious play. A diverse but interlocking set of signs – the dramatic **text** and its particular voicing, the appearance of the actors, and their stylized gestures – convey such states, according to rasa theory.

Rasa theory arose specifically from the *aesthetic* philosophers of the Indian tradition, writing about the ideal spiritual response that Sanskrit drama-in-performance should create. Although a range of semiotic forms draw out rasa, the poetic lines uttered in sacred performance are salient among them. Bruce Sullivan, an expert on Sanskrit drama and its contemporary performance (B. Sullivan 1990), writes:

All forms of [Sanskrit] drama utilize speech: prose statements move the plot along through action and dialogue, but when a character expresses an emotional state with the intent of evoking a rasa experience in audience members, the character does this with a highly polished Sanskrit verse or two in an identifiable meter – in short, with poetry (personal communication, August 2007).

Thus the discourse on rasa is a metasemiotic model of poetic language and divine states of emotion (rasa), or, if you prefer, a theory of multimodal

textuality. That is, rasa theory is a model of the ideal affective response to dramatic performance, a complex whole that consists of discursive **texts** and **voice** effects, along with a repertoire of conventionalized gestures and other on-stage visual effects. The experience of rasa always entails "a sense of unity" in the presence of "disparate matter" (Gerow 1981: 250). If textuality is coherence, and rasa entails an ecstatic experience of the unity of a poem or play, we can think of rasa as a feeling of textuality, or an affect-laden apperception of textuality – keeping in mind that the sources treated that sort of feeling or affect as divine. What sort of aesthetic integration is the experience of rasa – e.g., the rasa evoked by Kalidasa's play, *The Sakuntala*? Gerow describes the rasa *Sakuntala* inspires as an experience that is both social and cosmic insofar as it involves the cosmic self (*paramātman*) of the actors (2002: 268) and, presumably, audience members.

The nature of the unity or integration of the various feelings that may be stimulated by shifting scenes in Sanskrit drama is the subject of intense scrutiny. Medieval arguments on this point hinge on the distinction between *sthāyibhāva* (the stable, dominant, defining emotion of a dramatic performance) and *vyabichāri-bhāvas* (emotions created in each passing dramatic moment) – up to thirty-three of them (B. Sullivan 2007). As is true in the medieval Christian theological representations of passions and affections discussed below, this Sanskrit literature names a fixed set of rasas (eight). Any one of them can function as the *sthāyibhāva* of a sacred play. Each particular poetic or dramatic work was understood to produce one of these eight (or, in other writings, nine) rasas. The ninth, a somewhat controversial addition, is *s; ānta*, the rasa of 'peace' (B. Sullivan 2007: 430) or 'quietude' (Timm 1991).

Although medieval writings that elevated rasa far above bhāva have been influential, later voices – particularly in the devotional tradition of Vaishnava Hinduism (i.e., devotion to Krishna) – celebrated certain bhāvas as divine gifts, signs of sainthood (McDaniel 1989). The experience of bhāva is usually described as personal, leading us to ask whether it, rather than rasa, is the closer counterpart of English 'emotion.' Rasa is impersonal. Rasa *is* the play's very meaning. The rasa-objective in aesthetic experience is "catalytic" rather than "**cathartic**" (Lynch 1990a: 17; compare Gerow 2002: 266). The peculiar sort of 'result' rasa constitutes is an "affect, never an effect" (Gerow 1981: 250); it is an awareness in the audience that is "immediate"; not the fruit of contemplation (ibid.). "The rasa [is an] integrating experience – partly cognitive, because generalized – partly emotional, because responsive; it is a whole in which the various elements of the psyche come to rest and which, by being a whole, defines them as cooperating parts" (Gerow 2002: 268). Paradoxically, although a particular performance elicits rasa in a particular audience gathered at a certain time, the rasa itself is "generalized," "universalized" (2002: 268). This capacity of Sanskrit drama to somehow convey a "generalized situation" "voids such aspects of 'partial awareness' as 'mine,' 'his,' or 'now'" (Gerow 1981: 250–251). Its spiritual potential lies precisely in this capacity to lift viewers out of themselves, out of the here and now. (Note the similarity to the Javanese *priyayi* avoidance of indexicals discussed in Chapter 6.)

Deployments of the term bhāva in the Indian aesthetic literature probably never call up notions of the human condition in terms of sinfulness or fallenness, as did invocations of Latin *passiones* in the classics or in medieval theological texts (see below). Instead, bhāva represented an innate human potential that becomes the ground on which transcendent 'emotional' experiences (rasa) can be created in the experience of sacred dramatic performance. "In Krishna *bhakti* [devotional practice], bhāva and rasa are reinterpreted, shorn of their aesthetic distance; emphasis is placed, instead, on emotional experience of Krishna and its spontaneous expression (*raganugabhakti*) in the devotee's life" (Toomey 1990: 161).

From the first chapters of this book, I have stressed the need to view emotion and emotive language in relation to metasigns that reflect, for example, on emotion words or the relationship of emotion to other sorts of signs-in-context (such as chanting Krishna's name, or contemplating a sacred image). Forms of metasemiosis, including discourse that constructs ideal selves by projecting a certain emotional persona, typically serve not just as representations of, but as models for. The Indian philosophical literature proposes such models; ethnographic evidence indicates their popular influence. In a contemporary setting, the Chaubes of Mathura (Uttar Pradesh, India), a Vaishnavite group, idealize a state of holy intoxication, *masta*, and speak of themselves as *mastram*. Lynch provides a "thick description" of the Chaubes and their model of emotion. Thus, although he explores what masta denotes, he is more concerned to provide an account of discursive practice, the pragmatics of discourse about masta. "A mastram is one who either is masta (intoxicated, drunk, proud, wanton, lustful, happy, overjoyed, careless) or experiences masti (intoxication, *joi de vivre*, carefreeness, passion, joyous radiance)" (Lynch 1990b: 91–92). The semantic intensions of these terms are just one resource in semiotic practice that involves not just **reference** but various forms of social **identification**; but it is in living contexts, moments when these terms are deployed for certain pragmatic ends, that we see their real meaning.

We shift now to ground more familiar to many readers.

Historical roots of Western theories of emotion: classical and Christian philosophy

Limitations of space preclude a thorough summary of the long history of scholarly thought that preceded the modernist naming of a single unified field, 'the emotions,' in the two centuries leading up to an experimentally oriented, atheological, scientific psychology, and the special role of Scottish moral philosophers in effecting this change (Dixon 2003). Still, it is important to offer some cultural-historical context for current theory.

Historians describe the fallacy of *presentism* in the historiography of what we now call 'emotion,' pointing out major shifts in labels and models of this semantic domain – even within the so-called Western philosophical (and, importantly, theological) tradition. Such twists and turns undermine (a) the widespread tendency, even among scholars, to treat their own cultural history as teleological, leading inexorably to a scientific view of such phenomena; and (b) the tendency to anachronism, projecting into the past a 'scientific' view that unites all subjective states under the single term 'emotion,' which only became dominant in nineteenth-century psychology. For centuries preceding the emergence of "atheological" scientific psychology, religious (and, from his Christian perspective, doctrinally "orthodox") and philosophical models of subjectivity differentiated "the passions" from "the affections" (Dixon 1999, 2003), respectively deemed dangerous and admirable, although in some way both emanate from, and index, God's love (1999, 2003). Certain strands of this tradition rejected a simple dichotomy between reason and feeling and the straightforward valorization of reason over affect.

The contrasts between classical Greek and medieval Sanskrit models of emotion that we have already encountered is one that recent ethnographers have built upon. In *On the Soul* and *Poetics*, Aristotle laid out a theory of motion, *anima* (soul), and **catharsis**. These imaginings of the soul, its motion, and God as Unmoved Mover influenced Christian theologians like Thomas Aquinas. Some nine centuries before Aquinas, Augustine developed a theory of the soul based on his reading of the Neoplatonists alongside Christian scripture. Augustine located the *imago Dei* (image of God) in what was incorporeal in humanity, namely the soul. This *imago* is reflected in human reason, but also in the proper uses of 'the affections' (*affectiones*). *Passiones* – 'the passions,' Augustine's overarching term for affective states – fell into four classes: 1) perturbations of the soul that one should control by means of reason, 2) "inappropriate desires (*cupiditas, libido, concupiscentia*) and lusts," 3) diseases (*morbi*) of the soul reflecting the body's rebellion against its Creator, and 4) passions that were "appropriate to this probationary earthly state but ultimately to be shed in the future life" (Dixon 2003: 41). Like Aristotle, Aquinas distinguished passions from affects, i.e., *passiones* construed as "involuntary passions of the soul, which were disturbances of the sensory appetite and had objects of sense for the objects," as opposed to *affectus*, or 'affect,' which was a voluntary act "without passion" (Dixon 2003: 46).

Affects, considered 'movements of the soul' at least through the time of Aquinas, were reimagined as 'mechanisms' in the Age of Reason (2003: 62). The eighteenth-century trend was toward replacing traditional Christian models of affects and passions with more naturalistic, secular models. Even in the Christian thought of revivalists Jonathan Edwards and Isaac Watts, Dixon sees a departure from earlier theologies of the passions, and the triumph of Cartesian dualism (2003: 92). The secularizing drive toward a scientific psychology reached an early peak in the works of eighteenth-century British moralists whose work foreshadowed that of David Hume (1711–1776) and Thomas Brown (1778–1820).

Hume's *Treatise of Human Nature* (1739–1740) provided "the earliest sustained use of the term ['emotions'] in the English language in a way that is similar to present-day usage" (Dixon 2003: 104). About a century later, Edinburgh philosopher Thomas Brown's publication of *Lectures on the Philosophy of the Human Mind* (in 1820, the year he died) made him "the first major mental philosopher to replace 'passions and affections' with [the single encompassing category] 'emotions' in his lectures" (Dixon 1999: 305). Brown is a central figure, first because he broke with the prevailing theological orthodoxy, and second because his lectures on 'the emotions' were embedded in what he variously referred to as "'Science of the Mind' …'physiology of the mind,' 'mental chemistry,' and 'mental science'" (1999: 306). The secular psychology that arose after the 1850s would soon cite Brown as a foundational thinker.

With the rise to hegemony of the category of 'emotion,' consciousness of 'emotion' in the West has greatly increased. We can chalk this up to the emergence of "the psy disciplines" (N. Rose 1996) that make emotions their object and ascribe to this domain a new integrity. But this history is particular. Any projection of such history onto the broader world represents the long and unfortunate tendency to "deprovincialize Europe" (Chakrabarty 2000), pretending that Europe, uniquely modern and somehow transcending its locality, represents the whole world – a kind of semiotic imperialism.

Europe's self-invention as modern and the Otherization of emotion

What the theologian Dixon fails to provide, beyond the history of taxonomies, is the historical context needed in order to understand European thought in relation to early English modernism and its relationship with colonialism. Emotion plays a central role in the history of (meta)discursive tools enabling Europe's modern invention of itself. Reflecting contemporary political tensions, Bacon and Locke worried about "interest, passion, emotionality, and belief," which they connected with "rhetoric" and contrasted with rationality and knowledge (Bauman and Briggs 2003: 45). Their heirs in the next generation were the forebears of anthropologists, folklorists, and linguists. These "philologists" (such as Blackwell, 1701–1757, and Wood, 1717–1771) and "antiquarians" sharply distinguished their own society's discursive rationality from the "cries of passion" from which language evolved. Such primitivizing was part of a larger set of metadiscursive strategies by which early English moderns (elites) set themselves apart from non-Europeans as well as the non-elites in their midst – women and peasants. Philologists like Robert Wood ascribed a certain inherent passion to the state of orality and the poetics associated with it and with "the language of Nature" (Bauman and Briggs 2003: 107). By contrast,

Wood and other early moderns associated their own literate society with a certain coldness (Bauman and Briggs 2003: 112).

This theme played a central role in Europe's deprovincialization of itself, and thus in its imperial project, as Bauman and Briggs point out. The repeated association of passion with spatiotemporal and sociocultural Others – 'Orientals' being the philologists' favorite – and the equally strong insistence that contemporary Europe was home to a discursive rationality (even if its rational discourse was said to be cold, lacking vitality) – became a ready trope widely available, even difficult to unthink, today. Early modern European rhetorical acts of self-invention have had consequences, shaping European imperialism and channeling its energies in particular directions. The semiotic practices of the British Raj, and of Indian elites most influenced by the British in India and their ideologies of language, performance, and emotion, helped reshape colonial-era Bengal – a theme foreshadowed in the second myth in the Introduction.

Darwin

By 1872 when Darwin first published *The Expression of Emotion in Man and Animals*, a scientific consensus had emerged as to the utility of viewing 'the emotions' as a coherent unit. Darwin offered a startlingly new explanation as to why certain expressive features consistently characterized human – and animal – emotions. Opening the eyes and mouth wide in surprise may, for example, help animals both see and respond to potential threats, while the intensity or loudness of angry cries by animals may index their strength. Thus some of the shared expressive features humans have inherited, Darwin argued, help the expresser adapt physically to the circumstances to which the emotion responds, while others are more purely indexical.

Darwin shared Herbert Spencer's hunch that musicality emerged in our species before language. In Chapter 4, I presented a critique of arguments that distinguish too sharply between language and human musicality, primitivizing music. Take the musicality out of language and you have what we all know as a computer attempting to talk (although breakthroughs in artificial speech are proceeding rapidly). These reservations aside, Darwin rightly recognized the prosodic features of speech as affectively charged, and helpfully emphasized timbre and resonance, as well as "pitch and intervals," i.e., both the average of a person's speech (with or without affect, as Darwin thought of it) and the intonational dynamism that conveys a particular affect (Darwin 1998: 90–93).

Freud, Elias, Foucault, and the repressive hypothesis

Freud's work is significant to the history I am constructing. Freud is one important inspiration for postmodern moves to decenter the self, and to recognize the multivocality of any utterance; however, his work has also inspired universalists.

Breuer and his patient "Anna O.," or Bertha Pappenheim, were the true creators of the "**talking cure**" (Showalter 1985), which in the hands of Freud and Breuer became psychoanalytic psychotherapy. As was true in many contemporary branches of medicine, more than it is today, talk was central to this form of psychiatry. Freud's later interest in slips of the tongue or pen – a class of errors Freud called parapraxes – testifies to his abiding interest in discourse. Slips of the tongue, Freud claimed, reveal unconscious feeling, though they certainly also become objects of emotions, especially embarrassment (Freud 1965[1916]). The analysis of parapraxes and dreams – more accurately, the analysis of patients' dream reports – legitimized Freud's claims that psychoanalysis was not only relevant to the treatment of neuroses but to the 'normal' lives of individuals and societies (Strachey 1965: 7). The "psy disciplines" (N. Rose 1996) – which claim knowledge of, and thus authority over, normal life – changed bereavement (for example) from a communal challenge addressed by magical lament (as in Karelia) into a challenge to the self; "bereavement counseling" thus "entails the translation of whatever discourse the client originally produces into a discourse of feeling" (Árnason 2001: 307).

This book has emphasized **identification** – over identity – as a dynamic process, one that is in part accomplished (and not only manifested) in discursive acts. This pursuit is indebted to Freud. We must remind ourselves of Freud's utter reliance upon discourse in the conduct of analysis when we consider his writings on identification. Freud and his students represented identification as a psychological, rather than discursive, process defined vis-à-vis affect, including desire, hostility, and ambivalence. In what might be called Freud's myth of the self and its emergence, desire for the parent in the "first sexual period" of psychic development (Freud 1962[1923]: 26) gives way to "identification." That identification – e.g., a boy's with his father – is ambivalent from the start, but that ambivalence surfaces (at least in 'the unconscious') at a later psychosexual-developmental stage, the Oedipal phase.

For Freud, language hides as much as it reveals about affect; crucial to this hiding is his notion of repression. Repression is a "watchman," standing ready at the doorway between the unconscious and conscious systems of the mind to exclude any matter with which the conscious self would be uncomfortable (Freud 1989[1915–1917]). Freud suggested that the psychic burden created by repression of our more primal instincts was substantial. Middle class European socialization produces a level of guilt or shame that weighed so heavily on individuals, Freud argued, that it produces occasional horrific backlashes. To him, WWI was just such a backlash against repression.

The discursive psychologist Billig, while sympathetic to Freud's psychological project and the notion of repression, resituates repression in the realm of conversation. "The business of everyday conversation provides the skills for repressing, while, at the same time, it demands that we practice those skills. In this respect, language is inherently expressive and repressive" (Billig 1999: 1).

The theme of repression resurfaced in different form in Elias's *Civilizing Process* (2000 [1939]), which traces a gradual cooling of feeling on one level, together with the rise of one feeling – shame – at another. Over the past few centuries of European history, 'civilized' people – particularly the nobility – concluded that they ought not to express feelings. On the other hand, to be 'civilized' is to feel a concern for honor, and the anxiety of being shamed. Cultivation of such sensibilities becomes a policing of boundaries between social classes. The same nobility who, in the early Medieval period, evinced no particular disgust at lower-class habits, came to "reprove" them, as in this line from an early manners guidebook by William Caxton: "Thingis sometyme allowed is now repreuid" (as quoted by Elias 2000[1939]: 70), i.e., "Things once allowed are now reproved." Elias calls this "a motto for the whole movement that [was] ... coming" (2000: 71). Eventually, the highest elites developed a strong distaste even for the speech of the lower classes, including the bourgeoisie (2000: 421). Scheff summarizes Elias's achievement: "Unlike Freud or anyone else, Elias documents, step by step, the sequence of events that led to the repression of emotions in modern civilization" (Scheff 2000: 90).

Today Elias's argument must contend with Foucault's strong qualification of the repressive hypothesis and his assertion of the productive (rather than repressive) role of modern power, which calls into being new subjectivities. Freud saw "Civilization" producing masses of "discontents" (Freud 1961), unconsciously resentful of the burden repression placed on them as biological entities. Foucault sought to correct what he perceived as an imbalance in this argument. Like Billig, Foucault reconceived repression as a social and discursive process. At the same time, discourse in the Victorian era (or ours) not only represses, but – through institutions like psychology and psychiatry – helps to incite or produce (new forms of) sexuality, and subjectivity more broadly (Foucault 1997: 126, as cited by Zhang 2005: 5).

Wittgenstein and Sass, discussed below, represent a very different approach to the self.

Schizophrenia and modernism

Diehard traditionalists who prefer representational painting, rhyming poetry, selves that are not decentered – and artistic works that do not produce vertigo in the observer – will not be surprised that serious analyses have linked "modernist"[1] subjectivity as manifest in certain defining works of art, philosophy, and literature with subjectivities produced by schizophrenia. Sass (1992) argues that, in both schizophrenia and modernist works, the quest for intense experience leads, paradoxically, to self-distancing and an attenuation of experience. "Avant-gardism" in literature led to a rebellion against convention, form, and genre, until finally language itself became suspect. Literary devices once hidden become overt objects of play. "Since the turn of the [twentieth] century, the revelation of the inadequacy of standard meanings and habitual constructions of reality, including conventional language ... have become prominent themes" in philosophy and literary criticism (1992: 55). In schizophrenia and in modernist philosophy, inner experience becomes ineffable, and authentic expression impossible. What Sass calls modernism (and others might call postmodernism) "glorifies the being of language itself rather than its presumed connection to something inward, personal, or primal" (1992: 198).

The last decades of the nineteenth century saw a "move toward [envisioning thought as] a kind of *inner speech... more authentic than conventional language*" (Sass 1992: 184; emphasis added). V. N. Volosinov, a Soviet-era linguist who has influenced recent linguistic anthropology, indeed described thought as inner speech. Although thought is (to Volosinov) a kind of speech, speech may have but an unsure connection with mind. Volosinov inverted normal understandings of the relationship between expression and experience:

It is not experience that organizes expression, but the other way around – expression organizes experience. Expression is what first gives experience its form and specificity of direction. ... expression-utterance is determined by the actual conditions of the given utterance – above all, by its immediate social situation (Volosinov 1973: 85, 91).

Wittgenstein, a giant of twentieth-century philosophy, can be considered a kindred spirit who doubted the possibility of a "private language." This doubt carried over in regards to the knowability of others' inner states (even via their expression in outward signs). Wittgenstein thus argued that we ought not to conceive of "feeling" as behind or underlying speech; "feeling is [instead] the expression with which the sentence is said" (1960: 35). He continues: "I have been trying... to remove the temptation to think that there '*must* be' what is called a mental process of thinking, hoping, wishing, believing, etc., independent of the process of expressing a thought, a hope, a wish, etc." (1960: 41). Therefore, we should limit our focus to the expression itself rather than speculating about any veridical relationship it might have to inner states.

With Sass, I situate Wittgenstein's rejection of "private languages" in the light of the twentieth century's loss of confidence in language in general, and particularly in its capacity to bear witness to inner states. Between writing the *Tractatus* and *Philosophical Investigations*, Wittgenstein abandoned a truthconditional account of language – i.e., that the meaning of a sentence is determined by its relation to the conditions under which it is true. In its stead, he propounded a pragmatic theory of meaning, widely cited as a precedent by those in the field of linguistic pragmatics and linguistic anthropology. But in this transition, Wittgenstein adopted, and furthered, the twentieth-century's decoupling of language and 'real' emotion.

Admittedly, Wittgenstein balances caution about subjectivity and language – his "disappointment with language" (Das 1998: 187, citing Cavell [1994]) – with an affirmation of the urgency of human connection through speech-in-inter-action. His famous exploration of the possibility of "*my* pain being located in *your* body" (Das 1998: 192) can be understood as a way of affirming that "to say 'I am in pain' is to ask for acknowledgment from the other, just as denial of another's pain is not an intellectual failure but a spiritual failure" (ibid.) Yet, the attitude of sympathy, for Wittgenstein, helps constitute the imagination of another's feeling. We do not take such a stance "toward a sufferer" because of "a belief 'in something behind the outward expression of pain'" (Kripke 1982: 138, citing Wittgenstein without attribution). Behaviorism held a strong attrac-tion for Wittgenstein (1982: 125–126). Thus, "psychological language stands in need of outward, rather than inner, criteria" (Billig 1997: 140). "There is no such thing as a private inner object to which a private language may be found to give expression" (Das 1998: 187).

Twentieth-century philosophers' skepticism concerning language and mind parallels linguistic anthropologists' skepticism regarding a core self, and the 'actual' emotions that discourse might invoke. Pointing out this parallel will no doubt be controversial. As we have seen, Edward Sapir – one of the fathers of linguistic anthropology – understood ordinary linguistic judgment to be oriented toward aesthetics rather than rules per se. This is no innocent development, unrelated to broader cultural trends. Rather, the apotheosis of the aesthetic in Sapir reflects not only his acknowledged indebtedness to Italian philosopher Croce, but a much broader cultural shift regarding language. Sapir's emphasis on "the *sensory* presence of [the] signifying vehicle … and the elusive multivalence of meaning" (Sass 1992: 199 [emphasis added]) puts him in league with the modernists we have been discussing.

Agnosticism about any sure link between language and subjectivity has shaped more recent anthropological investigations as well. Merleau-Ponty, who has had an impact on anthropology perhaps as great as Wittgenstein's, wrote "Truth does not 'inhabit' the 'inner man,' or more accurately, **there is no inner man,** man is in the world, and only in the world does he know himself" (1962: xi). Linguistic anthropologist William Hanks appears to endorse this state-ment and the phenomenological insistence that "the relations between self and other" are grounded in both being "in the world" and thus being able to come to "mutual interpretation" of it (Hanks 1996: 136). This larger claim strikes me as more reasonable than the claim that "there is no inner man," something not even Wittgenstein would have said. Yet it appears to reflect a stance of radical agnosticism common in linguistic, as opposed to psychological, anthropology.

Rejecting the referential transparency of language (its ability to neutrally represent), and thrusting it into the dimness of the unconscious self – a 'high modern' critique – was only one step toward contemporary positions. 'Late modern' or 'postmodern' views of language go even further, famously decon-structing the autonomous subject. Such views appear to influence even those anthropologists – such as Jane Hill, whose work I describe below – who do not identify with postmodernism or deconstructionism. Whatever our view of various 'isms' or ideological commitments, *postmodernity* – the dissolution of boundaries that had appeared firm in the era of modernity, the rise of (and responses to) radical doubt, apparent slippage in taken-for-granted forms of global hegemony (Mascia-Lees, Sharpe, and Cohen 1989; Friedman 2003) – has become the defining reality in the West, to one extent or another.

From Sapir to Ochs

As an anthropologist of Wittgenstein's generation, a product of the twentieth century, Edward Sapir wrote of the ill fit between language, suited for "ideation," and raw emotion,

> The emotions, on the whole, seem to be given a less adequate outlet [in language than the need and ability to issue commands]. Emotion, indeed, is proverbially inclined to speechlessness. … On the whole, it must be admitted that ideation reigns supreme in language, that volition and emotion come in as distinctly secondary factors. … [Emotions] are, strictly speaking, never absent from normal speech, but their expression is not of a truly linguistic nature (Sapir 1921: 38–39).

Sapir goes on to describe the "feeling-tones" associated with words that we can place along a cline of increasing emotional force, such as 'storm,' 'tempest,' and 'hurricane.' But "the feeling-tones of words are of no use, strictly speaking, to science" (1921: 40–41). Although speakers find them useful, given that "mental activities are bathed in a warm current of feeling," such facts are of more use to the writer of fiction or poetry than the linguist (1921: 41). Such statements reflect twentieth-century skepticism over the adequacy or capacity of speech to reveal 'the inner world.' As we shall see, they contrast strikingly with late twentieth-century work.

Signs, wrote Sapir, must be emotionally denuded in order to enter the domain of true language:

> Shaking the fist at an imaginary enemy becomes a dissociated and finally a referential symbol for anger when no enemy, real or imaginary, is actually intended. When this emotional denudation takes place, the symbol becomes a comment, as it were, on anger itself and a preparation for something like language. What is ordinarily called language may have had its ultimate root in just such dissociated and emotionally denuded cries, which originally released emotional tension (1949b [1934]: 565).

So, to become language, communicative signs had to be stripped of passion. Although language has its roots in cries and emotional gestures, Sapir makes it stand for civilization, a development far beyond emotion's primitivity.

Sapir's attempt to excise what seems to others to be the very "heart" of language – emotion (Ochs and Schieffelin 1989) – reflects the **intellectualism** that informs the **structuralist** approach to language. Late twentieth-century work on language and emotion by Ochs, Schieffelin, and Besnier, reflects 'the pragmatic turn' in linguistic anthropology, its return to ethnography, and its determination to use the tools of linguistic analysis to address the major theoretical concerns shared by all social scientists – e.g., socialization, ideology, and the self (Duranti 2003).

The title of one of Ochs' early essays on language and emotion – "From Feelings to Grammar" (1986) – oddly belies her consistent demonstrations that grammar (as well as every other structural-functional dimension of language) conveys feeling. The title echoes Sapir's separation of feeling from language per se. Given Ochs' clear rejection of this facet of Sapir's thought, perhaps this is an example of "the return of the repressed" (Freud 2003 [1909]: 111). Apart from the title, however, Ochs' concern with the pragmatic meaning of emotion talk reflects Wittgenstein.

Indian and Greek models of emotion and language: recent anthropological invocations

Although I have stressed the influence of Western philosophy on anthropologies of language and emotion, quite a few anthropologists reflect critically on our tradition – e.g., on Aristotle's *Poetics* and his notion of **catharsis** – and engage indigenous philosophical traditions from their fieldsites. Aristotle attributed an emotional function to dramatic plot structure: the linear unfolding of events leads to emotional catharsis. For several decades, ethnographers of communication have argued that indigenous theories of emotion, discourse, and text provide models that guide local actors and ritual action. The rejection of the catharsis model in some ways continues the trend toward skepticism vis-à-vis authentic self-expression.

Don Brenneis exemplifies this trend. His (1987) study of the work done by the *pancayat* or 'council of five' among Fijian Indians takes Aristotle's notion of catharsis as its rhetorical foil, and explores whether the *pancayat* can be considered "therapeutic." Whatever Aristotle might have meant by *katharsis*, Western social scientists have exploited it in constructing what Brenneis critiques as a psychodynamic (and reductionist) understanding of social processes. In particular, Brenneis rejects Gibbs's (1963) argument that "the genius of" an informal dispute resolution meeting like the pancayat (i.e., a *moot*) "lies in the fact that it is based on a covert application of the principles of psychoanalytic theory which underlie psychotherapy" (1963: 1). Gibbs claims that the possibility of cathartic venting of personal feelings make the moot a sort of group therapy.

The *pancayat* as Brenneis describes it is not unemotional, and indeed he calls the Fijian Indian moot "therapeutic." The therapy, however, entails achieving a level of group satisfaction, rather than the personal satisfaction ostensibly experienced through individual participants' venting. The meeting is important not only insofar as it achieves what all such informal conflict negotiations should achieve – a common, public narrative of the disputed event. Beyond that political function, Fijian Indians find satisfaction in their pancayats as aesthetic achievements. Understanding just what sort of satisfaction this is requires an analysis of Fijian talk of "emotion, expressiveness, and experience" – i.e., an analysis of their ethnopsychology.

To some extent, that local psychology reflects rasa-bhāva theory. The classical Indian discourse on poetics and aesthetic experience opened the possibility of transcendence through the shared experience of a *depersonalized* feeling, rasa. In the discussion above I noted a kind of cyclical shifting in how bhāva was represented vis-à-vis rasa and spiritual achievement, how the medieval Vaishnava bhakti literature rehabilitated bhāva as a category of spiritual feeling. Likewise, in the Fijian-Indian village of Bhatgaon, *prembhaw* (*prembhāva*, 'love-bhāva') is a religiously valorized emotional state, understood as impersonal and universal. And that is the state that actors claim, conventionally, to produce and experience in successful *pancayat* meetings.

Although Bhatgaon residents do not use the word rasa, the way they use bhaw not only reflects some of the medieval Sanskrit descriptions of bhāva – it also shares some features of rasa, classically defined. It is the impersonality and universality of bhaw in Bhatgaon metadiscourse on the pancayat that becomes a resource for Brenneis's argument against the individualistic interpretation of the moot. Brenneis's departure from Western philosophical models in analyzing his field data reflects the broader twentieth-century skepticism I have been describing.

Recent linguistic anthropological theory

How does the 1987 Brenneis argument look in the grander view of the history of theory? Why is it, for example, that in the whole print run of the *Journal of Linguistic Anthropology* since 1991, the word "ethnopsychology" never appears, and "ethnotheories" only once? Why is it that all six instances of the phrase, "construction of self," occur since 1999, and likewise (since 1998) with all mentions of Derrida in the journal? These trends coincide with a loss of faith in "the self," the stable centered subject – a loss apparent in accounts calling themselves postmodern (or accounts of the postmodern), and probably in the wider culture. Thus, a brilliant 2005 *Journal of Linguistic Anthropology* examination of therapeutic discourse per se – of Rogerian therapy in particular – refuses to take the notion of therapy as a given, concluding that the very experience of "something interpretable as a 'real self'" arises from a "peculiar conjunction of semiotic factors" produced in Rogerian therapy, if not other contexts (Smith 2005: 270).

In place of centered selves, linguistic anthropology has recently focused on the multiple voices (Ronkin to appear), even multiple "selves," projectable, for example, through the different codes a bilingual narrator uses. Linguistic and psychological anthropologist Michèle Koven (1998) critiques a tendency that she sees still as plaguing anthropology – the "lurking folk belief in the neat, one-to-one correspondence of person, language, and culture" (1998: 410–411). In contrast with that "folk belief," Koven advocates analytic strategies that will uncover in a woman's narrative "an implicit and emotionally compelling commentary on the relevant voices embodied by herself and others in the narrated and narrating events" (1998: 417). Koven's stance typifies more recent approaches to the linguistic construction of emotion, no longer conceived as leakage from an authentic, stable, self, but as a blooming, buzzing confusion of affects, stances, voices, or 'selves.'

If the reader sees in these trends a postmodern turn in linguistic anthropology, that is my point. Few if any linguistic anthropologists, however, proudly call themselves postmodernists. Still, it is important to situate any activity – including scholarship – in a broader sociohistorical context, if we are to understand its significance. This motivates the reanalysis and historical contextualization, below, of an essay I (and many others) admire greatly – the essay by Hill introduced in Chapter 2.

Analyzing a Mexicano (i.e., Nahuatl) speaker's story of his son's murder, Hill uncovers layer upon layer of **voicing**. She distinguishes voices in Don Gabriel's narrative based on features including **syntax** and intonation, but – separate though they are – these other voices interact with each other. Voices of an involved and a neutral narrator, an evaluator, and a father, fade and return, and comment on various other voices made present in "reported speech." This complex interaction of voices Bakhtin called multivocality or **heteroglossia**: "Language is heteroglot from top to bottom: it represents the co-existence of socio-ideological contradictions" (Bakhtin 1981: 291).

Hill asserts that this richly heteroglossic narrative reveals not the single, centered, authentic emotional self that Freud envisioned struggling (in psychoanalysis) to overcome repression, but "a veritable kaleidoscope of 'emotional selves,' which are all art" (Hill 1995: 139). These selves are all narrative creations. "Dysfluencies" – particularly "accounting dysfluencies" – punctuate Don Gabriel's narrative. However, Hill's assessment departs radically from psychoanalytic interpretations of dysfluencies. Dysfluency arises in Don Gabriel's mostly eloquent moments, when he speaks of that which he viscerally opposes – "business for profit." Rather than grief (signaled by choking on words related to his son's murder), these stumbles index the author's self-conscious attempt to be extremely accurate in narrating the climactic events of his story. "The self which produces these [accounting dysfluencies] is a responsible self" (Hill 1995: 137). This "'responsible self' ... [, which] we may call consciousness ... allows us a privileged glimpse of ... moment[s] of 'active choice'" (1995: 139). Whatever affect Don Gabriel's narratorial voice evinced, Hill claims, reflects his control rather than an upwelling of uncontrollable emotion. The chances of language revealing real emotion are unclear. Even as I embrace Hill's analysis I am reminded that it reflects a historical trend toward skepticism far beyond the confines of linguistic anthropology.

Such an argument may open the way to the next stage in a history of increasing reflexivity in anthropology; I certainly do not presume that this is the case. Perhaps it serves to underscore the emotional as well as ritual nature of our own scholarly discourse (Wilce 2009). In any case, as with any history, the history of scholarly theories of language and emotion in and beyond anthropology leads not to a final truth, but to more history.

SHIFTING FORMS OF LANGUAGE AND EMOTION

Introduction: historical problems

The titles of this and the previous chapter entertain the illusion that "theory" (in focus in Chapter 9) belongs to academe, and is somehow distinct from "the world," which occupies us in this chapter. But this book has presented 'culture,' 'language,' and 'emotion' as moving targets whose existence in the world is inseparable from dominant theories. Neither 'a language' nor 'synchronic' linguistic 'facts' are fixed entities, or explicable apart from history. This includes apparent facts about any particular language-emotion nexus in any particular population. Because cultural ideologies of mind and language are in a constant state of flux, we can expect significant changes as centuries pass. Note the stark contrast between two cultural discourses on emotion in two declarations from British courts across four centuries: "The thought of man is not triable; the devil alone knoweth the thought of a man" (1477), and (from 1889) "The state of a man's mind is as determinable as the state of his digestion."[1] (Rosen 1995: 5).

Later in this chapter I describe early modern transformations that shook English society, but let me start with more familiar, recent events. Linguistic, emotional, and social change has certainly accelerated. We can hardly miss changes in communication that are going on around us, brought about by or accompanying the use of technology. Insofar as it appears to be creating phenomena like the intimate stranger, mobile phone use, at least in Japan, may be socio-emotionally significant (Miller 2006: 1051). Email, chat, and instant-messaging are famous as channels for the evolving use of new emotional lexemes, so to speak – emoticons. Jones and Schieffelin (2009) describe an emerging grammatical rule in "reported speech and thought" in a sample of instant-messaging records of students at a large city university in New York. Students in their sample (18–22 years of age) used traditional quotatives like "said" for relatively careful renderings, and reserved the newer "be + like" quotative for use in "demonstrations of attitudes and emotions in narrated situations" (see also Barbieri 2008). They regarded emoticons as either out of date or juvenile.

Religious practices are *technologies of the self*. Remaining at least temporally close to home, we move next to the twentieth-century religious movement, Pentecostalism.

The explosive growth of Pentecostalism

Chapter 9 touched on the apparent disappearance of theological psychologies. That appearance holds only if we focus on such religious psychologies in mainstream academic settings. "Modernization theories" popular in the 1960s and 1970s (but deriving from such earlier thinkers as Weber) have fallen on hard times. They falsely predicted the end of '**tradition**,' 'peasant societies' – and the power of religion in people's lives, at least in 'modern' societies. Instead, we have witnessed a resurgence of religious zeal, and religion's assertiveness in the political realm; moreover, there are millions who take theological psychologies very seriously.

Within global Christianity, churches that either are Pentecostal or share Pentecostalism's emotional fervor are growing rapidly. Pentecostalism is the fastest growing segment of Christianity by far, shaking up even secularized northern Europe. "'The Danish church is boring,' says [Stendor] Johansen, 45, who left the state-run Danish Evangelical Lutheran Church three years ago and joined this high-octane interdenominational church run by a [Pentecostal] missionary pastor from Singapore. 'I feel energized when I leave one of these [Pentecostal] services'" (K. Sullivan 2007).

Attending carefully to discourses on emotion and subjectivity, we find that certain "keywords" (Williams 1983), representing attempts to give structure to subjectivity, dominate modern reflections. Some keywords with broad circulation index what Williams calls "structures of feeling," an emerging "social experience ... related to ... forms ... conventions ... art and literature" (Williams 1977: 132–133). For at least the contemporary English-speaking world, one such keyword is *experience*. Subjective experience – even the experience of God (as in the 'experience meetings' typical of eighteenth- and nineteenth-century Methodism) – becomes "the most authentic kind of truth" (Williams 1983: 128). This experience-grounded approach to truth explains both the attractiveness of Pentecostalism to many, and its controversial status in the eyes of more established Protestant groups.

Robin Shoaps studies Pentecostalism and the salience of emotion in its worship. She describes the pastor of an Assemblies of God (Pentecostal) church in the US who "once described his congregation, in comparison to mainline churches, as 'having fun, doing cartwheels in the aisles'" (Shoaps 2002: 39). To worshippers, such emotion is a sign of the Holy Spirit's presence. In order to help worshippers experience this spiritual affect, Pentecostal churches foster a high degree of personal involvement, including ample opportunities to speak during services. Intense affect and participation are foundational to

Pentecostalism, and help explain its separation from mainstream Protestantism in the early twentieth century. At the same time, Pentecostal discourse subjects emotion to God's sovereignty: "The emphasis must always be on the inner filling ["the inner work of the Holy Spirit"] rather than on the emotional experience" (Assemblies of God 2007a, 2007c).

Pentecostal **language ideologies** center on the concept of "earnestness," especially "earnest *language*," which is speech that is "seen as emotionally true" (Shoaps 2002: 43). Although Shoaps does not discuss the use of the term "earnest" in the US congregation she studied, a search for the term on the Assemblies of God website (2007b) yields 157 occurrences – some indication of its salience for this group. ("Experience" yields 7070 occurrences!)

Pentecostal emotionalism appears not just in words alone but also in bodily movement (sometimes "dancing in the spirit") and vocal intensity. Both Shoaps (2002) and Krancus (2007, analyzing Pentecostal sermons available as podcasts) deal with "implicit voicing phenomena, that is, nonmetapragmatically explicit speech that indexes another's perspective" (Shoaps 2002: 49) in Pentecostal sermons. Both examine sermons in which the preacher animates two distinct voices – that of the believer (or preacher, or even God), and that of either a nonbeliever or a less-than-enthusiastic believer. (Note that English "enthusiasm" derives from Greek εν θεοσ [en theos], "possessed by [a] god.") Following Kulick and Schieffelin (2004), Krancus designates these two voices as the "good subject" and the "bad subject." They are created in large measure through different affect marking. Given Pentecostalism's embrace of a highly emotional relationship with God, it is hardly surprising that the good **subject**'s voice in Krancus's data is markedly emotional, while the voice of the bad **subject** is unenthused.

Transcription key

"words" = reported speech
word-word-word = faster speech
CAPITALS = Louder speech
@ = Audible inhalation (or "in-breath")
Transcript 2: Excerpt from Sermon, "Empty to Receive," Pastor Ed Jorgenson, August, 2006

14 "Blessed are the poor in spirit,
15 for theirs is the kingdom of heaven"
16 But they never quote it that way …
17 I-usually-hear-it-quoted,
18 "Well-blessed-are-the-poor-for-theirs-is-the-kingdom-of-heaven,"
19 and they move on and they go on
20 and it's used as an excuse for
21 "well I ya know I don't got a lot in life
22 but thank God someday I'll have the whole kingdom"
…

97 Every time I get in my own private devotion
98 I, I get my hands on this book
99 and I open it up
100 and I begin to let the black and white sink into my head and I begin to pray
101 "god let it become more than just words on a page@
102 BUT LET IT BECOME A REAL LIFE EXPERIENCE @"[2]

After quoting the biblical passage "blessed are the poor in spirit," Pastor Jorgenson introduces the voice of the bad subject. That voice of relatively low affect/involvement he animates (in part) via the discourse marker, hedge, or downtoner *well* in lines 18 and 21. Later (lines 97–102) Jorgenson animates the voice of the good subject, in which *well* is absent. Instead, the good subject's enthusiasm (high affect/involvement) is marked by a much higher intensity (volume), and by the audible in-breaths at the end of each line or "intonation unit" (Chafe 1993). This forms an indexical icon of the model subjectivity Jorgenson presents his congregation.

Linguistic and semiotic anthropologists' attempts to analyze what makes rituals tick have centered on their indexical iconicity.

Rituals work… by both pointing to or reminding participants of preexisting sacred features of the surround and effectively bringing others into being [i.e., two possible manifestations of indexicality], … [and] through [iconic] signs that individually or collectively (as a "diagram") imitate the cosmic end being ritually enacted (Wilce 2006: 894).[3]

Pastor Jorgenson's model prayer-speech fits this ritual pattern precisely. His speech both points to (indexes), and embodies (is iconic of) the goal toward which his audience should strive, the emotionally involved speech members should use in addressing God. In doing so, it effectuates the transformation it aims for. This in effect drags the audience into the "subject position" it performs.[4]

Emotionalism defines the Pentecostalism movement worldwide, in part because North American Pentecostals, who were Pentecostalism's pioneers, have traveled extensively as missionaries. The North American style influences the practice of emerging Pentecostal churches and pastors around the world, such as Sakapultek pastor Don Domingo in Guatemala, one focus of Shoaps' more recent work. Local manifestations of Pentecostal emotionalism offend Catholic Sakapulteks. Although Don Domingo would shun some 'traditional' **speech events**, he participates in many others that allow some emotional expression. Perhaps the most 'traditional' of these events is a wedding *pixab'* 'ritual offering of advice,' which the pastor attended as the paternal uncle of the bride. We see his Pentecostal style, his embrace of emotion as a valid socio-moral guide, in several features of his *pixab'*: his claim that emotion comes "from his heart"; his voice, which chokes up at one point; and his direct counsel that the bride and groom rely on their own judgments, coming from the "'inner self,' where the experience of God resides" (for Pentecostals).

This last feature contrasts sharply with the emphasis in local Catholicism on conventionally defined roles and obligations, conceived as outside of – and transcending – the individual. Although parents often fight back tears during *pixab'*, Don Domingo's open reference to his emotion "produces a counsel that departs from the norm and reflects some of the international Pentecostal discursive regimes of emotional expression and sincerity" (Shoaps 2003).

At stake here is not only emotion, or the particulars of advice at one wedding, but a new way of being, a new self, constituted in and through discursive practices, especially emotional talk. Could it be that Pentecostal emotionalism offends Sakapultek Catholics in part because it seems that – claims of dialogue with the Holy Spirit aside – Pentecostal emotionality is cut off from traditional social contexts? Established forms of power do not simply stop change in its tracks – who is to silence Pastor don Domingo, particularly when his message is clothed in the style of traditional verbal art? Sakapulas is no longer an undivided 'Catholic' emotional-discursive regime in which emotional expression is restricted – i.e., one with an ideology like that which often accompanies grammaticalized honorifics, in which a low-affect style can be other-elevating (see Chapter 6). It is now a community in which some speakers stake a claim to moral authority by making explicit reference to emotion.

Of course, there is an older, broader, Protestant context to such change.

Sincerity, modernity and Protestant prayer

All societies have strong, often uncritical, notions of the role of language in the world – **language ideologies** (Schieffelin, Woolard, and Kroskrity 1998). The idea that speech can and should make inner states transparent, that this is one of language's chief ends, is in many places closely associated with Protestantism (Keane 2002: 24). Bauman and Briggs (2003) point to an association of certain ways of speaking with Protestant modernity – a language ideology with a clear historical origin. The early modern move that demoted language to a "transparent" (instead of magically performative) medium, they argue, made the modern form of knowledge-of-the-world possible. This reinvention of language as a transparent medium has a profound bearing on questions surrounding language and emotion, as well as their relationship to class. Locke consigned non-elites to a premodern linguistic muddle; they were incapable of clear, rational, efficient discourse. We should keep in mind such classism, and the class-based distribution of ideologies of language and emotion, as we delve further into language ideologies connected with Protestantism.

For more than a decade, Webb Keane (1997) has been exploring the Protestant origins of modernist language ideology on the island of Sumba, Indonesia, supplementing his ethnographic fieldwork with an archival investigation of Dutch Calvinist missionary records. Sumbanese conversion hinged on Dutch missionaries effectively challenging their notions of language,

agency, and prayer. The missionaries came to Sumba with the same "refer-ential model of language function" (1997: 682) we have revisited again and again in this book. They confronted a very different concept of the agency of language, even its coercive force, among "*marapu* followers" (followers of ancestral spirits). "When Dutch Calvinists look at *marapu* prayer, they coun-terpose the sincerity of Christian prayer as expressions that arise from individ-ual and internal sources against what they take to be a fetishistic displacement of agency onto objectified forms" (1997: 682). Today, Sumbanese Christians embrace the notion of prayer coming from the heart, in contrast to "the highly formal and supposedly fixed canon of couplets used in Sumbanese oratory and *marapu* ritual" (1997: 683, 679).

The phrase "praying from the heart" neatly encapsulates an ideology of lan-guage. Although many so-called 'traditional societies' maintain a different per-spective, the drive to make language a tool for sincere, truthful **reference**, and close the gap between self and speech, continues apace. Although Shoaps and Keane locate that drive within two forms of Protestantism, the same motivation animated the scientific metadiscourse of early English modernity.

Coffeehouses, language, intimacy, and rationality

Historical trends do not float above the material realm, disconnected from it, as social histories of emotion demonstrate. The materiality of culture – e.g., the culture of food – interacts with structures of feeling dominant in any given "emotional regime" (Reddy 2001). Drinking alcohol in particular ways, quanti-ties, and settings has helped constitute ways of life. More importantly perhaps, the influx of coffee into Europe around the sixteenth century coincided with the invention of accurate timepieces and the spread of ideologies and practices necessary for the take-off of capitalism (Weinberg and Bealer 2001).

Discourse plays a central role in constituting malleable social sentiments; but coffee, conversely, contributed to the emergence of a "public sphere" (Habermas 1987) defined largely by a modern form of talk. Coffee did not affect European subjectivity simply because of its effects on bodies; Europeans came to drink coffee in coffeehouses, which became sites of a new sort of dis-course. Habermas has located in these coffeehouses the discursive foundations of bourgeois democracy. Although he makes it appear as though the coffee-house was from the start the birthplace of a rational public sphere, rules had to be posted to maintain order, because in fact they could be chaotic, smelly, "wildly energetic" places (Pendergrast 1999: 13) – home to much emotion, apparently. Coffee drinking played a role; conversation in these coffeehouses was known to be "lively." Over time, however, *coffeehouse* and *salon* could be used in the same breath, as they are in claims by Habermas about the estab-lishment of the rational European public sphere, the wellspring, if you will, of public opinion. Habermas's claim reflects the fact that coffeehouses came to be sites not only of lively but of sophisticated, literary discussion; they were favored sites of the new bourgeoisie (Gaudio 2003).

Yet the roots of "the art of conversation" (P. Burke 1993) are undemocratic, writes Gaudio (see also Bauman and Briggs 2003). Elias (2000[1939]) located those roots in the "courtly classes" of the absolutist era in European monarchy. He also uncovered the emotional stakes of the conversational art – those found to be speaking or otherwise acting like those of lower status were at risk of "embarrassment" (see the discussion of shame in Chapter 7). Sensitivity to the aesthetics of speech (as pleasing sound, and pleasing juxtapositions of words) marked the elite (Elias 2000: 422). Despite the narrow class-base of the original advice manuals, their influence spread to the growing bourgeoisie (Gaudio 2003: 672, citing P. Burke 1993: 116–17; Elias 2000[1939]: 79–85).

Globalization, emotion, and linguistic transformations

Our path in this chapter has already taken us to Guatemala and Indonesia, although thus far my concern has been to contextualize changes occurring there in relation to European, and Christian, history. The following case studies shed light on local agency in globalization.

Two monasteries, two forms of Tibetan Buddhism

Michael Lempert (2007) has studied Tibetan Buddhist monks in two monasteries – *Sera Monastery* (SM) at Byllakupe in southern India, and the "self-consciously modernized" *Institute of Buddhist Dialectics* (IBD) in Dharamsala in the north. The IBD celebrates the Dalai Lama, known as a modernist reformer. Despite Sera Monastery's ultimate allegiance to the titular head of Tibetan Buddhism, in fact it does not share his modernist orientation. Lempert finds an **icon** of these two temporal orientations in the way the two monasteries organize the task of discipline. Juxtaposing the two offers a window on "affect in projects of local modernity," and the analysis of disciplinary rhetoric at SM illustrates the importance of orders of indexicality in affective discourse (Lempert 2007).

"Disciplinarian" monks at SM like Geshe-la, Disciplinarian during Lempert's recent fieldwork, offer apparently angry "public reprimands" and "advice"-giving talk directed at "(re)form[ing] the moral dispositions of others." These reprimands always target generic "derelict monks," never real names. And they must "dissimulate – sever affect from 'intention,'" indexing hearts that are free of anger (Lempert 2007: 3). Such dissimulation, which presupposes a distinction between an inner and outer self, has until recently been a stable cultural category; now, officials at the modernizing IBD judge such a separation of display from self to be premodern. The IBD's original charter declared that there was no need for a disciplinarian. Even though the office was later created, its occupants have had much less authority than at SM. The IBD's egalitarian ethos contrasts with the hierarchical ethos at SM. IBD disciplinarians offer "only 'advice,' not 'reprimand'" (Lempert 2007: 9). The preference for advice indexes the IBD's commitment to producing the "**liberal subject**," i.e., the sort of self suited for modern capitalist society – construed as autonomous and held accountable for sincerity. The IBD's approach to affect and discipline eschews conscious dissimulation.

Lempert had been acquainted with the austere monk, Geshe-la, before he became the Disciplinarian at SM. Dissimulation frames his angry speech as "histrionic," *not* coming from his heart. Despite the salience of histrionic anger at SM, monks have no explicit metapragmatic label for it. Lempert addresses the question of the recognizability of "histrionic wrath" at two levels, which we will call **co-text** (or **entextualized** structure) and the "independently pre-supposed" context.

The affect performed in public reprimands is marked as histrionic and not vulgar, first, in relation to certain event-independent signs (e.g., the post of Disciplinarian in itself). Other indexes of histrionic anger are contextually emergent, and constitutive rather than presupposing of context. The avoidance of attacks on named persons constitutes an index of the impersonality and purity of the anger. But the most important index of dissimulation is a complex metasign, less available to metapragmatic awareness: The emergent, entextualized structure of reprimand speech becomes, in itself, a "**metapragmatic icon**." Icons resemble their objects. Pragmatic, or indexical, signs point to or constitute contextual features. Metapragmatic signs point to "some pragmatic dimension of language" (Silverstein 1993: 39).

Frames (Bateson 1972) are both indexical and meta-indexical (metapragmatic), reflecting the (pragmatic) function of the signs they frame. Ritual speech is often characterized by pervasive metasigns indicating not only ritualness but efficacy. The structure of ritual discourse typically emerges as an iconic metasign (Silverstein 2004), 'resembling' (for participants) the cosmic process it enacts.[5] A pattern of linguistic parallelism – "poetic juxtapositions of paired elements" (Fox 1988: 3) – that intensifies over the course of a ritual exemplifies "how changes in linguistic form may realize the progression of the ritual action by resembling it, an instance of a '**metapragmatic** icon'" (Keane 2004: 436, citing Silverstein (1981) or "**diagrammatic icon**" (Silverstein 2004, Wilce 2006). The emergent, entextualized speech structure of displays of histrionic anger

figuratively 'contains' the affect indexicals of anger, framing them fore and aft with conspicuous (even hyperbolic) displays of deference and benevolence … [T]his text-metrical pattern diagrammatically figurates [i.e., is a **metapragmatic icon** of] affective 'containment', as if the Disciplinarian had this anger under volitional 'control.' It is displayed, not felt (Lempert 2007: 8).

This emergent structure is apparent in a reprimand event in which Lempert sees three parts. In the first and third, Geshe-la spoke in an unmarked voice, whereas a harsh voice quality characterized the "encompassed" middle section. This emergent structure coincides with somewhat incongruous use, in the first and third sections, of honorifics toward the voiced, virtual figure of the "derelict monk." This sandwiching, encompassing, or containment of the markedly wrathful discourse is an icon of one of the meta-emotional practices these monks most value, viz., containing the "afflictive emotions," or *nyon rmongs*, like anger. The unfolding textual structure of the Disciplinarian's speech serves as an icon of valued practice, a metapragmatic icon of dissimulated anger.

The IBD's collapsing of the inner-outer distinction upheld at SM seems to replicate the peculiarly modern transformation occurring in many other parts of the world. However, Lempert gives no hint that Sera Monastery or its approach to affect will vanish any time soon.

Globally circulating images of self and language: clashing models

At least in some contemporary global instances of cultural change, two models of self, two models of emotion, struggle for dominance – one that is communally oriented and dialogically engaged, and another in which the self is an autonomous actor and emotional **subject**. Wardlow (2006) describes an apparent shift from one to the other among the New Guinean Huli people. Two emotion terms help define the Huli emotional terrain – *madane* (a violation of one's sense of entitlement to something, leading to resentment [2006: 31]) and *jelas* (overwhelming desire). The fact that "everyone is 'jelas' now" (2006: 30), filled with desire, means that people can no longer be counted on to give. In times past, Huli individuals could count on relations of reciprocity, on another's sense of obligation to respond to a request; the self was conceived as the sum of his/her relationships and the product of various physical and social inputs from birth through initiation, etc. (2006: 6–7). As Huli increasingly conceive of selves as autonomous, and potential givers do in fact refuse suppliants, humiliation becomes possible. Overwhelming desire and assertive requests are now likely to encounter potential respondents who feel separate from, and able to disappoint, suppliants. This is not just a representational or ideational change; change in the dominant model of self and emotion is causing pain and distress.

Such a shift characterizes our second case from Melanesia.

Humiliation, anger, and shifting ideologies of language

Sahlins (1992: 24) had Pacific island societies in mind in asserting a controversial claim regarding a cultural prerequisite of development: sociocultural humiliation: "[I]ndigenous senses of worth, both the people's self-worth and the value of their objects, have to be depreciated." Robbins (2005) attempts to reconcile this with another of Sahlins's contributions. This is his notion of "structure of the conjuncture," "a set of historical relationships that at once reproduce the traditional cultural categories and give them new values out of the pragmatic context" (Sahlins 1985: 125). Sahlins is arguing, in other words, that, in order to be adopted, foreign concepts must be recontextualized in relation to indigenous concepts.[6] With this – as well as Sahlins's argument about the necessity of humiliation – in mind, Robbins writes:

> Humiliation [too]… must first arise *in traditional terms*, since these are the only terms that exist at that point in the lives of the people whose humiliation is at issue. It is only once humiliation arises in traditional terms that it can work to dislodge the very culture that first made it sensible (2005: 15, emphasis added).

Another recent response to Sahlins's claims comes from Besnier, who argues that some indigenous discourse on 'humiliation' in the Pacific has been misconstrued. Only careful attention to discourse, and the play of multiple voices therein, allows an accurate grasp of the meanings – particularly the *pragmatic* uses – of talk of 'humiliation.' Besnier is unique in exploring the affective tone of real, everyday narratives of modernity recorded in his field site, Tuvalu.

Modern technologies recently introduced on Tuvalu can frustrate and mystify islanders. Older women are particularly likely to tell stories depicting themselves as overcome by the technology, but can also be the butts of joking stories told by others. Some of these may even make their way onto *Tala Fakkata*, "Stories that Make One Laugh" – one of the most popular programs on Radio Tuvalu. Whereas central authorities determine radio content in most 'modernizing' contexts, the opposite is the case with Radio Tuvalu, for which callers' stories constantly feed broadcast content (Besnier unpublished manuscript).

Besnier's analysis of a narrative produced by Sunema, an older woman, is of special interest here. Sunema had recently visited her cross-cousin, Fagauta, who lives in the capital of Tuvalu, Funafuti; he has a son named Donny. Sunema's trouble with the bathroom, and the bath in particular, is the heart of the narrative Besnier presents. CAPS indicate loud voice, colons indicate a lengthened sound:

Transcript 3: **Heteroglossic** "humiliation" in Tuvalu

9 **Sunema:** Vau a Donny. Aku muna hh, (creaky) "Teehee te paipa e:: hai ei a:: hhh vai
10 kee- aka- hhhh kee kii aka kee koukou au?" "Donny comes over. I go, 'Where is the tap
11 where the water comes out of, so I can take my bath?'"
12 (falsetto) Muna a tou tagata! "VALEA PULALIFUULU! peenei EILOO mea!"
13 "He goes, '[YOU] STUPID BLOODY FOOL! It's like this!'"
14 (falsetto) Aku muna! "He aa!" "Kiloko ki te paipa teelaa e kii!"
15 "I go, 'Uh?' 'Look at that tap, you turn it on!'"
16 (mid-falsetto) Aku muna, "Maalie ua laa hh, e kii ki te (paipa) hhhh! (falsetto) "KII
17 MAI KIAA KOE!"
18 "I go, 'Hold it, so you turn on (tap) hhhh?' 'TURN IT RIGHT TOWARDS YOU!'"

...

...

...

22 **Sunema, ctd.** (whisper, deliberate tempo) Aku muna, "Ttaapaa ee!, Peenina!, kiloko! koe loo haa fakamatala kia::: kia Peifaga, i au laa nei heki kau iloaaga lele he mea hh peehhhnei!"

"I go, 'Hey!, Penina!, look, don't you go and tell this to Peifaga, it's just that I have no idea about any of this!'"

Note: Peifaga is the host of the national radio program mentioned earlier.

Besnier subjects the narrative to two readings. The first, "self-deprecating" reading reflects people's expectations that they will be humiliated in dealing with modern contraptions. However, in the second, ironic, reading, we can hear implicit moral condemnation of Donny, Sunema's cross-cousin's son, "calling his classificatory mother *pulalifuulu* 'bloody fool,' like a colonial officer berating a native." The irony, says Besnier, is well marked by the overdramatized features of the narration – the conspiratorial whisper (in fear that she [Sunema] be overheard) and the falsetto, for example. In the second reading these affective markers function metapragmatically – commenting on the voiced experience of humiliation, or indicating who ought to speak humbly. Some affective signs (indexes of fear, or of irony) serve as metasigns that frame or contextualize another set (indexes of humiliation).

Rather than confirming a simple experience of humiliation, ostensibly necessary to engaging with development, such narratives manifest layerings of meaning and emotion. As Fanon argued decades ago (1967), encounters with development, colonialism, or any of the more violent or racist facets of globalizing modernity, are as likely to engender rage as humiliation.[7] Such encounters may also provoke humor.

We see shifting metasigns in the next case, too.

Literacy and shifts in meta-emotion, Junigau, Nepal

Cultural attitudes toward emotions can change quite rapidly. This is the case of the appearance of romantic love in Junigau, a change that took many centuries in Europe (Reddy 2003).

As unproblematic as romantic love may appear to us, it has neither been with us forever nor attracted much scholarly attention. Its rise in medieval Europe at a time when the church condemned desire and pleasure even within marriage met with the same sort of reductionist response with which Reddy charges the church through the centuries, and scholars today. To the medieval church, "clothing desire in the language of chivalrous love was a transparent self-deception that required no special comment from theology" (Reddy 2003: 4–5).

Until recently, many South Asian communities (Raheja and Gold 1994, Wilce 1998) expected a son's affection and loyalty, even after marriage, to continue to be toward his parents, brothers, etc., rather than toward his wife. On an embroidered proverb I saw hanging on a wall during my fieldwork in rural Bangladesh, these words appeared:

Bhai-bhai boro dhon,	The greatest treasure is the brotherly relationship –
rokter bodhone,	because of blood,
jodio prithok hon,	even though they are separated –
narir karone	because of Woman

In the early 1980s Junigau, Nepal, was a fairly isolated and 'traditional' village, where – as in Bangladesh – parents negotiated marriages for their children, and children were expected to obey. According to Ahearn (2001a: 4), one can perceive "romantic love" even in old folksongs sung in the village; it is neither new nor an import. However, in dialogue with globally circulating notions in the 1990s, villagers reconstituted their visions of "desire" (2001: 173). Romantic love became both the object and ground of development. That is, modern desire came to be desirable, and love relationships were reconceived as enabling couples' economic advancement. How did love/desire become entangled in development discourse which, to many critics, represents the hegemony of a world system insensitive to the needs and goals of local groups? The key was literacy, a technology capable, in this case, of remaking both language and the self.

During the 1990s, rates of school attendance and female literacy rose sharply, the latter aided especially by evening literacy courses. This meant young men could do something previously unheard of – engage in exchanges of letters with young women toward whom they had romantic feelings. Both school books and materials used in women's night classes "were saturated with 'development discourse'" (Ahearn 2003: 109). With this change came new magazines about film actors and actresses and their romantic lives and relationships, which young people in Junigau read (particularly young men, who had relatively more spare time).[8]

Exchanging love letters is still something of an "illicit" activity (2003: 109). As if to underscore the reasons for this, the loyalty of husbands in newly formed romantic couplings does indeed sometimes shift from their parents to their wives, "because of the strong emotions engendered by a love letter correspondence" (2003: 116). Parents' worst fears are thus confirmed. For our purposes it is more important to note another lesson from Ahearn's case study: At least some affects (e.g., romantic love) only become fully formed feelings under the constructive influence of particular, culturally contextualized discourse.

These passages from letters by Bir Bahadur "to his eventual wife Sarita" exemplify the linking of romantic love or desire with development: "The 'main' meaning of love is 'life success.'" "When love and affection have become steady, one will certainly be able to obtain the things one has thought and worried about." "May our love reach a place where we can in our lives overthrow any difficulties that arrive and obtain success" (2003: 112–113). Education – epitomized in literacy – as one facet of development, can also be called both the object and ground of desire. That is, literacy enabled the romantic letter exchanges, and letters refer to writers' desire for a highly literate spouse. Concomitant with the spread of literacy, young people in Junigau – responding to newly circulating understandings – placed new value on marriages and spouses that are *bikāsī*, 'developed.'

We have wrestled in this book with issues of indexicality and of language ideologies, coming to see that these are connected. Chapter 8 discussed Inoue's (2006) claim that historical processes of *indexicalization* underlie (lower order) indexes (at least those involving *human semiosis*). I close this chapter by exploring Japanese 'women's language' as a case study in indexicalization.

The case of Japanese 'women's language'

Nowhere does the historical dialectic among orders of indexicality become clearer than in the nexus of linguistic form, affectivity, and reified identity in the story of "'Japanese women's language' (*onna kotoba* or *joseigo*)" (Inoue 2006: 1). This is a case in which widely cited 'facts' turn out to be historical constructions.

Until very recently, scholars working on the Japanese language agreed that, even if Japanese women speak more 'like men' today, Japanese interaction still draws on 'women's language' – and 'boyish' and 'girlish' styles, too – as useful resources (Maynard 2002). Distinct uses of certain pronouns and utterance-final particles, some of which are understood as 'blunt' and others as 'polite,' are said to index a "'masculine' voice" and "women's language," respectively. The same forms carry meanings related to emotion and empathy. Maynard's manual of expressive forms for Japanese learners (2005: Ch. 2) notes how gendered use of pronouns and final particles is shifting. Some 'feminine' forms, such as the self-lowering first-person singular pronoun *atakushi*, are simply disappearing. The question, however, is how polite endings -*desu* and -*masu*, and the 'feminine' ending -*wa*; and the "masculine" (or "assertive") particles -*zo*, -*ze*, and -*na* (Maynard 2005: 23)[9] came to be gendered. Before we answer that question, in order to clarify the argument over these matters, we review Ochs' claims regarding gender and affect in Japanese, and Inoue's critique of those claims.

Ochs' (1990, 1992) concept of "indirect indexicality" has greatly enriched studies of affect in the context of language-in-interaction. She argued that the Japanese final particles -ze and -wa are direct indexes of two kinds of affective intensity. -Ze indexes what she labeled a "coarse" form of affective intensity; -wa indexes "gentle" intensity, or softness. What -ze and -wa indirectly index, and thus constitute, is gender – "male" and "female" respectively (Ochs 1992: 341). By signaling a stance of affective and epistemic assertiveness, one indirectly indexes a male "gender identity." Discursive indexing of a "gentle" affective and epistemic stance indirectly signals and constitutes, a "female gender identity" (see Inoue's [2006: 76–77] discussion of Ochs 1992).

Inoue attributes this analysis to the "history effect" (Inoue 2006: 76), which calls to mind Bourdieu's (1977b) vision of history as self-effacing. The story of "women's language" as a first-order index is even more complex than its "two-tiered" rendering by Ochs (direct, indirect; Inoue 2006: 76) lets on. At the dawn of the nineteenth century, examples of Japanese popular and serious literature were in wide circulation. None, however, reflected the particular commitment of the Western realist novel, bent on a truthful depiction of the ordinary lives of ordinary persons. While Anderson (1991) has uncovered the novel's role in constituting national social imaginaries (*Selves*), it played an equally important role in evoking an *Other* by which national selves came to be defined. Confronting the challenge posed by Western literature, nineteenth-century Japanese literary figures undertook a campaign of linguistic-literary 'reform' that would help to constitute Japanese modernity and the modern (male, middle-class) Japanese **subject**. The dialogue of this emerging subject with Otherness led quickly to a focus on an *internal* Other – Japanese women.

But how to represent these women as Other? How to constitute women in "the discursive space of the nation-state" (Inoue 2006: 81)? The *gembun'itchi* movement – a highly institutionalized literary reform aimed at making a colloquial style the new Japanese standard[10] – found, or created, models for the new 'women's language' in what was ostensibly *jogakusei-kotoba*, contemporary 'schoolgirls' speech.' This speech, at least as the reformist writers represented it, was characterized by the set of final particles that are "identified today as women's language" (2006: 98).

What appeared, not to Ochs alone but to many, to be a "stable indexical order of affect and gender on the one hand, and of gender and speech forms on the other ... did not exist until the late nineteenth century" (2006: 77). Inoue's comparison of sentence final particles from two literary works – the 1813 piece of popular fiction called "*Ukiyoburo* (The bathhouse of the floating world)," and the 1909 "prose narrative" *Sanshiro* (Inoue 2006: 93–5, citing Komatsu 1988) – reveals a striking change. The 1813 source represented men and women using a far greater number of particles that were part of a shared repertoire. By 1909, particles in the shared repertoire had been divided up and assigned exclusively to male or female characters. That is, these affect-laden particles now appeared to be part of a gender-exclusive pattern.

Lest we think that this shift was merely a construction of affectively differentiated gendered voices, Inoue points out that the quoted, represented voice of women became a "'quoting' voice as young women claimed their new modern Japanese identity and constructed their virtual speech community" (2006: 102). Thus what had been something of a fiction became a sociolinguistic fact, as the construction served as a magnet to draw to itself the previously different reality, i.e., speech practices. Recalling Kulick's work on language and desire (Kulick 2003, Cameron and Kulick 2003), early twentieth-century novels like *Makazekoikaze* (Inoue 2006: 101) became objects of desire in two ways. First, women readers were led to desire the sort of speaking selves they found in female characters, i.e., desiring to speak like they did. Second, the novel also served to introduce such Western notions as romantic love, a form of desire that was made desirable.

This is a classic case of indexicalization. What had come to be a commonly accepted indexical connection – namely, between gender and particular linguistic forms (said to function as a sort of female register) – emerges instead from the interface of fiction, construction, and sociohistorical fact.

Conclusion

A major goal of this book, and particularly Part IV, has been to historicize cultural connections between language and emotion. Other historically oriented anthropologists have described case after case involving transformation in discursive practices, forms of subjectivity, aesthetic sensibilities concerning speaking and other forms of action, and ideologies that link language to social groups and histories in unique ways. Profound shifts are afoot, many brought about by globally circulating modernist notions and values. Globally circulating nationalist visions influenced Tamil linguistic nationalism in South India. Catholic missionization, which led to the conversion of Gapun villagers in the 1940s, eventually contributed to the near abandonment of their indigenous language – a change mediated by new ideologies of language and their effect on how Gapuner parents interact with children, and thus far from inevitable. The global advance of Protestantism, in its Pentecostal or Dutch Calvinist forms (for example), has spread notions of language and emotion some of which we can call Protestant per se, and others local hybrids.

Chapter 11 presents ethnographic, historical, and linguistic evidence of how other technologies of self – "the psy disciplines" (N. Rose 1996) – shaping discursive practices and ideologies in many societies around the world.

I I

LANGUAGE AND THE MEDICALIZATION OF EMOTION

Introduction

In Part II, I explored the relations of language, power, and emotionality. Some say that power relations determine the bounds of sanity and madness, but this is an oversimplification. In this chapter I explore a Foucaultian theme – claims that the "psy disciplines" (N. Rose 1996, i.e., psychiatry, the first to emerge, and allied disciplines) have a growing, global influence on conceptualizations of emotion, and even on subjectivity. This impact is mediated through the treatment of ostensibly pathological states and patterns of feeling.

Before proceeding, I acknowledge a debt to Gregory Bateson (1972), whose insight into reflexivity (metacommunication, framing) and schizophrenia make him an important ancestor for a linguistically sensitive anthropology of mental illness.

The psy disciplines, writes Rose

have not only been able to supply a whole variety of models of selfhood but also to provide practicable recipes for action in relation to the government of persons by professionals in different locales. ... It has become impossible to conceive of personhood, to experience one's own or another's personhood, or to govern oneself or other's without psy (N. Rose 1996: 34).

Rose writes with the peculiar confidence of those who are not in the business of ethnographically, or cross-culturally, testing such questions of influence. Are there good grounds to believe Rose?

As my discussion of what I call "psychiatry's magic complex" (later in this chapter) indicates, there are reasons to doubt Rose's claims. Yet many share his perspective. More and more communities are encountering a new **register** that deals not only with emotion, but with politics, ritual traditions, etc. The register signals what philosopher Alasdair MacIntyre calls "emotivism," a plague on modern logic (1980). Emotivism is a popular philosophy that confuses statements of moral judgment – which at least attempt a transcontextual relevance – with statements of personal feeling or evaluation. However, we might wish to adapt the term for a broader obsession with emotion that tries to reduce not just moral judgments but rituals and other social phenomena to their putative emotional function. "We live in a specifically emotivist culture" (MacIntyre 1980: 21), despite the easy availability of "devastating hostile critiques" of particular emotional-therapeutic techniques.

What MacIntyre labels emotivism, others describe as **"therapization"** (Olivier de Sardan 1994) or "therapeutization" (Szasz 1975, see Foucault 1975) – signs, we are told, of our "therapy culture" (Furedi 2003), or "therapeutic culture" (Yates 2001). Conservative commentator David Frum, welcoming the critique offered in *One Nation Under Therapy* (Sommers and Satel 2005), added his own. What sort of evidence is available for a careful analysis of changes in the relationship of language and emotion, both in practice and ideological conception?

To query the intersection of language, emotion, and madness is to inquire into the nature of our fundamental humanness. Although the fields of religion or philosophy have staked a claim over questions of human nature, anthropologists have certainly also worried over them. Despite the problematic history of comparative studies of psychopathology, especially those involving Native Americans (Waldram 2004), anthropologists claim a unique perspective – systematic access to evidence from many societies, and well-tested paradigms for comparing those societies.

Class and distinct "individualisms" in the US: evidence of the therapy culture

Let us invoke another pioneering American anthropologist. Since Margaret Mead, some fieldworkers have returned from far away places to study their own society. Recently, an increasing number of American ethnographers study 'at home.' Some of these have produced studies of class in the United States – typically a taboo topic. Psychological anthropologist Adrie Kusserow's work in New York City (2004), introduced in Chapter 3, is particularly important for our purposes. Kusserow's findings lead us to believe that the American parents most likely to socialize their children to use language to accurately refer to and thus 'express' their feelings – i.e., to speak like Protestant moderns described in Chapter 10 – are upper middle class.

Kusserow describes her interest in inequality and class as a lifelong obsession; eventually, it led her to carry out fieldwork in three neighborhoods in New York City. Given the salience of the task of childrearing in every community, and the difficulty of collecting data on class in the United States by asking about it in interviews, Kusserow focused on parents' discourse on what sorts of selves their children should become, and on childrearing strategies cued to those aims. "Parkside" is her pseudonym for "a wealthy, mainly white, upper east side neighborhood in Manhattan." The other two communities, working class neighborhoods in Queens ("Kelley" and "Queenston" – again, pseudonyms), will concern us less.

Kusserow conducted interviews with Parkside parents, and observations in a "Parent Guidance Workshop." Parents paid $40 per session for ten group workshop meetings with a nationally known parenting expert (2004: 151).[1] In addition, she recorded public discourse. For example, a preschool in Parkside wrote a self-description that, for Kusserow, matches the sort of "psychologized individualism" that is the goal of parenting in Parkside. (Preschools, she argues, reflect, rather than trying to change, the values of the communities they serve (2004: 7)). Psychologized individualism, which she also labels "soft," contrasts with the "hard individualism" valued in Kelley and Queenston. Hard individualism stresses the difficulties of life and, in that context, the need to stand up for oneself.

Parkside parenting, and the ideologies of language and emotion it embodies, differ markedly from parenting styles common among previous American generations. Evidence for the shift comes in the form of comments by older adults (especially women, in public places) expressing some shock at the extent to which Parkside parents encourage children's verbalizations in general, and emotional verbalizations in particular. At the Parent Guidance Workshop, one mother said "One of my problems comes from the looks I get, the people who don't accept [my parenting style]" (2004: 155).

What does that style entail? Workshop participants present the sorts of challenges they currently face with their children. One mother had felt obligated to invite a girl to her house, although as the visit progressed, her son made clear that he did not like the girl. He told his mother flatly that he did not care about her, or her feelings, and thus did not understand the problem entailed in hurting those feelings. Such discussions indicate the balance that these parents seek between encouraging honest talk of feelings, and encouraging empathy and politeness. The expert suggested the mother should have said, "I know this is a pain for you. You didn't invite her over, but she's a guest in our house, and for an hour I need you to help." Another mother – 'April' – whom the counselor had asked to role-play the mother's part, responded to the counselor's suggested words with approval: "Yeah, yeah, 'cause then you're validating their feelings, that you don't have to like everybody. I think you have to respect his feelings, because you don't have to like all of your neighbors" (2004: 154–155).

Apparently April also had a child who was 'going through a stage.' Lately, her daughter seemed to hate everything. The counselor suggested

They're not developed enough to say, "You know, it really makes me angry when …" And I think parents overreact too. What they mean at that moment is "yuck." It's an expression of an immediate negative feeling (2004: 156).

These exchanges indicate the degree to which the culture of Parkside (and who knows how many other US communities) is a "therapy culture." Parents unreflectingly accept the legitimacy of therapy and its relevance to intimate life settings. Parkside promulgates the contemporary form of confessionalism, involving "incitement to discourse" about the self, a peculiarly modern self that – Foucault argues – is constituted by such discourse (1990). Kusserow presents the sort of empirical evidence of naturally occurring discourse that is lacking in Foucault's oeuvre. April's comment about "validating the feelings" of the child echoes expert discourse. The expert implies that mature persons should make statements like "it really makes me angry when ..." – while admitting that children cannot. Most relevant here is the valorization of a certain kind of feeling statement. Therapy culture encourages lexicalizing feelings – 'I feel [emotion lexeme]' – *not* what it calls 'acting out.' Acting out can involve one child hitting another; but it can also involve verbally acting out anger by raising the voice – and failing to 'own' that feeling through rendering emotion-talk a kind of referential practice. Value is not attached to performing feelings in any form of action, including vocalization, but to referring to them.

Note here the material grounding of linguistic ideologies. We can reinterpret Kusserow's argument thus: capitalist classes produce persons and discourses that are most likely to embrace an 'ownership' model of emotion talk. Note, too, the importance of the referentialist ideology of language, especially to those classes whose power to excuse we have seen in relation to 'hate speech' (Chapter 5). Finally, keep in mind the social-economic histories under which language ideologies of authenticity (Trilling 1972, Taylor 1991) emerge (viz., the spread of the culture of therapy, particularly in comfortable classes who can afford therapy). Relative to millennia of human history Parkside is unique – but not so vis-à-vis "late modernity" (Fischer 1999).

Culture and medicine: essentializing Latinos and their language

Like Kusserow, Santiago-Irizarry (2001) carried out fieldwork in the United States, focused on a set of powerful agents – psychiatrists and psychiatric care facilities. The result is a fascinating case study with a damning title – she discovered that the psychiatrists, almost all of them Latino, like the patients in the special programs designed to serve Latinos, were in effect *Medicalizing ethnicity*. 'Medicalization' denotes the spreading influence of the medical profession and its pathologizing of normal life events. In the twentieth-century United States, pregnancy and childbirth were declared pathologies, or at least conditions that fully warrant biomedical intervention. Santiago-Irizarry studied three institutions – two in New York City, one outside, run by New York State. Despite good intentions, all three ended up medicalizing Latino ethnicity.

Of particular interest is the way the psychiatrists conceived of the role of the Spanish language. Oddly, although bilingualism is pervasive among New York City Latinos, the psychiatrists drew lines around Spanish, as if their patients could only "abreact" – or speak the truth from their "gut" – in Spanish, because (ostensibly) Spanish was the language of their childhood. Given this distorted image, Santiago-Irizarry describes the psychiatrists' ideology as one of "linguistic regression;" they encouraged regression to the language of child-hood. Such mythologizing involved visual and verbal imagery that effectively surrounded one language (Spanish) with warmth and generalized emotionality. Such imagery undergirded arguments central to at least the local psychiatric **register** (i.e., local to the three institutions). Staff psychiatrists thus made Spanish a key sign of Latino "character" – again, warm and emotional, but also feminized, associated with maternality (Santiago-Irizarry 2001: 114).

Pathologies of language and emotion at two poles

In what sort of cultural context can we situate psychiatry, and psychiatrists such as these? Psychiatric models of emotion and psychopathology like the International Statistical Classification of Diseases and Health Related Problems (the ICD) – and the more psychiatrically focused, but also more Americanist, *Diagnostic and Statistical Manual* (the DSM, the handbook of the psy professions [American Psychiatric Association 2000]) – are cultural products. By pathologizing conditions that involve either 'too much' or 'too little' emotion, the DSM figurates (discursively constructs, without referring to) a golden mean. In this section I discuss the DSM and related pathologizing discourses.

Control is a paramount virtue in psychiatry, the DSM, and the Northern European cultural perspective that produced both (Gaines 1992). The DSM is built on covert racial, ethnic, and gender stereotypes:

Certain categories of people have been and are putatively 'inherently' unable to exercise control over themselves because of their emotional character. This is said of emotional others who might be 'uncivilized' (i.e., culturally different), or of a 'different' gender, age or putative 'race' … Unable to control their emotions, they are suspect (Gaines 1992: 16).

Such categories of people become covert models for pathologies of 'excessive emotion' or lack of control.

'Flat affect' is also pathologized in the DSM and elsewhere, because Northern Europeans view both "emotional extremes as problematic" (Gaines 1992: 20). The label *alexithymia* (from three Greek roots that, together, mean 'having no words for feelings,' coined by Sifneos [e.g., 1973]), pathologizes the putative inability to engage in emotion talk. Other diagnostic categories can embody both excess and absence. In schizophrenia we find

the 'Kretschmerian paradox' – the fact that schizophrenia-spectrum patients can simultaneously experience both exaggerated and diminished levels of affective response (Sass 2007: 351).

If schizophrenia involves trouble with affect, 'autism,' too, is said to primarily involve trouble with processing and expressing emotion. Autistic spectrum disorders (including Asperger syndrome at the 'high functioning' end of the spectrum) involve "impaired perceptual and especially perceptual-affective capacities" (Hobson 1993: 207). Linguistic anthropologist Ochs and her colleagues (Ochs et al. 2004) point to the challenge autistic children face in processing "socio-cultural indexicality." This refers to indexical expressions whose semiotic objects or interpretive keys are matters of particular social knowledge, such as allusion through telegraphic or indirect means to complex scenarios. For example, when 11-year-old 'Adam,' who has Asperger syndrome, reports all the questions his grandmother asked him, his family says she could have been "a detective." But Adam doesn't understand the emergent contextual reason for the label – the link between his description of grandmother's questioning, which his parents call "interrogating," and their contextual inference, construing such activity vis-à-vis a social stereotype.

Ochs, Solomon, and Sterponi (2005) have explored possible improvements in families' ability to help children with autism spectrum disorder, by shedding light on the relevant *habitus*, a particular nexus of language, emotion, culture, and embodiment. *Habitus* denotes sensibilities and "dispositions [that are] unquestionably the product of social determinisms, [but] are also constituted outside the spheres of consciousness and constraint" (Bourdieu1991: 51); these sensibilities and dispositions generate a particular sets of 'choices' related to class-specific patterns of conduct. Ochs and her colleagues

demonstrate how certain features of the habitus associated with [middle-class] Euro-American [Child-Directed Communication] may limit the communicative potential of certain children with autism spectrum disorders (Ochs, Solomon, and Sterponi 2005: 560).

These features include a preference for caregivers to interact with children *face-to-face* with many signs of "positive affect" such as *praise* delivered with "exaggerated intonation" (2005: 562).

Building on this research, Mangano and Engelke (2006) document interactional breakthroughs between an expert who immigrated from India as an adult, and a child with autism, involving a tightly controlled affective style foreign to middle-class American parents. Therapeutic progress apparently hinged on the expert timing of her praise to directly coincide with the child's stepwise progress and suppressing the intonational dynamism of praise utterances. The expert's goal was to train the child's mother, who could continue helping the child learn to communicate. Unfortunately, the Euro-American mother, in accord with her habitus, continued to offer diffuse, frequent, and intonationally dynamic praise. This study may encourage caregivers to try dampening their affect, accommodating the needs of their low-affect children.

Capps and Ochs' (1995) study of a contrasting disorder – panic disorder, involving emotional excess – offers advice to therapists dealing with the disorder. They unearth discursive processes contributing to constructing and maintaining the disorder. Capps and Ochs

track on a linguistic plane how [a panic disorder patient's] narratives construct theories of a world in which emotions creep up on, invade, and sometimes overwhelm the present rather than being contained at a distance. In this sense, agoraphobia can be seen as an outcome of theories individuals develop [and keep *speaking*] as they act and interact with others in the world (Capps and Ochs 1995: 21–2).

The patient in question, Meg, uses a "grammar of abnormality" involving marked use of mental verbs and place adverbs.

The discursive structures through which Meg maintains her relationship to panic include the following (1995: 75–76):

Transcript 4: Excerpts from panic disorder patient's narratives (ellipsis shows my omission of four lines)

Mental verb+ emphatic stress	1 And – and then I *realized*
Voice quality	2 *((desperate, pleading tone))*
Present tense + halting delivery	3 Well what *can* I – ?
Intensifying adverb+ emphatic stress	4 I felt real *helpless.*
…	
Present tense + negative modal auxiliary	9 *I can't leave*

Capps and Ochs fault therapists for failing to identify the kinds of "habitual linguistic forms and discourse patterns that actualize debilitating portraits" of those with panic disorder (1995: 179). They recommend attention to weaknesses and strengths clients iconically signal by means of the "sentential position" and "semantic roles" they assign to the self in narratives (1995: 187). Without challenging the notion of panic disorder or the authority of the psy disciplines, Capps and Ochs suggest ways in which suffers can be empowered. This is in keeping with the increasingly applied dimension of Ochs' work.

How did the DSM and all of its illness labels, together with other features of psychiatrese, emerge?

Enregisterment: the emergence of 'psychiatry' and a 'psychiatric register'

Words like 'psychiatry' have existed since Romantic-era physicians like Johann Christian Reil (1759–1813), who coined the term *psychiatrie* in 1808 (Opitz, Schultka, and Göbbel 2006: 119), whence it was almost immediately borrowed into French (Goldstein 1987: 4). The word made its way into English around 1846. The very coinage indexes medicalization, an institutional power-grab over the domain of the soul – *psyche*, in Greek, seat of the emotions. *Psychiatrist* entered the aforementioned languages some decades later. The former label – 'mad doctor' – scarcely helped to remove the reputation for involvement with magic. In the following sections I offer evidence of the psy disciplines' impact on language and people in Europe and Asia.

Foucault's classic work *Madness and Civilization* may not be an ideal historical guide to the details of psychiatric history, but it is a bold, imaginative presentation of its outlines. Seventeenth- and eighteenth-century "Classicist" doctors offered visions of madness and of particular conditions and helped set the terms, literally, in which some subjectivities were pathologized – for some centuries to come, if not into our own time. "Hysteria" and "hypochondria," for Classicists, meant nearly the same thing – dangerous excesses of feeling (Foucault 1988: 165).

We can look at the influence of early psychiatrists as operating through metadiscourse – e.g., foregrounding preexisting linguistic distinctions between thoughts and feelings. The nineteenth-century French *Idéologue* doctors – practitioners of "the science of ideas," "medicine of the imagination," or "moral treatment," such as Philippe Pinel [1745–1826] – cemented the thought-feeling distinction. They treated (in both senses of the word) "ideas" and "passions" as two, radically distinct, potential loci of pathology (Goldstein 1987: 49, 84, 89, 94).

J. E.-D. Esquirol (1772–1840), Pinel's student and later his patron, introduced a new psychopathological category in 1810 – "monomania" (pathological obsession). *Monomanie* became the French forerunner of the psychobabble in our languages and in the titles of our self-help books. Whereas the French word *nostalgia*, "a late seventeenth-century medical coinage," took "almost a century and a half to win" the approval of the Académie Française, *monomanie* was in widespread use among "the nonmedical French intelligentsia" by 1820, and accepted by the Académie by 1835 (Goldstein 1987: 153). The reason for the different treatment seems to have been the rapid rise of prestige associated with the medical, or psychiatric, **register**.

Professional registers appear to reflect the prestige of professions. Some scholars have depicted prestigious professional registers as especially esoteric – as though only doctors speak like doctors. Actually, members of the public tend to borrow from medical and psychiatric registers, as the French example and the current glut of self-help books filled with psychobabble illustrate.

A psychiatric register was just emerging in English at the very time England came to dominate India. In the eighteenth and nineteenth centuries, the **enregisterment** of medical and psychiatric English – i.e., the process by which this register emerged[2] – was no more cut off from popular usage than was the case with psychiatric French. However, certain phrases increasingly came to index the ever more prestigious medical profession – particularly the construction, "you are suffering from (some illness)." This usage came to index medicine more clearly after a shift in the denotative meaning of "to suffer," from the vague "to undergo" to the more particular "endure pain or disease" (Oxford English Dictionary, second edition, "suffer").

By the end of the nineteenth century, the particular resonances of the progressive form 'you are suffering from' were strong enough that literary instances of the phrase were consistently medical. The phrase appears in the fiction of Conan Doyle, Kipling, and George Eliot either in the mouths of medical doctors, or in apparent parodies of the medical voice. Dr. Tertius Lydgate speaks thus to Rev. Causabon in *Middlemarch*: "I believe that you are suffering from what is called fatty degeneration of the heart" (Eliot 1986 [1871–2]). Note that the progressive aspect emphasizes the immediacy (though, perhaps, short-term duration) of what the semantic patient is enduring.[3] (The same holds true of the Bangla word for "suffering," as we shall se below. The full Bangla-English dictionary entry for *bhug-* is to "suffer, experience, undergo, be troubled with," Ali, Moniruzzaman, and Tareq 1994: 616.)[4]

The classifying urge

To use the psychiatric register today is to invoke diagnostic categories from a scientifically authoritative source like the DSM, whose taxa are known as Research Diagnostic Categories or RDCs. Psychiatrists and psychologists assign patients diagnostic labels in 'initial assessment' interviews. Such assessments and labels become written parts of patient records (case histories) – a complex genre with a complex history (Berkenkotter and Ravotas 1997: 264). "The initial assessment interview is very important to the client's role and identity because they are constructed in the lexicon of the psychiatric profession" (1997: 259). Berkenkotter and Ravotas call RDCs "membership categorization devices" (MCDs) – Harvey Sacks's (1972) term for the families or category sets by which people routinely describe others. Noun phrases that follow the key declaration, "You are suffering from …" are MCDs. Properly invoking MCDs that stand a chance of being recognized as rigorous is crucial to science, medicine, and psychiatry (in descending, nesting order). The title of Berkenkotter and Ravotas's article, "Genre as Tool in the Transmission of Practice Over Time and Across Professional Boundaries," points to their claim that the initial assessment – as genre – helps reproduce the psy disciplines. MCDs are crucial to this task.

There is obviously a bigger picture here. Classifying is not just central to culture, to what languages perform as semanticoreferential systems, or to what speech-interaction does (Silverstein 2004). Nor is the bigger picture limited to the fact that *self*-conscious development of a set of labels, knit together in hierarchies, uniquely characterizes the modernist self-invention of the sciences. Rather, what Charcot (1892) called "practicing nosography" was, in Freud's words, a sort of recapitulation of "the myth of Adam, who must have experienced in its most perfect form that intellectual delight so highly praised by Charcot, when God led before him the creatures of Paradise to be named and grouped" (Freud 1924–1953 as quoted by Goldstein 1987: 384).[5] From this perspective, the very taxonomic obsession that has produced the psychiatric register, in all of its scientism, is actually a thoroughly hybridizing practice, reflecting the pull that myth and magic exert on psychiatry.

Peculiar to modern psychiatric nosologies is the special attraction of *natural kinds*, first discussed in Chapter 4. From its very origins, psychiatry has been a profession plagued by magical associations (Foucault 1988: 276, and compare 250).[6] This helps explain its serious case of science-envy, also reflective of the fact that psychiatry deals in interactive kinds, whereas the natural sciences deal with natural kinds. Natural kinds (e.g., water) are indifferent to being classified as such. Interactive kinds are conscious of and affected by being classified as they are; they change in response to labeling (Hacking 1999: 105). The ever-frustrated drive to emulate the natural sciences becomes envy, given the resources whose distribution today depends on the competition to claim the mantle of science.

A single register may be performed in, and circulate by means of, many discursive genres. When the English medical (and later, psychiatric) register emerged, it embraced narrative in the form of single case histories and the new genre of *medical research article*. Medical writing did not shun references to the author's thought processes and emotions – indexes of subjectivity common to most narrative (D. Atkinson 1992: 348). An "involved" or affective style, marked by high counts of second-person pronouns and "private" verbs [think, feel], etc.]), typified the register. However, as Atkinson discovered by analyzing 250 years of research articles in the *Edinburgh Medical Journal*, the register drifted from its roots. Article style shifted steadily from the "involved" pole toward the "informational" (i.e., highly focused on propositional content, longer words, more nouns [1992: 350]). This trend, and related transformations, culminated in the 1980s. At that time, editors of such discursive institutions as the *American Journal of Psychiatry* pronounced the single case history obsolete "because its *n of one* precluded generalization across population groups and because case histories could not be replicated" (Berkenkotter 2008: 29). Note here that, even as various affects continued to serve as psychiatric symptoms, psychiatric and medical writing became ever more affectively removed.

From Kraepelin to the neo-Kraepelinian revolution

Psychiatry's focus on classifying illnesses as natural kinds emerged with the publication of the 1899 edition of Kraepelin's textbook on clinical psychiatry, though precedents can be found in Pinel's 1801 textbook and throughout the nineteenth century. In the 1899 edition Kraepelin elevated "*dementia praecox*" – which Eugen Bleuler would later (1908) **baptize** "schizophrenia" – "to the status of a major disease, formed by fusing all these degenerative processes into one category" (Barrett 1998: 621).[7] (American psychiatrists followed these European developments closely, quickly adopting Kraepelin's labels [Noll 2004]).

Kraepelin, who first baptized the now well-known illness *manic-depressive disorder*, displayed concern to accurately classify mental diseases:

Experience shows that this condition is very characteristic of an entirely different disease, to which we will give the name of *maniacal-depressive insanity*, for reasons to be discussed immediately. This disease generally runs its course in a *series* of *isolated attacks*, which are not uniform, but present either states of depression of the kind described or characteristic states of excitement... (Kraepelin 1985: 12–13; emphasis in original).

Kraepelin dealt in his own way with what I have called psychiatry's "**magic complex**," "its need to convince a skeptical public that its ... associations with magic and religion were finished, vanquished in part by discursive measures, focused on a scientizing drive" (Wilce 2008: 91). "As a complex or neurosis this involves attraction ... and a need to deny the attraction" (2008: 92). The scientism of recent editions of the DSM has influenced discursive genres that pervade psychiatric practice.

These historical strands help contextualize the Bangladeshi iteration of the story of the enregisterment of psychiatric discourse.

The psychologization of suffering in Bangla psychiatric discourse

The influence of English, and the English psychiatric register, appear quite strong in relation to the discursive practices of Bangladeshi psychiatry, and particularly the discourse of the recently launched magazine popularizing a psy perspective on the self – *Manabigyān* (a pseudonym), or *Psychology*.

Early in my experience with Bangla, I learned to use the very handy impersonal construction x-*lāge*, 'something strikes,' or 'something affects.' (Here, NP means 'noun phrase,' AP means 'adjective phrase,' OV means 'object[noun phrase]-verb[phrase],' i.e., 'head-final' languages in which 'direct objects' precede verbs.)

$(NP_{genitive/"dative"})_{optional\ experiencer}\ NP\ (or\ AP)_{experience}\ lāge$
as in [*āmār*] *lajjā lāge.*
Shame affects [me].

Note that in Bangla *and in English*, "it strikes/struck me" is ambiguous, denoting either a physical or a subjective event. In everyday Bangla, the vast majority of feeling statements make use of *lāg-* ([it] affects).[8]

Although I also learned the verb phrase, x-*bhug-*, 'to suffer,' I found it used less often, and very rarely in referring to the suffering of illness. One doesn't normally "suffer from a cold" in Bangla; instead, "[a] cold/catarrh affects" [one].

tʰānḍ -ṣardi lāge (tʰanḍa / ʃɔrdi lāg-e)
cold – catarrh strikes/affects

Bangla, a head-final language, has an OV verb phrase structure. The x in "x-*lāg*" and "x-*bhug*" denotes some experienced object or state preceding the verb in each case. In the case of *lāg-* constructions, the phrase preceding the verb is often an adjective that qualifies the nature of the experience. Two NPs may optionally precede the adjective. One is in either the nominative case, or – if the NP is a personal pronoun – the 'objective' case, and indexes the thing that 'affects' the experiencer, for example, for the 'good.' An optional NP preceding that one encodes the experiencer and occurs in the so-called dative case (a 'dative-' [Klaiman 1980] or 'experiencer-subject' construction, Verma and Mohanan 1991).[9]

āmār tomāke bhālo lāge
my you-Obj good strikes
'I like you'
(adapted from Klaiman 1980:276).

The second line in the letter in Transcript 5, below, is a complex example.

Speakers of Bangla and other South Asian languages (Verma and Mohanan 1991, Bhatt 2003, Pappuswamy 2005)[10] use this construction to index the domains we call experience, emotion, and illness, but also to perform a number of tasks beyond indicating subjectivity. Many things – crowds, flying objects, clothes fitting too tight, nausea, as well as feelings translatable as psychiatric symptoms – can 'strike' or 'affect' a person.

This at least has been the status quo. Recently, however, psychiatrists have markedly departed from the *lāg-* construction. They may not even be aware of it, but their verbal practice is clear enough. I claim this based on analyzing 111 letter exchanges in the advice column of the only domestically produced magazine circulating in Bangladesh that treats (and popularizes) *Manabigyān* '*Psychology*' (the magazine's pseuodymous name) and psychiatry. The readership of *Manabigyān* is impossible to count, since each copy would likely be read by several people, but surely well above the 9,000 copies of each monthly issue being printed in 2000 when I interviewed its entrepreneurial founder and publisher. Dr. Minaj (a pseudonym) is a psychiatrist who completed postgraduate training in England. He has gathered around him a circle of former students who assist him with the publication. Readers send letters to its *Parāmarśo Pātā*, advice page, from all over Bangladesh, seeking help with their own or their loved ones' problems. The psychiatrist-editors responding to them reframe *samasyā*, 'problems,' as *mānasik rog*, 'psychiatric illnesses.'[11] Dr. Minaj is shaped by his engagement with global psychiatry (through his training and later attendance at regional conferences) and by his scouring of the internet for articles (importantly, in English) to translate for *Manabigyān*.

Manabigyān's implicit challenge to *lāg-* constructions as the traditional means of referring to affective states involves consistent replacement of that construction with *bhug-* constructions.[12] This is significant in several ways. First, the context in which the editors deploy these constructions is psychiatric diagnosis based on the stories and complaints readers send in their letters. The construction is thus crucial to the **enregisterment** of psychiatric Bangla, the invention of this new scientific language variety. And note that the shift from *lag-* to *bhug-* offers (it cannot impose) a new means of discursively construing emotion, and a new linguistic construction of self.

'Depression' and its Bangla counterpart, *biaṣnnatā* (*biʃɔnnɔta*), are late arrivals on the Bangladeshi scene, but global pharmaceutical manufacturers are making up for lost time with advertising campaigns that propel the circulation of the diagnostic labels. Another **metacultural** force adding accelerative 'umph' to the new cultural category *biaṣnnatā* is *Manabigyān*. So a new set of illness labels – closely and intentionally matched with the ICD or DSM (the diagnostic manuals guiding mental health workers around the world) – accompanies *Manabigyān*'s insistence on a psychologizing grammatical construction based on *bhug-* "suffer."

Transcript 5: *Lāge*-grammar in letter vs. bhugchen in editors' reply (letter#25)

1 *sab samay-e   sarīr-e   ekṭā klānti bhāb thāke.*
  all time-LOC body-LOC   DET tired feeling stays
  "My body always feels tired."
2 *[āmār] kono   kāj-e-i   bhālo lāge nā.*
  [my] any   activity-LOC good strikes not
  "No activity makes me feel good."

  Editors' reply
3 *āpni depression bā biṣannatā roge bhugchen*
  "You are suffering from depression or dejection illness."

The original letter left the experiencer NP [which would have been something like āmār, "my," (loosely translated, "I")] implicit, which is extremely common. That sentence encodes an additional NP not in the nominative or objective but the locative case – *kono kāj-e-i*, "no activity" – in this case, the experienced object, the /e/ being the locative case suffix. /i/ is a stress marker.

The semantic range of *bhug-* is far narrower than that of *lāg-*. An anxious young psychiatric profession might feel the need to discipline itself by restricting how it communicates with patients and families about their suffering. For the psychiatric register, *lāg-* has the disadvantage of being grammatically impersonal – always third person, never inflected to agree with the experiencer. Things just 'strike.' *Lāg-* is thus a very poor candidate for a psychologizing idiom. Finally, *lāg-* almost never occurs in the progressive form that is so well suited to indexing ongoing subjective states, whereas only 9 out of a total of 64 tokens of *bhug-* are *not* progressive.[13]

To summarize: *bhug-* is not an impersonal verb, but is always inflected to agree with the experiencing subject. In the psychiatric register it typically occurs in progressive aspect, denoting the immediacy and flux of experience.

There is nothing foreordained about the particular changes in Bangla that Bangladeshi psychiatrists are at least modeling. Indeed their chances of success in changing linguistic practice throughout the country are slim indeed. Despite these caveats, "the psy disciplines" – "psychology, psychiatry, and their cognates… have brought into existence a variety of new ways in which human

beings have come to understand themselves and do things to themselves"
(N. Rose 1996: 2). Despite findings that psychiatry receives far less respect
than other medical specialties (Rosoff and Leone 1991), and that international
peers may disdain Asian psychiatrists (Lee 1999), psy disciplines increasingly
affect people around the world.

Conclusion

The reach of biomedicine and the psy disciplines, i.e., the breadth of their
influence, corresponds with the depth of their roots in the West, but perhaps
nowhere more so than in the United States. In the author's home country, it
is hard to discuss emotion without somehow engaging its conceptualization
within the psy disciplines. What is needed is more ethnographic work analyzing both micro-level, face-to-face interactions in which emotion is constructed
or pathologized, and broader patterns in the construction and circulation of
discursive categories that underlie and enable those micro-processes.

12

CONCLUSION

Having come this far, are we any clearer about what emotion is? Emotion's ontological status or precise denotation – its semantic intension – did not claim most of our attention. But I hope I have clarified emotion in its relation to language, by demonstrating the breadth of its semantic extension and the range of pragmatic effects that follow emotion talk.

Throughout previous chapters, I have described not only emotion talk, but reflections on it – be they everyday, philosophical, or anthropological – as forms of social action. We have explored the implications of this claim for how such action might be, in various forms, efficacious, performative, or powerful. No emotion-related discourse is more transformative than those metadiscourses that reframe emotion talk. Perhaps the central example of this is what Foucault (1990) calls the "incitement to discourse," starting in a church-confessional context where sins of feeling and thought needed confessing, passing into a medicalizing context that solicits and pathologizes emotion-talk (the famous **talking cure** was just the beginning) or its absence (the category "alexithymia"), and thereby produces the modern, individuated self.

The previous paragraph, and the consistent invocation throughout it of *emotion* – a single lexeme indexing what, to us, appears as a transparent category with natural integrity – points to, but also masks, a history: Each generation, in every society, produces and uses its own taxonomy organizing various facets of subjectivity. This may involve one umbrella term – or several major, inclusive categories – as well as myriad labels for the entities envisioned as nodes included under those inclusive terms. Some of these resist simple equation in comparing different cultural systems. We have dwelt on the historical dimensions of this variability, in part because previous treatments of language and emotion have, to a great extent, neglected history.

In what follows, I retrace highlights of this book's argument.

Reflexivity

In regards to language and emotion and in general, the relationship between metadiscourse and discourse (between higher-order indexes and the lower-order indexes the former take as their object) is not merely reflective but creative (Silverstein's unpublished lecture "Metaforces of Power in Traditional Oratory" delivered to the Anthropology Seminar, Yale University 1981, Silverstein 1993; Agha 2007). This claim underlies my assessment of the impact of all accounts of emotion-language, whether spontaneously produced local folk accounts, or academic accounts like histories and ethnographies. A similar relational vision motivates an examination not just of language as it makes emotion its referential object, but of feelings, sensibilities, etc. that make some variety of language their object. There is a dialectical relationship between emotional language and *linguistic feelings* (any feelings about any form of language). We see the same dialectic at work in cases where forms of language come to be evaluated, sensed, feared, or loved as 'emotional.' Members of one group may say they "recoil in horror" when they hear another group's speech, while the latter may fear such reactions, and fear the dismissal of their speech as irrational. That is, feelings that target linguistic forms include feelings about ostensibly feelingful language. We live in this kind of hall of mirrors, amidst reflections on reflections. Some of these higher order indexes or reflections have the potential to reshape ostensibly emotional language. Thus, whole codes that are, for example, stigmatized – codes whose speakers come to feel some degree of shame regarding them – may well undergo 'reform.' The particular structures (phonological, morphosyntactic, etc.) speakers use to index or perform emotion might shift. Ideological accounts might figure such shifts as individual 'choices,' or 'seeing the linguistic light.' Yet those 'choices,' practices, and structures inevitably reflect material rewards accruing to some forms and not others in a linguistic economy. They also interact with the very ideological accounts that seek to describe – or prescribe – them.

It is for such reasons that neither emotion nor emotion talk can be reduced to a straightforward working out of an evolutionary program of natural selection leading to (always-shifting) genetic distribution in a population. Admittedly, our genetic, neuranatomical, and neurophysiological makeup *do* fix the outer limits of our emotional and linguistic potential. Within that range, however, the sort of reflexivity described above can have relatively profound influence. It could well be that no genetic fact with an impact on linguistic or emotional function is so autonomous as to be totally resistant to shame, pride, or any of the language passions described in Chapter 7. And whatever the universals that have been, or have yet to be, uncovered vis-à-vis some relatively fixed human subjective palette, they have not prevented successive generations even in the West from either favoring their own particular paint (think of the suffering celebrated by the Romantics, or by Buddhists [Obeyesekere 1985]) or dividing the world of subjectivity differently.

Simply because we qualify the extent to which our biological evolution tells the final story about our capacities for language and emotion does not allow us to neglect real bodies in real situations. Far from excluding embodied actors from our consideration, I hope to have opened new paths of inquiry vis-à-vis embodiment, affect, linguistic performance, and culture. Depending on the severity of my case of 'linguistic insecurity' – which I prefer to conceive of as shame – my face may blush, my palms may sweat, and I might even lower my head ever so slightly. Yet this set of acts-and-experiences reveals not just emotions that are easily named and probably universal, but context-specific cultural sensibilities. And those sensibilities not only reflect, but motivate acts that garnish, symbolic capital. The capacity to realize errors, including just when it is that my speech has crossed the line to become 'too emotional' or 'too cold' may well be a desideratum in every human community. In many communities, people who habitually speak unguardedly may be called *shameless*. Such opprobrium points to no universal reason for shame, like nakedness, but to having or lacking a particular set of cultural and aesthetic sensibilities. These are also feelings, and they offer us guidance vis-à-vis our speech-conduct – one of the several kinds of relationship we have explored between language and emotion.

For Charles Peirce, action per se involves what he called Secondness, while "conduct ... sympathy, flesh and blood, that by which I feel my neighbor's feelings, is third [Third]" (1931–1958: 1.337, p. 171). Firstness is unqualified fact or presence, as in a feeling that has gone on forever and will last forever, and exists on its own without relation to anything else – clearly an **ideal type** that exists nowhere in our world. In a less rigorous sense, iconicity is Firstness. Secondness involves the action of some force upon another. Thirdness, however, involves regularities of action, relations mediated by convention, "order and legislation" (ibid.) Indexes may be Seconds. Yet, when viewed in the light of potentially infinite "orders of indexicality" in which (for example) ideological representations of sociolinguistic facts (i.e., 'lower-'order indexes) reflect on and potentially change them, we see that the sort of indexicality with which we are concerned is caught up in Thirdness. "Exaggerated language" – perhaps a random act of speech in a moment of passion – "is the furniture of minds which think of seconds and forget thirds" (ibid.) Yet even such moments may actually reflect larger patterns of "conduct." In any case, they are *judged* in relation to some law-like sociocultural order, i.e., Thirdness.

Culture, including particular 'cultures' of language and emotion, consists of interaction between Firsts (or [putative] icons), Seconds (prototypically, indexes), and Thirds (norms, laws, conventions and hence "symbols" in Peirce's sense). What does someone "speak like"? This way of posing the question – and, even if no one explicitly poses the question, we commonly hear answers to it – betrays the fact that we think in terms of icons. But any answer – "she speaks like x, y, or z" – will involve indexes, or more accurately, reflections (metaindexes) on some pattern (a purported first-level index) that is commonly enough represented (in a second-order index such as the statement I'm discussing) to be drawn on. Our ways of representing such ostensible patterns turn the chaos of ever-shifting speech forms associated with ever-shifting collectivities (and involving ever-shifting patterns of identification by speakers with collectivities and speech forms) into norms, rules, generalizations (Thirds). And language reveals cultural concepts (Silverstein 2004) precisely in such interactions of iconicity, indexicality, and symbolicity. Ritual language moves us (emotionally, but also in cosmic terms) in part pbecause – precisely through its **entextualized** pattern, emerging in relation to its non-linguistic context – it "paints a picture [iconicity] of what it accomplishes in relation to that context [indexicality$_1$] and can change our experience of the context [indexicality$_2$] to the degree we accept the picture" (Silverstein 2003b: 38). Indexicality as first understood (designated indexicality$_1$) involves signs reflecting their immediate, ritual context. In the second understanding, indexical signs point to a context that is coming-to-be as a result of their very work – in close conjunction with the iconicity entailed in "figurating" (Silverstein 2004, Wilce 2006) the very goal of the ritual discourse, a transformation whose significance is both more-or-less cosmic and personally engaging.

I have described a number of *genres* of emotional performance, from discursive displays of wrath (the Gapuner *kros* [Kulick 1992, 1998]), to love letters as an emerging genre in Junigau (Nepal; Ahearn 2003), to Karelian laments (Tolbert 1990). *Kroses* and laments appear to be fading away, while love letters play an increasingly important role in Junigau. By the time we – or, more importantly, local actors – have designated a particular performance with a genre label, or in any other way invoked the genre, the performance has already been influenced by the histories of discourse associated with it. "Already" means before and during the performance as well as during any post facto labeling and evaluation. Reflexivity is inherent in the relationship among performances, labels, and metadiscourse. Metadiscourse about the *kros*, associating it with women, backwardness, irrationality, and paganism, helped seal its doom in the modernizing Gapun village. Globally circulating discourses on modernity and education constitute the context in which love letters flourish in Junigau, while the letters also add momentum to those very discourses. Love is thus married to development; the letters perform the ceremony.

Language ideologies and the contextualization of emotion

A broad range of phenomena can be considered reflexive and, as we have seen, influence the ongoing evolution of language and emotion. The denunciation of women's *kroses*, which were often prompted in some way by men – though that was rarely talked about – reflects a **language ideology**. These notions of language and its connection to social categories (e.g., women) are always partial and distorting. They form the link between linguistic form and practice on the one hand, and structures of power and authority on the other – in the case of the ideological representation of *kroses*, helping to solidify the authority of men and the Catholic Church in Gapun village.

The fact that the very words "emotion" and "language" – or, more accurately, their uses in certain contexts – do some ideological work of their own is no doubt less transparent to us. It is all too easy to dismiss some discourse as emotional. Such acts of labeling typically signal concern and disapproval. The dismissive use of the label "dialects" (as in "all the dialects of Africa" – "dialects," apparently, because they are unwritten, or 'primitive') carries its own subtle affective stance, enabling the contrasting word "languages" to take on an air of legitimacy. The reality that our concept of languages – including, perhaps, the assumption that real ones are written and not only oral, and that they thus have a standard version that must be learned at school – is both an ideology and a possible source of strong (and dare we say, irrational?) feelings about languages is a hard pill to swallow.

All of these insights flow from the claim that, in order to understand the scope of all significant relations between language and emotion, we must take into account the fundamentally reflexive nature of languaging as a form of **semiosis**. Whether it be the immediacies of face-to-face interaction or larger scale cultural formations, we have gained insight into the workings of language and emotion by examining the ways in which each may provide context to the other, and by grounding their interaction in the particulars of context.

The ideologies of language and emotion discussed above – visions of language (etc.) in the world that are particular to a society or segment thereof (e.g., a social class) – shape the context of speaking emotionally and of feelings for language. We have seen how this kind of contextualization functions over time and over generations, as children learn to speak and to do so with appropriate emotions. The language socialization literature we reviewed demonstrates how cultural notions of the self, of children's selves in particular, of language, and of emotion shape what children learn and thus what is, and is not, reproduced. Gapuners in the 1980s understood children to be naturally endowed with *hed*, or assertiveness, but were concerned that they acquire *save*, or cooperative social skills. Contextualizing particular performances and genres – the *kros* and men's house oratory – as Kulick does, involves uncovering their ties to the ideologies motivating changing adult practices, particularly their linguistic practice with children. Parents hope children will **identify** with proper conduct.

Language(s), emotion, and identification

At least since Kenneth Burke (1969[1950]), theories of society, language, and rhetoric have accorded the notion of **identification** a central place. For example, Kroskrity's ethnographic study of the "multiethnic identity of the Arizona Tewa" (1993: 178) focused on "the active and creative role that speakers" (1993: 205) and speaking play in managing shifting moments of identification. With a nod to Burke, Kroskrity aimed at a "general model of identification" (1993: 190, 192). Situated language use – specifically, using the codes that

Arizona Tewas controlled when Kroskrity's book was published, viz., Tewa, Hopi, and English – is central to his model.[1]

We have examined cases in which affect crucially mediates the indexical relationship between language and modes of identification. Studies like Samuels' (2004) ethnographic and ethnomusicological investigation of processes of identification among the San Carlos Apache complicate common understandings of indexicality. Previous ethnographic accounts of Apache semiosis (Basso 1996) have depicted traditional linguistic practices, like place-naming and place-oriented story telling, as direct indexes of Apache identity. Other examples that depict "speaking like an x" as a straightforward index of "x-ness" abound.

Samuels offers a sort of triangulated model of identification, inserting a mediating element between a semiotic form and the 'identity' it ostensibly indexes. That mediating element is affect. Singing country western songs with Apache emotion – albeit in English – indexes Apacheness. As a mode of identification, affect, and particularly affective singing, mediates between semiotic form and identity category.

Describing Gapuner "identities" changing, in connection with shifting practices involving language and emotion, would leave us with the notion of some fixed repertoire of these identities, viewed (despite the best of intentions in the literature) as things. In contrast, to describe rapid change in Gapun village in the 1980s and 1990s in terms of patterns of identification reminds us that indexical connections linking practices to people enter their lived experience as emotional processes. Whether we are discussing language shift in Gapun village, or the embarrassment over working-class or immigrant speech patterns that leads some in the United States to pay large sums of money to "dialect coaches" (Cameron 2001; also called "accent reduction" coaches, Lippi-Green 1997), we are trying, in effect, to capture a moment of change in patterns of identification that are at once linguistic and cultural, personal and social, emotional and ideological.

This book's approach to affect as a force that plays a mediating role between linguistic forms and modes of identification is an extension of my notion of "triangulation" in moments of discursive identification (Wilce 1998: 35). During my Bangladesh fieldwork I was struck by a pattern I had seldom heard in my own middle-class American community's discourse. Bangladeshi individuals would tell me (person A) about others' feelings towards them, "So-and-so (B) loves me" (C) – depicting self to an interlocutor through the mediating invocation of another. This contrasts with many Americans' urgent concern to let others know their *own* feelings and, perhaps more tellingly, their apparent concern to establish their self-worth on the basis of feelings they say they are experiencing (e.g., love for their children or spouses). Bumper stickers abound in the United States on the pattern of "I love my wife," or "I (heart symbol) Colorado," etc. Adopting a triangulating strategy, or a triangulated subject position, involves discursive/affective identification with a valued other.

Language passions, and politically charged affects like tamilparru, signal modern, collective forms of identification with a language, newly objectified, and newly construed as an index. Mitchell (in press) describes "how specific languages have gone from being understood and portrayed as natural features of particular local landscapes and environments, available to be used as local resources and mediums of communication, to being experienced as inalienable attributes of human beings that constitute a fundamental basis of their identities". In fact such 'identities' are phantoms, masking the realities of shifting subject positions, shifting linguistic identifications. As this book has shown, these identifications are linguistic in two senses – we engage in identification through linguistic forms, and toward linguistic forms. Ironically, we sometimes identify with linguistic forms that are not our own. This is what Labov (1972) described in the case of lower-middle class speakers of English in New York City, and what Bourdieu described as "symbolic domination" (1991: 51). We gain more clarity by calling this particular affective identification "shame" rather than "linguistic insecurity."

For some, this book may spend too much time presenting matters of brain, biology, bodies, and evolution – and for others, too little. What we derived from wading through such matters was the insight that intersubjectivity is fundamental to our being; on this, those who assiduously avoid matters of biology agree with neuroscientists. Intersubjectivity is surely a form of mutual engagement and identification. We are hard-wired for intersubjectivity, not for private emotional experience. Mirror neurons are part of that hard wiring (Gallese, Eagle, and Migone 2007). And phenomenological sociologists (Schutz 1962–1966) and ethnomethodologists – and their offspring, conversation analysts – remind us that talk-in-interaction is the primordial site for the ongoing achievement of intersubjectivity.

The big picture of emotion, language, and the world

Our journey has taken us to many sites of ethnographic investigation, but also to many histories, many intersections of the local and global. Outposts of Protestant missionization, often in partnership with colonialism, have spread modernist language ideologies that in some cases have helped to shut down traditional genres of emotive speech. They have spread an ideology of sincerity that has proven central to producing liberal subjects, displacing premodern understandings of emotion, meaning, and self (Wilce 2009). We have seen how the psy disciplines have gained ground in their countries of origin but also in places like Bangladesh. The enregisterment of psychiatric discourse forms in Europe and elsewhere has helped pathologize 'extremes' of emotion ('too little' and 'too much'). The global spread of the sciences of the self, its diseases, and its treatment has in some cases worked together with Christianization (Halliburton 2005). Even where mass conversions to Christianity have not taken place, ideas that emerged along with Protestantism in Europe have grown powerful.

The invention of a language of emotion – i.e., Scottish moral philosophers' promotion of 'emotion' as a unified, inclusive category – helped the psy disciplines to take root, creating a "culture of therapy." Although few Bangladeshis live in a so-called culture of therapy, speak the language of 'psychobabble,' or even talk about emotion in such a way that foregrounds the experiencer, Bangladeshi psychiatrists are co-opting old linguistic resources like *bhug-* (the verb denoting suffering) to encourage that very sort of shift.

The increasing hegemony of a very few languages, like English and French, is one factor threatening indigenous languages around the world. Nostalgic identification with indigenous languages does not suffice to reverse language shift. Work by linguistic anthropologists on endangered languages that has uncovered such nostalgia constitutes an exception to the generalization that the phenomenon of languages as objects of affect is undertheorized in our discipline. What the present book has done is to promote this sort of case to a more central position in the theory of language and emotion, and to draw out the consequences of such cases for theory in general.

Linguistic anthropology has not fully acknowledged the extent to which its distrust of language as an expression of inner life reflects the larger cultural milieu, e.g., the influence of Wittgenstein and the increasing technological mediation of experience. Situating theories of language and emotion in their historical context reflects a much older metatheoretical project. Mascia-Lees, Sharpe, and Cohen (1989), for example, described the efflorescence of postmodern anthropologies as a symptom of the new and radical challenges world histories were posing to Western males in particular. Still, my claims in this arena will be controversial. My assertion that the increasing doubts of linguistic anthropologists over any direct connection between the inner life and ostensibly 'expressive' language reflects broad currents of modernist thought and cultural production (Sass 1992) may provoke argument. The reason probably lies in the implication that we have been less than fully aware of this influence, and that places us with our consultants, those whose cultural systems and linguistic practices are partially unconscious. But this claim, as disturbing as it might be to some, is simply an extension of widely accepted understandings of ideologies – namely, that there is no privileged position from which to analyze them, no stance (academic or otherwise) that is free of ideological influence. No doubt this book's critics will shine a light on some of *my* blind spots.

In describing cultural visions of language and emotion vis-à-vis the broadest possible contexts (material, ideological, etc.), we remind ourselves that both language and emotion participate in the political economy. As Irvine pointed out (1989), there are many instances in which people pay others for some bit of language, and in the case of the Senegalese Wolof, payments are made for emotional language. Likewise, American presidents pay speechwriters not just for pretty words, but **textual** crafting that stirs listeners. The linguistic insecurity or shame some lower-middle-class speakers of New York English evince is an indication not of some personal flaw or vulnerability, but of the close relation between forms of language and forms of wealth and status. Feelings about language, and the social distribution of 'taste' in general and aesthetic sensibilities touching language in particular, index socioeconomic status – sometimes creatively (as in *Pygmalion* and its movie adaptation, *My Fair Lady*).

Looking back, looking ahead

Each particular argument summarized above builds on work by predecessors, especially in linguistic anthropology. In fact, ethnographic, linguistic, ethnomusicological, psychological, philosophical, and historical investigations have each contributed bricks I have used to build my argument. Yet, the explicit theory of language and emotion I have adduced through engaging these literatures has broken new ground.

Future empirical work on language and emotion might engage the vision I've laid out here. Ethnographies of local linguistic-emotional practices ought to take account of the positioning of those practices vis-à-vis relevant histories, i.e., representations of how those local practices evolve in dialogue with globally circulating metadiscourses (values and ideologies focused on discursive practices) and structures of feeling. They should attend to the microinteractional engagement of bodies, and to economies of language, feeling, and embodiment – that is, to the contextualization of local interaction vis-à-vis the distribution and circulation of linguistic, emotional, and bodily signs.

This is a tall order, but not an impossible task.

NOTES

Introduction

1 On the "waning of affect," see Jameson 1991, and for the countervailing view, see Massumi 2002.
2 See Nussbaum 2004 on shame, disgust and the law; see Saurette 2006 on shame and international relations. Both advocate an increasingly emotion-centered approach.
3 I'm playing with the Latin theological expression, *extra ecclesiam nullam salus* – "outside the church there is no salvation," and am using this twist on the old expression to mean "outside of affect there is no salvation [or culture, more accurately]."
4 Context is not a thing. We no longer regard language (or emotion) as the pawn of something ostensibly more important or fundamental – a powerful 'context' – but rather recognize language and other sign modalities, as well as features we might call structure, as all contributing to their joint *contextualization*. Context unrolls, scrolls, or dynamically unfolds in interaction (Lindstrom 1992, and other contributors to Duranti and Goodwin 1992).

> Context is a field of power relations. It is not, however, a frozen field. Context rolls as people talk. Preexisting discourses and discursive conditions do set limits but they are never totally determinant. People can occasionally say the unsayable. They can contest the context, by evoking available alternative or competing discourses (Lindstrom 1992: 103).

5 On cultural intimacy see Herzfeld 1997 and Shryock 2004.
6 Two of the anthropologists who have contributed the most to our understanding of language and emotion, Ochs and Schieffelin, have explored histories relevant to their field sites, Schieffelin in recent work on Kaluli or Bosavi (2007), and Ochs in earlier work (1986). For both, missionization provides a historical context central to their ethnographic investigations.
7 I.e., "indexicality," to which I return in a few paragraphs.
8 In transliterating South Asian words I have followed regional convention, which preserves the recognizability of Sanskrit roots. *Bhadralok* in IPA representation would appear as $b^h \jmath dr \jmath lok$.
9 Representations of human emotional expression often involve metaphor, particularly likening such expression to the sounds of animals, like cats or birds.
  The words, "has become ... the mew of a pussy," are those of the mid-nineteenth-century novelist, Bankim Chandra Chatterjee, from his essay, *Pracheena O Nabeena* (The Old and the New), as translated and cited by Banerjee 1989: 168. The words about the *bhadralok* feeling "ashamed" are Banerjee's (1989: 136).
10 Bangla is the name now preferred for the language commonly known as Bengali, with some 170 million native speakers, spoken in Bangladesh, India, and Nepal

(Gordon 2005). It is the language in which the author has done most of his field-work – in Bangladesh. Bengali is still used to designate the people, and the culture, of greater Bengal.

11 Semiosis refers to the production and circulation of signs. Although 'communication' is an adequate designation for some semiosis, few would call cell division, or the turning of a sunflower toward the sun, communicative, but these *are* examples of semiosis.

12 "I prefer the term 'sentiment' to related ones like 'emotion' or 'affect' because it carries connotations of cultural and even artistic shaping while the latter two suggest psycho-biological states" (Abu-Lughod 1985: 259, endnote 2).

13 Again, there are exceptions, e.g., Matoesian 2005.

14 It goes without saying that no mechanical recordings of discourse during the French Revolution are available for analysis.

15 Indexicality in the human world, in other words, involves "interactive kinds" (Hacking 1999).

16 There has admittedly been substantial work on nostalgia vis-à-vis what appear to be vanishing languages (e.g., Hoffman 2008, Cavanaugh 2009). I intend my generalization, however, to apply to work that specifically theorizes language-and-emotion per se.

17 Although some associate the term 'madness' with opprobrium, I prefer it because the world's peoples (e.g., Bengalis) do not necessarily represent madness as illness.

18 Metaculture consists of reflections on culture, be they local or scholarly – or some combination.

Defining the domain

1 These words are widely ascribed to Anton Chekhov in two letters to Lydia Avilova, written on March 19, 1892 and April 29, 1892.

2 The original saying about revenge is attributed to Stalin.

3 The embodiment of language may play a relatively small role in writing and mediated discourse, but is important to acknowledge. The fact that my shoulders are sore from my habitual bad posture as I hunch over my laptop to produce the discourse you are now reading – or that very young children, unaccustomed to telephones, sometimes nod their heads silently in answer to a question posed on the other end of the call – would often go unnoticed.

4 If emotion was once a step-child in anthropology, this probably reflected twin misperceptions: (a) that it was not a very social, or political, phenomenon, and (b) that it was a biological, or embodied matter. In either case, this meant (to many) that emotion was of secondary interest to the social sciences. I thank Mara Buchbinder for her suggestive comments along these lines.

5 ...as Neill Hadder of Texas State University, put it (personal communication, May, 2005).

6 See Lyon (1995), Lock (1998), and Wilce (2003).

7 "The raw and the cooked" is Lévi-Strauss's famous couplet (1983[1969, 1964]), signifying nature and culture. Thanks to Michael Lempert for prompting such comparisons.

8 The work of C. and M. H. Goodwin certainly grounds affect and language in embodied talk-in-interaction, and Ochs and Schieffelin's pioneering work in language socialization argued that patterns of language use with and around children correlate

with the direction in which caregivers hold babies (facing outward, or inward toward the caregiver), patterns with strong implications for the socialization of emotion.

9 Note that Stern (2000: 137) affirms the likelihood that "different societies could maximize or minimize [the] need for intersubjectivity," as I have argued (Wilce 2004a).

10 It was Kanner (1943), in explaining autism, who first pointed out the importance of this disruption in personal-affective relatedness.

11 The popularity of the idiom that persons or groups experiencing emotion are "moved" may indicate that the e-motion concept is an old idea in new scientific garb.

12 See the discussion of Sanskrit *bhāva*, the root of the Hindi word, in Chapter 9 of the present work.

13 I return to this issue in relation specifically to *histories* of thought in Chapters 9–11.

The relationship of language and emotion

1 As cited in Chapter 1, this definition includes "emotion, feelings, moods, dispositions, and attitudes associated with persons and/or situations" (Kulick and Schieffelin 2004: 352).

2 "Vitality affects" or "background feelings" are "changes or modulations in" the "continuous [background] music of being alive" (Stern 2000: xvii, xix).

3 Precedents for such an approach are strong. These include, from the field of psychological anthropology, Geoff White's affirmation that emotion ought to be seen as simultaneously category, metaphor, event schema, and discourse.

4 They use both terms, without discussion.

5 Colons are the standard way of representing the lengthening of the immediately preceding consonant or vowel.

6 This phrase is both the title of Matoesian's article, and that of a famous essay by Charles Frake (1972). Matoesian explores the literal, embodied meaning of the phrase.

Approaches to language and emotion

1 I have borrowed some of the following text from my own contributions to the Wikipedia article on linguistic anthropology.

2 The scenario Flom and Bahrick describe presumes the infants and adults are using a spoken, not signed, language.

3 Here I adapt, and make more consistent, Corwin's representation of the pronoun usage of genderqueer individuals, who describe being referred to as both 'she' and 'he' in growing up, and finally hitting upon *zhe* as an index of genderqueer selfhood.

The panhuman and the particular

1 We now recognize that the very notion of 'a language' is to some extent a reification, given the dynamism of language processes, and our recognition of how notions of language or 'a language' are always shaped by ideologies (Schieffelin, Woolard, and Kroskrity 1998; Kroskrity 2000).

2 I am following the convention in cognitive linguistics to represent metaphors in all caps.

3 For Aristotle, the natural site of poetics was not abstracted from performance (i.e., not written poems per se), but Greek drama and the like.
4 Ironically, universalist Ekman (1992a) provides scientific support for this phenomenon, whereby outward manifestation leads to (a transformation of) subjective experience.
5 Goodwin's work on distributed cognition is indebted to Vygotsky and Bateson.
6 This bias becomes clear when we scan one of Wierzbicka's articles (e.g., 2003) and find numerous tokens of "refer" and "reference," and no mention of "act," "action," or "interaction."
7 Whorf was describing "the ways of analyzing and reporting experience which have become fixed in [any] language as integrated 'fashions of speaking' and which cut across the typical grammatical classifications, so that such a 'fashion' may include lexical, morphological, syntactic, and otherwise systemically diverse means coordinated in a certain frame of consistency" (1956b).
8 A boon companion may be a drinking companion, or simply a close friend.
9 Compare Gaudio 2003, on the slippery, ideologized relationship between "conversation," equality, and affectivity.

Language, emotion, power, and politics

1 Homer's two lines exemplify "chiasmus" as "a grammatical figure by which the order of words in one of two parallel clauses is inverted in the other" (Oxford English Dictionary, second edition, "chiasmus.")
2 I am indebted to Matthew Basham (Northern Arizona University) for this presentation of parallelistic features of the President's declaration of the onset of hostilities.
3 I have rearranged the utterance vis-à-vis Atkinson's presentation thereof in order to display its verse-like parallelistic structure.
4 Saurette is a political scientist whose specialty is International Relations.

Status, honorification, and emotion for hire

1 Fahd (1993: 64), citing al-Tabarī, Appendix, and extract from the Dhayl al-Mudhayyal, iii, 2387; Ibn al-Ahthīr, Usd al-ghāba, I, 299.
2 Fahd 1993: 65.
3 Nigerian Hausa Muslims have been enthusiastic consumers of imported Indian films (Inda and Rosaldo 2002).

Language, affect, gender, and sexuality

1 My interlinear glossing follows Agha 2005: 48.
2 "In other words a woman came to be called 'one' in Seneca and Cayuga but 'it' in Huron," writes Chafe (1997: 20).
3 The *ade* term may also be used to call forth empathy for the older sibling (B. Schieffelin 1990: 121).
4 The table reflects Kulick's description (1992: 20).
5 In 2007 (Kulick, personal communication) it appeared as though Taiap had made something of a comeback.

A history of theories

1 I side with those who, while recognizing important differences between 'modernism' and 'postmodernism' (or between 'modernity,' 'late modernity, and 'postmodernity'), see significant links between them as well (Lyotard 1984: 77).

Shifting forms of language and emotion

1 Rosen (1995: 5) attributes the first, from 1477, to "C. J. Brian, Court of Common Pleas," and the second to the record of a case called "Edgington v. Fitzmaurice, 1889, 29 Chancery Division 459."
2 Transcript excerpt from Krancus 2007: 18.
3 Such indexical-iconic figuration is also known as **metapragmatic iconicity**.
4 Foucault (2005: 56–57) defines a *subject position* as "the subject's singular, transcendent position, as it were, with regards to what surrounds him, to the objects available to him, but also to other people with whom he has a relationship, to his body itself, and finally to himself."
5 For example, a ritual-textual achievement of "a Sumbanese aesthetic of completeness and balance … [is] iconic of the desired ritual outcome – sacred wholeness," Keane 2004: 436).
6 At the same time, as Sahlins (1985) argued, acting in ways that make sense vis-à-vis indigenous concepts (and this includes responding to new sorts of events in indigenous ways) often unwittingly undermines those very concepts. Sahlins has asserted that the Hawaiians who killed Captain James Cook believed they were simply sacrificing to the gods (an indigenously sensible idea), but in doing so indirectly paved the way for trade with Europeans and the undermining of their indigenous culture. For a vigorous counterargument to the "European myth" of the apotheosis of James Cook, see Obeyesekere 1997.
7 The slave trade, after all, not only occurred well within modernity, but helped to underwrite much of what we have come to associate with it.
8 Young women used their literacy skills to read and produce a smaller range of genres (Ahearn 2003: 115).
9 Maynard (2005) draws her examples primarily from media, such as soap operas, and novels, rather than naturally occurring face-to-face discourse.
10 For a description of a similar trend in Bangladesh's history, see Wilce "Society, Language, History, and Religion: A Perspective from Linguistic Anthropology." In *The Sociology of Language and Religion: Change, Conflict and Accommodation*, T. Omoniyi and J. Fishman, eds. John Benjamins, in submission.

Language and the medicalization of emotion

1 Apparently, Kusserow sat in on all ten sessions, though she only says she attended "weekly" (2004: 151).
2 Agha defines enregisterment as the process "through which a linguistic repertoire becomes differentiable [and] … socially recognized" (2003: 231).
3 The overlap of the two senses of "patient" is no coincidence.
Thanks to Doug Biber (personal communication, June 2006) for this interpretation of progressive aspect in English.
4 A Google search indicates that the simple present in English, "You suffer from…," tends either not to be medicalized or, when it is, to occur in interrogative or conditional sentences.

5 Goldstein draws from two translations – the 1924 by J. Bernays, and the J. Strachey version in the *Standard Edition of the Complete Works of Sigmund Freud.*

6 "If we wanted to analyze the profound structures of objectivity in the knowledge and practice of nineteenth century psychiatry from Pinel to Freud, we should have to show in fact that such objectivity was from the start a reification of a magical nature" (Foucault 1988: 276).

7 Philosophers (Kripke 1972, Putnam 1975) and linguistic anthropologists (Irvine 1989, Silverstein 2004) have recognized that the meaning of technical terms (or any others) is indexical. That is, I do not make the statement "Water is H_2O" on my own authority. The statement instead indexes a chain of scientific authorities, going back to the discoverer. New scientific terms receive their initial meanings in ritualistic utterances in scholarly journals or meetings. Following Kripke (1972: 301–302), we call those performative utterances terminological "**baptisms**." See Glossary.

8 Klaiman [1980: 276] glosses the verb *lāg* as "to affect."

9 Given the fairly robust tendency for each of the multiple NPs in an experiencer-subject construction to take its own distinctive case marking, their order is flexible.

10 An example from Hindi follows:
mujhe is baat-kaa bahut dukh hai
I.Dat this thing-Gen great sadness be.Prs.Sg. (Bhatt 2003: 3)

11 Some letter writers refer to *rog* or *mānasik rog* (though never *manarog*, used 13 times by the editors), but the editors are responsible for 90% of the 50 tokens of the phrase *mānasik rog*.

12 The editors are responsible for 78% of all uses of the verb *bhug-* in my corpus.

13 I am grateful to Kathryn Woolard, who drew my attention to aspectual contrasts between *lāge* and *bhugchen* constructions when I presented a version of this section at the University of California, San Diego.

Conclusion

1 The reproduction of the Arizona Tewa language is threatened today, whereas it appeared to be secure in the early 1990s.

GLOSSARY

ā**ḍḍā**: Comforting/comfortable talk in a space of male homosocial intimacy.

agency: "The socioculturally mediated capacity to act" (Ahearn 2001b: 112) and thus to "affect other[s']" actions, a capacity that makes agents liable to others' evaluation (Duranti 2004: 453).

Bangla: The language often known as Bengali. Bangla is the local designation.

baptisms, terminological: Authoritative namings of entities; ritual moments in scientific discourse (see **Performative**).

Bengali: The culture, and the ethnic group predominant in greater Bengal, i.e., Bangladesh and West Bengal.

bhakti: South Asian devotional practice.

catharsis: Aristotle's model of the valued emotional release obtained by audiences of drama (falling under the rubric of "poetics").

context:Often used in contrast with **co-text** to denote the nonlinguistic 'surround' of discourse; both context and co-text unfold dynamically.

conversation analysis: A research tradition, mostly in sociology, influenced by **ethnomethodology** and the analysis of conversational interaction as "the primordial site of sociality," i.e., the activity context in which social structure emerges.

corpus analysis, corpus linguistics: A quantitative approach to the analysis of large bodies of texts, usually of several types or genres, often collected and made available for analysis by some entity other than the analyst; corpus linguists differ as to whether or not prosodic features may be successfully analyzed, and for some, lexical-grammatical features are the sole objects counted.

co-text: Linguistic context (as opposed to the nonlinguistic environment of speech).

cultural constructionism (or constructivism): The view that culture determines crucial aspects of human nature – in our case, emotions. See **social constructionism**.

cultural studies: An academic discipline that emerged in Great Britain in the 1960s and 1970s, focused largely on popular culture and associated with scholars like Stuart Hall (to be distinguished from cultural anthropology).

denotation: Semantic meaning, sense; meaning that is ostensibly context-free.

denotational text: The coherence, patternedness, or textuality of discourse at the level of the denotation of its words, phrases, and larger discourse units.

diagrammatic iconicity: A relationship in which the patterning of elements in a representation resembles the pattern of elements represented.

dialect: A linguistic variety associated with a geographical region. The term is sometimes used to encompass what are also called **sociolects** (see below). All humans speak dialects, be they 'standard' (also called 'elite-aspiring') or 'non-standard.'

emotive: first-person present tense feeling statements. See **Performative**.

enregisterment: Processes by which new registers emerge, coming to be recognized as distinct forms of speech (Agha 2003: 231). See **register**.

entextualization: Strategies, typically involving some form of parallelism, that render discourse text-like and thus memorable beyond its context. See **text**.

ergative: Refers to a morphosyntactic system in which noun phrases encoding agents receive a unique ("ergative") case marking that distinguishes them from another ("absolutive") case that marks both direct objects and subjects of intransitive sentences.

ethnography of communication: Movement originating in the 1960s, centered on Dell Hymes and John Gumperz, advocating a holistic, ethnographic approach to speech communities through their *speech events*, and classes of speech events.

ethnomethodology: A school of sociological thought, emerging out of phenomenological sociology and "associated with H. Garfinkel (b. 1917), which seeks to expose and analyze the methods by which participants in a given social situation construct their commonsense knowledge of the world" (Oxford English Dictionary).

genre: Regarded by linguistic anthropologists as a type of discourse, typically associated with more than one context and having some stereotyped formal features, that is recognized locally and often specifically named; or, in relation to a type of discourse, expectations guiding its production and reception. See **ideal type**.

hadith: Traditional accounts of the sayings of the Prophet Muhammad and his early followers.

heteroglossia: The juxtaposition of competing "voices," social personae or perspectives, in a single text; sometimes called "double-voicing," "dialogism," or "multivocality."

hypernym: A superordinate or inclusive term in a taxonomy.

icon, iconicity: Used in Peirce's sense, a sign that stands for something by means of resembling it, as an image or as a pattern or diagram.

ideal type: In Max Weber's (1999 [1904]: 248) thinking, an analytic category, a summing up of features members of a category often, but not always, possess.

identity, identification: In contrast with the fixity implied in the noun **identity**, the choice to write about **identification** indicates a commitment to look at dynamic processes that may never settle into fixed form.

ideology: Ideas, less fully formed notions, and evaluative stances that are a) shared by some social group, b) tied in significant ways to structures of power, and c) partial in their representations, and thus to some extent distorting. See **language ideology**.

index, indexicality: Used in Peirce's sense, a relationship in which a sign-vehicle, which we call an index, co-occurs with its object, in some sense pointing to (*indexing*) it, as when smoke points to fire, or a weathercock indicates the wind's direction.

intellectualism: A philosophical or theoretical commitment to ideas as the primary engines of history.

interactional text: The particular coherent, tellable outcome of discursive interaction in terms of the roles and identities of interlocutors, i.e., what they become (to each other) in an event of interaction.

interpretant: The effect of a sign or, commonly, its mental representation.

intersubjectivity: Shared feeling, mutual understanding, mutual attunement; the ground of cooperation, successful interaction, and the co-production of meaning.

lament: Sung-texted weeping; spontaneous improvised crying songs performed at leave-takings (prototypically, funerals).

language attitude: Typically refers to the values that subjects in "matched guise" experiments apparently ascribe to tape-recorded voices, and actually attach to the languages spoken on tape.

language games: Wittgenstein's phrase stressing the procedural knowledge necessary to successful linguistic interaction, and the possibility that, as in a game, users bring "differentiated understanding" to the task (Duranti 1997: 237).

language ideology: Ideas about language and its relations to the world, ideas that share the defining features of **ideology**.

language socialization: Socialization to and through the use of language.

magic complex (in psychiatry): Psychiatry's need to convince a skeptical public that its perceived associations with magic and religion are finished, vanquished in part by discursive measures, focused on a scientizing drive. As a complex or neurosis this involves attraction and a need to deny the attraction.

metaculture: Reflections on culture that are themselves cultural, and that influence the replication and circulation of the cultural phenomena on which they reflect.

metapragmatic: Refers to signs that either overtly reflect on the pragmatic meaning of other signs ("No shouting allowed!") or structure other signs in such a way as to signal their pragmatic meaning.

metapragmatic icon: A trope or semiotic configuration in which "changes in linguistic form may realize the progression of the ritual action by resembling it" (Keane 2004: 436).

mimesis: In any relationship, typically mediated by images, a mutual becoming the other, like the other, or like the other's image of oneself.

modernity: An ideological construct that views some relatively contemporary period as radically distinct from what came before, i.e., **tradition**.

naturalistic interaction: Talk-in-interaction that would be occurring whether or not a researcher is present, i.e., talk that is minimally influenced (and certainly never elicited) by the interviewer.

orders of indexicality: The potentially infinite series of metapragmatic reflections on indexicals.

parallelism: Whole or partial repetition of elements in discourse, or the poetic juxtaposition of paired elements (rhyme, alliteration, or more complex forms such as chiasmus); key to **entextualization**.

performative: Used of an utterance regarded as bringing about, in the act of performing it, the very state it apparently describes, as in "I declare this case closed."

personalism: A language ideology that locates meaning in speakers' personal intent.

political economy: A systematic organization and distribution of power and wealth.

pragmatic meaning of linguistic signs: The relationship of the signs to their context, i.e., their fit (appropriateness); or, what those signs accomplish in relation to their context (efficacy).

reference: The object of a linguistic sign, i.e., what some bit of language is about.

referentialism: An ideology of language that holds that reference is its sole function, and that linguistic signs simply refer to entities whose existence is outside of language.

register: A speech variety associated with a situation and with a class of persons associated with that situation, such as psychiatry and psychiatric practice.

semiosis: The production and circulation of signs.

semiotic: Of or pertaining to signs, or a theory of signs; the 'singular' form used by philosopher C. S. Peirce as a noun (the theory) but more commonly today as an adjective (pertaining to signs).

sense: Denotation.

social anthropology: The British anthropological tradition, which gives priority to the analysis of social process and structure over explanations based on culture.

social constructionism: Like ethnomethodology, the view that shared forms of thought or practice, or what is commonly perceived as reality, is in fact constructed in social life, be it routine interaction (see conversation analysis), ritual, or institutional encounters.

social reproduction: A term with a Marxist lineage, denoting both biological reproduction insofar as it reproduces, for example, workers (a social class), and more broadly, processes that ensure the continuation of social structure from one generation to the next, i.e., **socialization**.

socialization: Processes that enable novices (including children) to become competent participants in a sociocultural order.

sociolect: A variety of speaking associated with some social group.

speech event: Dell Hymes' term for an event defined by the presence of speech; a key concept in the **ethnography of communication**.

structuralism: An intellectual movement arising in France (Saussure), Prague, Russia (Jakobson), and the United States (Sapir) in the first decades of the twentieth century, arguing that no element (e.g., a color term in some language) has meaning in and of itself, but only in relation to its opposite or some other term to which it is juxtaposed in a system or structure.

subject, liberal subject, modern subject: Following Francophone philosophical work on *le sujet*, these terms refer to what the Anglophone tradition calls 'self' or 'person'; the **liberal** or **modern subject** is that constituted under capitalism, defined as autonomous, and responsible to produce sincere speech.

syntax: The structure of phrases and sentences, i.e., 'grammar'; regarded by linguistic anthropologists as a resource for entextualization (this applies in particular to grammatical parallelism).

talking cure: Coined by Freud's colleague Breuer and Breuer's patient, "Anna O," the term for the emerging therapy that came to be known as psychoanalysis.

text, textuality: Used in contemporary linguistic anthropology to refer to "discourse rendered decontextualizable" (Bauman and Briggs 1990: 73), i.e., structured in such a way that it is coherent and thus memorable.

therapization: Related to medicalization, the submission of increasingly large swathes of social life to the appropriate realm of psychotherapy; i.e., a culture of therapy.

tradition: An ideological construct for a time radically distinct from modernity, a construct that enables "voices of modernity" (Bauman and Briggs 2003) to claim that certain social groups do not inhabit the same (modern) time as they do.

voice: In Mikhail Bakhtin's (1981) sense, a speech form associated with a social group or ideological position. Bakhtin's concept contrasts with concepts like 'sociolect' in that he argued that any given utterance resonates with multiple 'voices.' Any given speaker's management of such voices in his or her discourse may represent his or her ideological position (Hill 1995).

zhe: Resistant form of third-person pronoun among English-speaking persons who identify as genderqueer.

REFERENCES

Abu-Lughod, Lila 1985. "Honor and the Sentiments of Loss in a Bedouin Society." *American Ethnologist* **12**: 245–261.

1986. *Veiled Sentiments: Honor and Poetry in a Bedouin Society.* Berkeley, CA: University of California Press.

Abu-Lughod, Lila, and Catherine Lutz 1990. "Introduction." In C. Lutz and L. Abu-Lughod, eds., pp. 1–23.

Agha, Asif 2003. "The Social Life of Cultural Value." *Language and Communication* **23**(3–4): 231–274.

2004. "Registers of Language." In *Companion to Linguistic Anthropology.* A. Duranti, ed., pp. 23–45. Malden, MA: Blackwell.

2005. "Voice, Footing, Enregisterment." *Journal of Linguistic Anthropology* **15**(1): 38–59.

2007. *Language and Social Relations.* Cambridge: Cambridge University Press.

Ahearn, Laura M. 2001a. *Invitations to Love: Literacy, Love Letters, and Social Change in Nepal.* Ann Arbor, MI: University of Michigan Press.

2001b. "Language and Agency." *Annual Review of Anthropology* **30**: 109–137.

2003. "Writing Desire in Nepali Love Letters." *Language and Communication* **23**(2): 107–122.

Aitken, Kenneth J., and Colwyn Trevarthen 1997. "Self/Other Organization in Human Psychological Development." *Development and Psychopathology* **9**(4): 653–677.

Ali, Mohammad, Mohammad Moniruzzaman, and Jahangir Tareq, eds. 1994. *Bangla Academy Bengali-English Dictionary.* Dhaka: Bangla Academy.

Althusser, Louis 1971. *Lenin and Philosophy and Other Essays.* B. Brewster, transl. New York: Monthly Review Press.

Alvarez-Cáccamo, Celso 2005. Línguas de Mar Adentro: Universalidade e Hierarquias Linguísticas. Unpublished paper available at www.udc.es/dep/lx/cac/escritos/maradentro.pdf (accessed January 16, 2006).

American Psychiatric Association 2000. *Diagnostic and Statistical Manual of Mental Disorders: DSM-IV-TR.* Washington, DC.

Anderson, Benedict R. O'G. 1991. *Imagined Communities: Reflections on the Origin and Spread of Nationalism.* London, New York: Verso.

Anttonen, Pertti J. 2005. *Tradition Through Modernity: Postmodernism and the Nation-State in Folklore Scholarship.* Helsinki: Finnish Folklore Society.

Árnason, Arnar 2001. "Experts of the Ordinary: Bereavement Counselling in Britain." *Journal of the Royal Anthropological Institute* **7**(2): 299–313.

Assemblies of God 2007a. "Holy Spirit Baptism: Frequently Asked Questions." In *Beliefs.* Springfield, MO, USA: http://ag.org/top/Beliefs/baptmhs_faq.cfm (accessed June 17, 2007).

201

2007b "earnest" (as search term). Springfield, MO, USA: Assemblies of God. http://ag.org/top/ (accessed December 27, 2007).

2007c "experience" (as search term). Springfield, MO, USA: Assemblies of God. http://ag.org/top/ (accessed December 27, 2007).

Atkinson, Dwight 1992. "The Evolution of Medical Research Writing from 1735–1985. The Case of the Edinburgh Medical Journal." *Applied Linguistics* **13**: 337–374.

Atkinson, J. Maxwell 1984. *Our Masters' Voices: The Language and Body Language of Politics*. London and New York: Methuen.

Bakhtin, Mikhail 1981 "Discourse in the Novel." In *The Dialogic Imagination*. M. Bakhtin, ed., pp. 259–422. Austin: University of Texas Press.

1984 *The Problems of Dostoevsky's Poetics*. C. Emerson, transl. Volume 8. Minneapolis: University of Minnesota Press.

Bandyopadhyay, Sreekumar 1988. *Bangasahitye upanashyer dhara*. Calcutta: Modern Book Agency.

Banerjee, Sumanta 1989. "Marginalization of Women's Popular Culture in Nineteenth Century Bengal." In *Recasting Women: Essays in Colonial History*. K. Sangari and S. Vaid, eds., pp. 127–179. New Delhi: Kali for Women.

Barbieri, Federica 2008. "Involvement in University Classroom Discourse." Unpublished Ph.D. Dissertation, Applied Linguistics, Northern Arizona University.

Barrett, Robert J. 1998. "Conceptual Foundations of Schizophrenia, I: Degeneration." *Australian and New Zealand Journal of Psychiatry* **32**: 617–626.

Basso, Keith 1990. "To Give Up On Words: Silence in Western Apache Culture." In *Western Apache Language and Culture*. K. Basso, ed., pp. 80–98. Tucson: University of Arizona Press.

1996. *Wisdom Sits in Places: Landscape and Language Among the Western Apache*. Albuquerque: University of New Mexico Press.

Bateson, Gregory 1972. *Steps to an Ecology of Mind*. Scranton, PA: Chandler.

Bauman, Richard 1999. "Genre." *Journal of Linguistic Anthropology* **9**(1): 84–87.

Bauman, Richard, and Charles Briggs 2003. *Voices of Modernity: Language Ideologies and the Politics of Inequality*. Cambridge: Cambridge University Press.

Beatty, Andrew 2005. "Emotions in the Field: What are We Talking About?" *Journal of the Royal Anthropological Institute* **11**(1): 17–37.

Becker, Alton E. 1991. "A Short Essay on Languaging." In *Research and Reflexivity*. F. Steier, ed., pp. 226–234. Newbury Park, CA: Sage.

Bendix, Regina 1992. "National Sentiment in the Enactment and Discourse of Swiss Political Ritual." *American Ethnologist* **19**(4): 768–790.

Berkenkotter, Carol. 2008. *"Patient Tales: Case Histories and the Uses of Narrative in Psychiatry."* Charleston: University of South Carolina Press.

Berkenkotter, Carol, and Doris Ravotas 1997. "Genre as Tool in the Transmission of Practice Over Time and Across Professional Boundaries." *Mind, Culture, and Activity* **4**(4): 256–274.

Berlant, Lauren 1999. "The Subject of True Feeling: Pain, Privacy, and Politics." In *Cultural Pluralism, Identity Politics, and the Law*. A. Sarat, ed., pp. 49–84. Ann Arbor, MI: University of Michigan Press.

Besnier, Niko 1990. "Language and Affect." *Annual Review of Anthropology* **19**: 419–451.

1992. "Reported Speech and Affect on Nukulaelae Atoll." In *Responsibility and Evidence in Oral Discourse*. J. H. Hill and J. T. Irvine, eds., pp. 161–181. Cambridge: Cambridge University Press.

1995. *Literacy, Emotion, and Authority: Reading and Writing on a Polynesian Atoll*. Cambridge: Cambridge University Press.

Manuscript. "Humor and Humiliation: Narratives of Modernity on Nukulaelae Atoll." Amsterdam: Department of Anthropology, University of Amsterdam.

Bhatt, Rakesh M. 2003. "Topics in the Syntax of the Modern Indo-Aryan Languages: Experiencer Subjects." Cambridge, MA: Massachusetts Institute of Technology. web.mit.edu/rbhatt/www/24.956/dative.pdf (accessed June 16, 2007).

Biber, Douglas 1988. *Variation Across Speech and Writing.* Cambridge: Cambridge University Press.

2006. "Stance in Spoken and Written University Registers." *Journal of English for Academic Purposes* **5**: 97–116

Biber, Douglas, and Edward Finegan 1989. "Styles of Stance in English: Lexical and Grammatical Marking of Evidentiality and Affect." *Text* **9**(1 (special issue on The Pragmatics of Affect, ed. by Elinor Ochs)): 93–124.

Biddle, Jennifer 1997. "Shame." *Australian Feminist Studies* **13**(28): 227–239.

2002 "Bruises That Won't Heal: Melancholic Identification and Other Ethnographic Hauntings." *Mortality* **7**(1): 96–110.

Bilaniuk, Laada. 2003. "Gender, Language Attittudes, and Language Status in Ukraine." *Language in Society* **32**: 47–78.

Billig, Michael 1997. "The Dialogic Unconscious: Psychoanalysis, Discursive Psychology and the Nature of Repression." *British Journal of Social Psychology* **36**: 139–159.

1999 *Freudian Repression: Conversation Creating the Unconscious.* Cambridge: Cambridge University Press.

Bilmes, Jack 1986. *Discourse and Behavior.* New York: Plenum Press.

Boas, Franz 1995[1911]. "Introduction to the Handbook of American Indian Languages." In *Language, Culture, and Society: a Book of Readings.* B. G. Blount, ed., pp. 9–28. Prospect Heights, IL: Waveland.

Bonner, Donna M. 2001. "Garifuna Children's Language Shame: Ethnic Stereotypes, National Affiliation, and Transnational Immigration as Factors in Language Choice in Southern Belize." *Language in Society* **30**(1): 81–96.

Bourdieu, Pierre 1977a. "The Economics of Linguistic Exchanges." *Social Science Information* **16**: 645–668.

1977b[1972]. *Outline of a Theory of Practice.* R. Nice, transl. Cambridge: Cambridge University Press.

1991. *Language and Symbolic Power.* J. B. Thompson, transl. Cambridge, MA: Harvard University Press.

van Brakel, Jaap 1992. "Natural Kinds and Manifest Forms of Life." *Dialectica* **46**: 243–62.

1993. "Emotions: A Cross-Cultural Perspective on Forms of Life." In *Social Perspectives on Emotion*, vol. 2. W. M. Wentworth and J. Ryan, eds., pp. 179–237. Greenwich: JAI Press.

Bråten, Stein 1998. "Infant Learning by Altercentric Participation: The Reverse of Egocentric Observation in Autism." In *Intersubjective Communication and Emotion in Early Ontogeny.* S. Bråten, ed., pp. 105–124. Studies in Emotion and Social Interaction (Second Series). Cambridge: Cambridge University Press/ Editions de la Maison de Sciences de l'Homme.

Brenneis, Donald 1987. "Dramatic Gestures: The Fiji Indian Pancayat as Therapeutic Discourse." *IPRA Papers in Pragmatics* **1**(1): 55–78.

1990. "Shared and Solitary Sentiments: The Discourse of Friendship, Play and Anger in Bhatgaon." In Lutz and Abu-Lughod, eds., pp. 113–26.

Briggs, Charles L. 1998. "You're a Liar – You're Just Like a Woman!: Constructing Dominant Ideologies of Language in Warao Men's Gossip." *In Language*

Ideologies: Practice and Theory. B.B. Schieffelin, K.A. Woolard, and P. Kroskrity, eds., pp. 229–255. New York: Oxford University Press.

Bucholtz, Mary, and Kira Hall 2004. "Language and Identity." In *A Companion to Linguistic Anthropology*. A. Duranti ed., pp. 369–94. Malden, MA: Blackwell

Budge, Sir Ernest Alfred Wallis 1972. *From Fetish to God in Ancient Egypt*. New York: B. Blom.

    1967. "Rhetoric – Old and New." In *New Rhetorics*. M.J. Steinmann, ed., pp. 59–76. New York: Scribner's.

    1969 [1950]. *A Rhetoric of Motives*. Berkeley and Los Angeles: University of California Press.

Burke, Peter 1993. *The Art of Conversation*. Ithaca, NY: Cornell University Press.

Cameron, Deborah 1995. *Verbal Hygiene*. London and New York: Routledge.

    2001. "Language: Designer Voices." *Critical Quarterly* **43**(4): 81–85.

Cameron, Deborah, and Don Kulick 2003. "Introduction: Language and Desire in Theory and Practice." *Language and Communication* **23**(2): 93–105.

Campos, Joseph J., and Craig R. Stenberg 1981. "Perception, Appraisal and Emotion: The Onset of Social Referencing." In *Infant Social Cognition*. M.E. Lamb and L.R. Sherrod, eds., Hillsdale, NJ: Erlbaum.

Capps, Lisa, and Elinor Ochs 1995. *Constructing Panic: The Discourse of Agoraphobia*. Cambridge MA: Harvard University Press.

Caton, Steven C. 1987. "The Contributions of Roman Jakobson." *Annual Review of Anthropology* **16**: 233–260.

    1990. *"Peaks of Yemen I Summon": Poetry as Cultural Practice in a North Yemeni Tribe*. Berkeley, Los Angeles: University of California Press.

Cavanaugh, Jillian 2009. *Living Memory: The Social Aesthetics of Language in a Northern Italian Town*. Malden, MA: Wiley-Blackwell.

Cavell, Stanley 1994. *A Pitch of Philosophy*. Cambridge, MA: Harvard University Press.

Chafe, Wallace 1993. "Prosodic and Functional Units of Language." In *Talking Data: Transcription and Coding in Discourse Research*. J.A. Edwards and M.D. Lampert, eds., pp. 33–44. Hillsdale, New Jersey, Hove and London: Lawrence Erlbaum.

    1997. "The Importance of Native American Languages." In *The David Skomp Distinguished Lectures in Anthropology*. Bloomington: Department of Anthropology, Indiana University.

Chakrabarty, Dipesh 1999. "Adda, Calcutta: Dwelling in Modernity." *Public Culture* **11**(1): 109–145.

    2000. *Deprovincializing Europe*. Princeton: Princeton University Press.

    2004. "Romantic Archives: Literature and the Politics of Identity in Bengal." *Critical Inquiry* **30**(3): 654–683.

Charcot, Jean Martin 1892. "La Foi Qui Guérit." *Revue Hebdomadaire 1892* (December 3): 112–132.

Charteris-Black, Jonathan *Men and the Expression of Emotions: Evidence from Illness Experience Gender and Language* (in submission)

Chattopadhyay, Sunitikumar 1979 [1913]. "Hostel Life in Calcutta." In *Jiban Katha*. Calcutta: Jijnasha.

Chrysostom, John 1886. "Homilies on the Epistle to the Hebrews." In *Post-Nicene Fathers of the Christian Church*. F. Gardiner, ed., vol. XIV.

Chung, Sandra, and Alan Timberlake 1985. "Tense, Aspect, and Mood." In *Language Typology and Syntactic Description: Volume III Grammatical Categories and the Lexicon*. T. Shopen, ed., pp. 309–348. Cambridge and New York: Cambridge University Press.

Clancy, Patricia 1986. "The Acquisition of Communicative Style in Japanese." In *Language Socialization Across Cultures*. B. B. Schieffelin and E. Ochs, eds., pp. 251–272. Cambridge: Cambridge University Press.

    1999. "The Socialization of Affect in Japanese Mother-Child Conversation." *Journal of Pragmatics* **31**(11): 1397–1421.

Crapanzano, Vincent 1992. "Glossing Emotions." In *Hermes' Dilemma and Hamlet's Desire*. V. Crapanzano ed., pp. 229–238. Cambridge, MA: Harvard University Press.

Croce, Benedetto 1992 [1902]. *The Aesthetic as the Science of Expression and of the Linguistic in General*. C. Lyas, transl. Cambridge: Cambridge University Press.

Crowley, Candy, and Deborah Potter 2005. "An Experiment Changed: TV Coverage of the 2004 Campaign." *Journalism Studies* **6**(2): 233–236.

Csordas, Thomas 1990. "Embodiment as a Paradigm for Anthropology" (1988 Stirling Prize Essay). *Ethos* **18**: 5–47.

Cvetkovich, Ann 1992. *Mixed Feelings: Feminism, Mass Culture, and Victorian Sensationalism*. New Brunswick, NJ: Rutgers University Press.

Damasio, Antonio 1995. *Descartes' Error: Emotion, Reason, and the Human Brain*: Avon Books.

    2003. *Looking for Spinoza: Joy, Sorrow, and the Feeling Brain*. Orlando: Harcourt Harvest Books.

Danforth, Loring, and Alexander Tsiaras 1982. *The Death Rituals of Rural Greece*. Princeton: Princeton University Press.

Darwin, Charles 1998. *The Expression of Emotion in Man and Animals*. Introduction and Commentary by P. Ekman. Chicago: University of Chicago Press.

Das, Veena 1998. "Wittgenstein and Anthropology." *Annual Review of Anthropology* **27**: 171–195.

Davidson, Iain 2003. "The Archaeological Evidence of Language Origins: States of Art." In *Language Evolution*. M. H. Christiansen and S. Kirby, eds., pp. 140–157. Oxford: Oxford University Press.

Desjarlais, Robert R. 1992. *Body and Emotion: The Aesthetics of Illness and Healing in the Nepal Himalayas*. Philadelphia: University of Pennsylvania Press.

    1996. "The Office of Reason: On the Politics of Language and Agency in a Shelter for 'the Homeless Mentally Ill.'" *American Ethnologist* **23**(4): 880–900.

    1997. *Shelter Blues: Homelessness and Sanity in a Boston Shelter*. Philadelphia: University of Pennsylvania Press.

Dimien, Muriel 1994. "Money, Love, and Hate: Contradiction and Paradox in Psychoanalysis." *Psychoanalytic Dialogues* **4**: 69–100.

Dixon, Thomas M. 1999. "Theology, Anti-Theology, and Atheology: From Christian Passions to Secular Emotions." *Modern Theology* **15**(3): 297–330.

    2003. *From Passions to Emotions: The Creation of a Secular Psychological Category*. Cambridge: Cambridge University Press.

Doi, Takeo 1973. *The Anatomy of Dependence*. Tokyo and New York: Kodansha International and Harper & Row.

Doostdar, Alireza 2004. "'The Vulgar Spirit of Blogging': On Language, Culture, and Power in Persian Weblogestan." *American Anthropologist* **106**(4): 651–662.

Dorian, Nancy 1980. "Language Shift in Community and Individual: The Phenomenon of the Laggard Semi-speaker." *International Journal of the Sociology of Language* **25**: 85–94.

Duranti, Alessandro 1988. "Intentions, Language, and Social Action in a Samoan Context." *Journal of Pragmatics* **12**: 13–33.

    1992. "Language and Bodies in Social Space: Samoan Greetings." *American Anthropologist* **94**: 657–691.

    1997. *Linguistic Anthropology*. Cambridge: Cambridge University Press.

2003. "Language as Culture in US Anthropology: Three Paradigms." *Current Anthropology* **44**(3): 323–348.

2004. "Agency in Language." In *Companion to Linguistic Anthropology*. A. Duranti, ed., pp. 451–473. Malden, MA: Blackwell.

2006. "Narrating the Political Self in a Campaign for US Congress." *Language in Society* **35**(4): 467–497.

2008. "Further Reflections on Reading Other Minds." *Anthropological Quarterly* **81**(2): 483–494.

Duranti, Alessandro, and Charles Goodwin, eds. 1992. *Rethinking Context: Language as an Interactive Phenomenon*. Cambridge: Cambridge University Press.

Durkheim, Emile 1965 [1915]. *The Elementary Forms of the Religious Life*. J. W. Swain, transl. New York: The Free Press.

Durst, Uwe 2001. "Why German's Don't Feel 'Anger.'" In *Emotions in Crosslinguistic Perspective*. J. Harkins, and A. Wierzbicka, eds. pp. 115–148. Berlin: Mouton de Gruyter.

Eastwood, Clint 2006. Film *Letters From Iwo Jima*. USA: Warner Bros Entertainment Inc and Dreamworks Pictures.

Eckert, Penelope, and Sally McConnell-Ginet 1992. "Think Practically and Look Locally: Language and Gender as Community-based Practice." *Annual Review of Anthropology* **21**: 461–490.

Eisenlohr, Patrick 2006. *Little India: Diaspora, Time, and Ethnolinguistic Belonging in Hindu Mauritius*. Berkeley and Los Angeles: University of California Press.

Ekman, Paul 1992a. "Facial Expressions of Emotion: New Findings, New Questions." *Psychological Science* **3**(1): 34–38.

1992b. "Are There Basic Emotions?" *Psychological Review* **99**(3): 550–553.

Elias, Norbert 2000 (1939). *The Civilizing Process*. Oxford, Malden: Blackwell.

Eliot, George 1986 *Middlemarch*. Oxford and New York: Clarendon Press, Oxford University Press.

Errington, J. Joseph 1988. *"Structure and Style in Javanese: A Semiotic View of Linguistic Etiquette."* Philadelphia: University of Pennsylvania.

Exporter's Association of Northern Greece 1997. "Europartenariat Hellas 1997: The Philosophy of Life." Thessaloniki: www.moneymarket.gr/gr03.html (accessed August 1, 2007).

Fahd, T. 1993. "Niyāḥ" In *The Encyclopedia of Islam*, new edition. E. J. v. Donzel, ed., pp. 64–65, Vol. 6. Leiden: E. J. Brill.

Fanon, Frantz 1967. *Black Skin White Masks*. C. L. Markmann, transl. New York: Grove Press.

Farnell, Brenda M. 1995. *Do You See What I Mean? Plains Indian Sign Talk and the Embodiment of Action*. Austin: University of Texas Press.

Feld, Steve 1990. *Sound and Sentiment: Birds, Weeping, Poetics, and Song in Kaluli Expression*. Philadelphia: University of Pennsylvania Press.

Feld, Steve, and Aaron Fox 1994. "Music and Language." *Annual Review of Anthropology* **23**: 25–53.

Feld, Steve, Aaron A. Fox, Thomas Porcello, and David Samuels 2004. "Vocal Anthropology: From the Music of Language to the Language of Song." In *A Companion to Linguistic Anthropology*. A. Duranti, ed., pp. 321–345. Malden, MA: Blackwell.

Feldman, Ruth 2007. "On the Origins of Background Emotions: From Affect Synchrony to Symbolic Expression." *Emotion* **7**(3): 601–611.

Feldman, Ruth, and Charles W. Greenbaum 1997. "Affect Regulation and Synchrony in Mother-Infant Play as Precursors to the Development of Symbolic Competence." *Infant Mental Health Journal* **18**(1): 4–23.

Fichtel, Claudia, Susan Perry, and Julie Gros-Louis 2005. "Alarm Calls of White-faced Capuchin Monkeys: an Acoustic Analysis." *Animal Behaviour* **70**(1): 165–176.

Fischer, Michael M. J. 1999. "Emergent Forms of Life: Anthropologies of Late or Postmodernities." *Annual Review of Anthropology* **28**(1): 455–478.

Flom, Ross, and Lorraine E. Bahrick 2007. "The Development of Infant Discrimination of Affect in Multimodal and Unimodal Stimulation: The Role of Intersensory Redundancy." *Developmental Psychology* **43**(1): 238–252.

Foucault, Michel 1975. *I, Pierre Riviere, Having Slaughtered My Mother, My Sister, and My Brother...: A Case of Parricide in the 19th Century*. Lincoln: University of Nebraska Press Review.

1988 [1965]. *Madness and Civilization: A History of Insanity in the Age of Reason*. New York: Vintage.

1990 (1978). *The History of Sexuality: An Introduction*. R. Hurley, transl. Volume I. New York: Vintage.

1997 *Michel Foucault: Ethics – Subjectivity and Truth (Essential Works of Foucault, 1954–1984, vol. 1)*. P. Rabinow, ed., New York: The New Press.

Foucault, Michel, and James J. Fox 1974. "'Our Ancestors Spoke in Pairs': Rotinese Views of Language, Dialect, and Code." In *Explorations in the Ethnography of Speaking*. R. Bauman and J. Sherzer, eds., pp. 65–85, 455–56, 482–83. Cambridge: Cambridge University Press.

1988. "Introduction." In *To Speak in Pairs: Essays on the Ritual Languages of Eastern Indonesia*. J. J. Fox, ed., pp. 1–28. Cambridge and New York: Cambridge University Press.

Frake, Charles 1972. "Struck by Speech: The Yakan Concept of Litigation." In *Directions in Sociolinguistics: The Ethnography of Communication*. J. Gumperz and D. Hymes, eds., pp. 106–129. New York: Holt.

Freud, Sigmund 1961[1930]. *Civilization and its Discontents*. J. Strachey, transl. New York: W. W. Norton.

1962[1923] *The Ego and the Id*. J. Riviere and J. Strachey, transl. New York: W.W. Norton.

1965 [1916] *The Psychopathology of Everyday Life: Forgetting, Slips of the Tongue, Bungled Actions, Superstitions, and Errors*. A. Tyson and J. Strachey, transl. New York: W. W. Norton & Company.

1989[1915–1917] *Introductory Lectures on Psychoanalysis*. J. Strachey, transl. New York: W.W. Norton.

2003[1909]. "Phobia in a Five-year-old Boy ['Little Hans']." In *The Wolfman and Other Cases By Sigmund Freud*. L. A. Huish and G. Beer, eds., pp. 1–122. London and New York: Penguin Classics.

Friedman, Jonathan 2003. "Globalizing Languages: Ideologies and Realities of the Contemporary Global System." *American Anthropologist* **105**(4): 744–752.

Friedrich, Paul 1986. *The Language Parallax: Linguistic Relativism and Poetic Indeterminacy*. Austin: University of Texas.

1991. "Polytropy." In *Beyond Metaphor: The Theory of Tropes in Anthropology*. J. W. Fernandez, ed., pp. 17–55. Stanford: Stanford University Press.

Furedi, Frank 2003. *Therapy Culture: Cultivating Vulnerability in an Uncertain Age*. London: Routledge.

Fuss, Diana 1993. "Freud's Fallen Women: Identification, Desire, and a Case of Homosexuality in a Woman.'" *Yale Journal of Criticism* **6**(1): 1–23.

1995. *Identification Papers*. London, New York: Routledge.

1996. "Look Who's Talking, or if Looks Could Kill." *Critical Inquiry* **22**: 383

Gaines, Atwood 1992. "From DSM-I to DSM-IIIR; Voices of Self, Mastery and the Other: A Cultural Constructivist Reading of US Psychiatric Classification." *Social Science and Medicine* **35**(1): 3–24.

Gal, Susan 1989. "Language and the Political Economy." *Annual Review of Anthropology* **18**: 345–367.

Galasinski, Dariusz 2004, *Men and the Language of Emotions*. London: Palgrave Macmillan.

Gallese, Vittorio, M. N. Eagle, and P. Migone 2007. "Intentional Attunement: Mirror Neurons and the Neural Underpinnings of Interpersonal Relations." *Journal of the American Psychoanalytic Association* **55**(1): 131–176.

Garcia, Ricardo R., and Francisco Aboitiz 2007. "Commentary on 'The Evolution of Human Speech: Its Anatomical and Neural Bases' (Lieberman 2007)." *Current Anthropology* **48**(1): 54.

Gaudio, Rudolf P. 2003. "Coffeetalk: Starbucks and the Commercialization of Casual Conversation." *Language in Society* **32**(5): 659–691.

Geertz, Clifford 1973a. "Person, Time, and Conduct in Bali." In *The Interpretation of Cultures: Selected Essays by Clifford Geertz*, pp. 360–411. New York: Basic Books.

1973b. "Thick Description: Toward an Interpretive Theory of Culture." In *The Interpretation of Cultures: Selected Essays by Clifford Geertz*: pp. 3–32. New York: Basic Books.

1984. "'From the Native's Point of View': On the Nature of Anthropological Understanding." In *Culture Theory: Essays on Mind, Self, and Emotion*. R. A. Shweder and R. A. LeVine, eds., pp. 123–136. Cambridge: Cambridge University Press.

Gerow, Edwin 1981. "Rasa as a Category of Literary Criticism: What Are the Limits of Its Application?" In *Sanskrit Drama in Performance*. R. V. M. Baumer and J. R. Brandon, eds., pp. 226–257. Honolulu: The University Press of Hawaii.

2002. "Rasa and Katharsis: A Comparative Study, Aided by Several Films." *Journal of the American Oriental Society* **122**(2): 264–277.

Gibbs, James L., Jr. 1963. "The Kpelle Moot: A Therapeutic Model for the Informal Settlement of Disputes." *Africa: Journal of the International African Institute* **33**(1): 1–11.

Giddens, Anthony 1979. *Central Problems in Social Theory: Action, Structure and Contradiction in Social Analysis*. Berkeley and Los Angeles: University of California Press.

Gilleland, Michael 2004. "This and That." In *The Growlery* [blog]. February 2004. www.mgilleland.com/feb2004.htm (accessed April 5, 2008).

Glenn, Phillip 2003. *Laughter in Interaction*. Cambridge: Cambridge University Press.

Goffman, Erving 1979. "Response Cries." *Language* **84**: 787–815.

1981. "Footing." In *Forms of Talk*: pp. 124–259. Philadelphia: University of Pennsylvania Press.

Goldstein, Jan 1987. *Console and Classify: The French Psychiatric Profession in the Nineteenth Century*. New York: Cambridge University Press.

Good, Byron J. 1994. *Medicine, Rationality, and Experience: An Anthropological Perspective*. Cambridge: Cambridge University Press.

Goodwin, Charles 1994. Professional Vision. *American Anthropologist* **96**(3): 606–633.

Goodwin, Marjorie H. 2006. *The Hidden Life of Girls: Games of Stance, Status, and Exclusion*. Malden, MA: Blackwell.

Goodwin, Marjorie H., and Charles Goodwin 2001. "Emotion within Situated Activity." In *Linguistic Anthropology: A Reader*. A. Duranti, ed., pp. 239–257. Malden, MA.: Blackwell.

Goodwin, Marjorie H., Charles Goodwin, and Malcah Yaeger-Dror 2002. "Multi-modality in Girls' Game Disputes." *Journal of Pragmatics* **34**: 1621–1649.

Gordon, Raymond G., Jr. ed. 2005. *Ethnologue: Languages of the World* (online version: www.ethnologue.com/). Dallas: SIL International.

Gottman, John M., Lynn Fainsilber Katz, and Carole Hooven 1996. "Parental Meta-Emotion, Philosophy, and the Emotional Life of Families: Theoretical Models and Preliminary Data." *Journal of Family Psychology* **10**(3): 243–268.

Graham, Mark 2002. "Emotional Bureaucracies: Emotions Civil Servants, and Immigrants in the Swedish Welfare State." *Ethos* **30**(3): 199–226.

Griffiths, Paul E. 1997. *What Emotions Really Are: The Problem of Psychological Categories*. Chicago: University of Chicago Press.

Grima, Benedicte 1992. *The Performance of Emotion Among Paxtun Women*. Austin: University of Texas Press.

Habermas, Jürgen 1987. *The Theory of Communicative Action: Lifeworld and Systems, A Critique of Functionalist Reason*. T. McCarthy, transl. Boston: Beacon Press.

Hacking, Ian 1999. *The Social Construction of What?* Cambridge, MA: Harvard University Press.

Halliburton, Murphy 2005. "'Just Some Spirits': The Erosion of Spirit Possession and the Rise of 'Tension' in South India." *Medical Anthropology* **24**(2): 111–144.

Hanks, William F. 1996. *Language and Communicative Practices*. Boulder, CO: Westview.

Harkins, Jean, and Anna Wierzbicka, eds. 2001. *Emotions in Crosslinguistic Perspective*. Volume 17. Berlin: Mouton de Gruyter.

Hatfield, Elaine, John T. Cacioppo, and Richard L. Rapson 1994. *Emotional Contagion*. Cambridge: Cambridge University Press.

Haviland, John B. 2003. "Comments on The Meanings of Interjections in Q'eqchi' Maya: From Emotive Reaction to Social and Discursive Action." *Current Anthropology* **44**(4): 480–481.

Hayton, James C., Gerard George, and Shaker A. Zahra 2002. "National Culture and Entrepreneurship: A Review of Behavioral Research." *Entrepreneurship: Theory and Practice* **26**: 22–52.

Herzfeld, Michael 1997. *Cultural Intimacy: Social Poetics in the Nation-State*. New York: Routledge.

Higgins, Kathleen 2003. Comparative Aesthetics. In *The Oxford Handbook of Aesthetics*. J. Levinson, ed., pp. 679–692. Oxford: Oxford University Press.

Hill, Jane H. 1995. "The Voices of Don Gabriel: Responsibility and Self in a Modern Mexicano Narrative." In *The Dialogic Emergence of Culture*. D. Tedlock and B. Mannheim, eds., pp. 97–147. Urbana and Chicago: University of Illinois Press.

2008. *The Everyday Language of White Racism in the United States*. Malden, MA: Wiley-Blackwell.

Hobson, R. Peter 1993. "Understanding Persons: The Role of Affect." In *Understanding Other Minds*. S. Baron-Cohen, H. Tager-Flusberg, and D. J. Cohen, eds., pp. 204–227. Oxford: Oxford University Press.

Hochschild, Arlie 1979. "Emotion Work, Feeling Rules, and Social Structure." *American Journal of Sociology* **85**(3): 551–575.

Hoffman, Katherine 2002. "Generational Change in Berber Women's Song of the Anti-Atlas." *Ethnomusicology* **46**(3): 510–540.

2008. *We Share Walls: Language, Space, and Gender in Berber Morocco*. Volume II. Malden, MA: Wiley-Blackwell.

Hoopes, James, ed. 1991. *Peirce on Signs: Writings on Semiotic by Charles Sanders Peirce*. Chapel Hill: University of North Carolina.

Hymes, Dell 1972. "Models of the Interaction of Language and Social Life." In *Directions in Sociolinguistics: The Ethnography of Communication.* J. Gumperz and D. Hymes eds. New York: Basil Blackwell.

Inda, Jonathan Xavier, and Renato Rosaldo 2002. "Introduction: A World in Motion." In *The Anthropology of Globalization: a Reader.* J. X. Inda and R. Rosaldo, eds., pp. 1–36. Malden, MA, and Oxford: Blackwell.

Inoue, Miyako 2006. *Vicarious Language: Gender and Linguistic Modernity in Japan.* Berkeley: University of California Press.

Irvine, Judith 1982. "Language and Affect: Some Cross-Cultural Issues." In *Contemporary Perceptions of Language: Interdisciplinary Dimensions.* H. Byrnes, ed., Washington, DC: Georgetown University Press.

    1989. "When Talk Isn't Cheap: Language and Political Economy." *American Ethnologist* **16**: 248–267.

    1990. "Registering Affect: Heteroglossia in the Linguistic Expression of Emotion." In Lutz and Abu-Lughod, eds.

    1998. "Ideologies of Honorific Language." In *Language Ideologies: Practice and Theory.* B. Schieffelin, K. Woolard, and P. Kroskrity, eds., pp. 51–67. New York: Oxford University Press.

Irvine, Judith, and Susan Gal 2000. "Language Ideology and Linguistic Differentiation." In *Regimes of Language: Ideologies, Polities, and Identities.* P. Kroskrity, ed., pp. 35–83. Santa Fe: School of American Research.

Jakobson, Roman 1985 [1960]. "Closing Statement: Linguistics and Poetics." In *Semiotics: An Introductory Anthology.* R. E. Innis, ed., pp. 145–175. Bloomington: Indiana University Press.

    1987a. "The Poetry of Grammar and the Grammar of Poetry." In *Language in Literature.* K. Pomorska and S. Rudy, eds., pp. 121–144. Cambridge, MA: The Belnap Press of Harvard University.

    1987b [1966]. "Grammatical Parallelism and its Russian Facet." In *Language in Literature.* K. Pomorska and S. Rudy, eds., pp. 145–179. Cambridge, MA and London: Harvard University Press.

    1987c [1965]. "Quest for the Essence of Language." In *Language in Literature.* K. Pomorska and S. Rudy, eds., pp. 413–427. Cambridge, MA and London: Harvard University Press.

James, William 1890/1918. *The Principles of Psychology. Volume II.* New York: Henry Holt and Company.

Jameson, Frederic 1991. *Postmoderism: Or, the Cultural Logic of Late Capitalism.* London: Verso.

Jones, Graham M., and Bambi Schieffelin 2009. "Enquoting Voices, Accomplishing Talk: Uses of *Be + Like*" in Instant Messaging. *Language and Communication* **29**(1): 77–113.

Jordan, Jay 2005. "Dell Hymes, Kenneth Burke's 'Identification,' and the Birth of Sociolinguistics." *Rhetoric Review* **24**(3): 264–279.

Kachru, Braj B. 1997. "World Englishes and English-Using Communities." *Annual Review of Applied Linguistics* **17**(1): 66–87.

Kanner, Leo 1943. "Austistic Disturbances of Affective Contact." *Nervous Child* **2**: 217–250.

Karunanidhi, M. 1989 [1975]. *Nencukku Niti (Justice for the Heart) 3rd edition, Volume 1.* Madras: Tirumakal Nilayam.

Keane, Webb 1997. "From Fetishism to Sincerity: On Agency, the Speaking Subject, and their Historicity in the Context of Religious Conversion." *Comparative Studies in Society and History* **39**(4): 674–693.

2002. "Sincerity, 'Modernity,' and the Protestants." *Cultural Anthropology* **17**(1): 65–92.

2004. "Language and Religion." In *A Companion to Linguistic Anthropology*. A. Duranti, ed., pp. 431–448. Malden, MA: Blackwell.

Klaiman, Miriam H. 1980. "Bengali Dative Subjects." *Lingua* **51**: 275–295.

Kockelman, Paul 2003. "The Meanings of Interjections in Q'eqchi' Maya: From Emotive Reaction to Social and Discursive Action." *Current Anthropology* **44**(4): 467–490.

Komatsu, Sumio 1988. "Tokyōgo Ni Okeru Danjosa No Keisei: Shūjosi o Chūsin To Shite [The Formation of Gender Differences in the Tokyo Dialect: Centering on the Sentence-Final Particles]." *Kokugo To Kokubungaku* **65**: 94–106.

Kövecses, Zoltán 2000. *Metaphor and Emotion: Language, Culture, and Body in Human Feeling*. New York: Cambridge University Press.

Koven, Michèle E. J. 1998. "Two Languages in the Self/The Self in Two Languages: French-Portuguese Bilinguals' Verbal Enactments and Experiences of Self in Narrative Discourse." *Ethos* **26**(4): 410–455.

Kraepelin, Emil 1985. "Depressed Stages of Maniacal-Depressive Insanity (Circular Stupor)." In *Lectures on Clinical Psychiatry*. E. Kraepelin and L. B. Adams, eds. Birmingham, AL: Classics of Medicine Library.

Krancus, Nathanael 2007. *Pentecostal Sermon Podcasts as Language Socialization: A Critical Analysis*. Unpublished Paper. Flagstaff: Northern Arizona University.

Kripke, Saul 1972. "Naming and Necessity." In *Semantics of Natural Language*. D. Davidson and G. Harmon, eds., pp. 253–355. Dordrecht: D. Reidel.

1982. *Wittgenstein on Rules and Private Language*. Cambridge, MA: Harvard University Press.

Kristeva, Julia 1982. *Powers of Horror: An Essay on Abjection*. New York: Columbia University Press.

Kroskrity, Paul 1993. "An Evolving Ethnicity Among the Arizona Tewa: Toward a Repertoire of Identity." In *Language, History, and Identity: Ethnolinguistic Studies of the Arizona Tewa*. Tucson: University of Arizona Press.

Kroskrity, Paul, ed. 2000. *Regimes of Language*. Santa Fe: School of American Research Press.

Kuebli, Janet, Susan Butler, and Robyn Fivush 1995. "Mother–Child Talk About Past Emotions: Relations of Maternal Language and Child Gender Over Time. *Cognition and Emotion* **9**: 265–283.

Kulick, Don 1992. *Language Shift and Cultural Reproduction: Socialization, Self and Syncretism in a Papua New Guinea Village*. Cambridge: Cambridge University Press.

2003. "No." *Language and Communication* **23**(2): 139–151.

Kulick, Don, and Bambi Schieffelin 2004. "Language Socialization." In *A Companion to Linguistic Anthropology*. A. Duranti, ed., pp. 349–368. Malden, MA: Blackwell.

Kulick, Don, and Charles H. Klein. 2003. "Scandalous Acts: The Politics of Shame among Brazilian Travesti Prostitutes." In *Recognition Struggles and Social Movements: Contested Identities, Agency and Power*. B. Hobson, ed., pp. 215–238. Cambridge: Cambridge University Press.

Kunene, Daniel P. 1978. "The Ideophone in Southern Sotho." *Marburger Studien zur Afrika- und Asienkunde, Ser. A, Afrika* **11**: 1–183.

Kusserow, Adrie Suzanne 2004. *American Individualisms: Child Rearing and Social Class in Three Neighborhoods*. London: Palgrave Macmillan.

Kuter, Lois 1989. "Breton vs. French: Language and the Opposition of Political, Economic, Social, and Cultural Values." In *Investigating Obsolescence: Studies in Language Contraction and Death.* N. Dorian, ed., pp. 75–90. Cambridge: Cambridge University Press.

Labov, William 1972. *Sociolinguistic Patterns.* Philadelphia: University of Pennsylvania Press.

Lakoff, George, and Mark Johnson 1980. *Metaphors We Live By.* Chicago: University of Chicago Press.

Lakoff, George, and Zoltan Kövecses 1987. "The Cognitive Model of Anger Inherent in American English." In *Cultural Models in Language and Thought.* D. Holland and N. Quinn, eds., pp. 195–221. Cambridge: Cambridge University Press.

Lakoff, Robin. 1975. *Language and Woman's Place.* New York: Harper and Row.

Lambert, Wallace E., R.C. Hodgson, R.C. Gardner, and S. Fillenbaum 1960. "Evaluational Reactions to Spoken Languages." *Journal of Abnormal and Social Psychology* **60**(1): 44–51.

Larson, Gerald James 1976. "The Aesthetic (Rasasvada) and the Religious (Brahmasvada) in Abhinavagupta's Kashmir Saivism Philosophy." *East and West* **26**(4): 371–387.

Lee, Sing 1999. "Diagnosis Postponed: Shenjing Shuairuo and the Transformation of Psychiatry in Post-Mao China." *Culture, Medicine and Psychiatry* **23**: 349–380.

Lempert, Michael 2007. "Affected Subjects: Histrionics and the Liberal Speaking Subject in the Tibetan Diaspora." Paper presented at the 106th Annual Meeting of the American Anthropological Association. Washington, DC.

Lengacher, C.A., M.P. Bennett, L. Gonzalez, D. Gilvary, C.E. Cox, A. Cantor, P.B. Jacobsen, C. Yang, and J. Djeu 2008. "Immune Responses to Guided Imagery During Breast Cancer Treatment." *Biological Research for Nursing* **9**(3): 205–214.

Lévi-Strauss, Claude 1974 [1955]. *Tristes Tropiques.* New York: Atheneum.

1983[1969, 1964]. *The Raw and the Cooked: Mythologiques. Volume I.* Chicago: University of Chicago Press.

Levy, Robert I. 1973. *The Tahitians: Mind and Experience in the Society Islands.* Chicago: University of Chicago Press.

1984. "Emotion, Knowing, and Culture." In *Culture Theory: Essays on Mind, Self, and Emotion.* R. Shweder and R.A. LeVine, eds., pp. 214–237. Cambridge: Cambridge University Press.

Lewis, Helen B. 1971. *Shame and Guilt in Neurosis.* New York: International Universities Press.

Lieberman, Philip 2007. "The Evolution of Human Speech: Its Anatomical and Neural Bases." *Current Anthropology* **48**(1): 39–66.

Lindstrom, Lamont 1992. "Context Contests: Debatable Truth Statements on Tanna (Vanuatu)." In Duranti and Goodwin, eds., pp. 101–124.

Lippi-Green, Rosina 1997. *English with an Accent: Language, Ideology, and Discrimination in the United States.* London: Routledge.

Lipset, David 2004. "'The Trial': A Parody of the Law Amid the Mockery of Men in Post-Colonial Papua New Guinea." *Journal of the Royal Anthropological Institute* **10**(1): 63–89.

Lloyd, A.L. 1980. "Lament." *In New Grove Dictionary of Music and Musicians.* S. Sladie, ed., Volume 10. London: Macmillan.

Lloyd, Michael 1996. "Review of F. Macintosh, Dying Acts: Death in Ancient Greek and Modern Irish Tragic Drama." *Classics Ireland* **3**: 208–215.

Lock, Margaret 1998. "Menopause: Lessons from Anthropology." *Psychosomatic Medicine* **60**(4) (Special Issue: Cross-Cultural Research): 410–419.

Lutz, Catherine 1986. "Emotion, Thought, and Estrangement: Emotion as a Cultural Category." *Cultural Anthropology* **1**: 287–309.

1988. *Unnatural Emotions: Everyday Sentiments on a Micronesian Atoll and their Challenge to Western Theory*. Chicago: University of Chicago Press.

1990. "Engendered Emotion: Gender, Power, and the Rhetoric of Emotional Control in American Discourse." In Lutz and Abu-Lughod, eds., pp. 69–91.

Lutz, Catherine, and Lila Abu-Lughod (eds) 1990. *Language and the Politics of Emotion*. Cambridge: Cambridge University Press.

Lynch, Owen 1990a. "Divine Passions: The Social Construction of Emotion in India." In *Divine Passions: The Social Construction of Emotion in India*. O. M. Lynch, ed., pp. 3–34. Berkeley: University of California Press.

1990b. "The Mastram: Emotion and Person among Mathura's Chaubes." In *Divine Passions: The Social Construction of Emotion in India*. O. M. Lynch, ed., pp. 91–115. Berkeley: University of California Press.

Lyon, Margot 1994. "Emotion as Mediator of Somatic and Social Processes: The Example of Respiration." In *Social Perspectives on Emotion*. W. Wentworth and J. Ryan, eds., pp. 83–108, Volume 2. Greenwich, CT: JAI Press.

1995. "Missing Emotion: The Limitations of Cultural Constructionism in the Study of Emotion." *Cultural Anthropology* **10**(2): 244–263.

2003 "'Immune' to Emotion: The Relative Absence of Emotion in PNI, and Its Centrality to Everything Else." In *Social and Cultural Lives of Immune Systems*. J. M. Wilce, ed., pp. 81–101. London: Routledge.

Lyotard, Jean-Francois 1984. "What is Postmodernism?" In *The Postmodern Condition: A Report on Knowledge*. G. Bennington and B. Massumi, eds., pp. 71–83. Minneapolis: University of Minnesota Press.

Macaulay, Ronald 1994. *The Social Art: Language and Its Uses*. Oxford and New York: Oxford University Press.

MacIntyre, Alasdair 1980. *After Virtue: A Study in Moral Theory*. Notre Dame, Ind.: University of Notre Dame Press.

McDaniel, June 1989. *The Madness of the Saints: Ecstatic Religion in Bengal*. Chicago: University of Chicago Press.

McLeod, J. R. 1991. "Ritual and Rhetoric in Presidential Politics." *Central Issues in Anthropology* **9**(1): 29–42.

Malinowski, Bronislaw 1923. "The Problem of Meaning in Primitive Languages." In *The Meaning of Meaning*: Supplement. I. C. K. Ogden and I. A. Richards, eds., pp. 296–336. New York: Harcourt, Brace & World.

Mangano, Dario, and Christopher R. Engelke 2006. "Using the World: A Language Socialization Study of Children with Autism's Apprenticeship into Semiotic Practices of Shared Meaning and Representation." Paper presented at the 105th Annual Meeting of the American Anthropological Association, San Jose, California, Friday, November 17, 2006.

Marsden, Magnus 2007. "All-Male Sonic Gatherings, Islamic Reform, and Masculinity in Northern Pakistan." *American Ethnologist* **34**(3): 473–490.

Martin, Emily 2000. "Mind-Body Problems." *American Ethnologist* **27**(3): 569–590.

2001. "Rationality, Feminism, and Mind." In *Feminism in Twentieth-Century Science, Technology, and Medicine*." A. Creager, E. Lunbeck, and L. Schiebinger, eds., pp. 214–227. Chicago: University of Chicago Press.

Mascia-Lees, Frances E., Patricia Sharpe, and Colleen Ballerino Cohen 1989. "The Postmodernist Turn in Anthropology: Cautions from a Feminist Perspective." *Signs: Journal of Women in Culture and Society* **15**(1): 7–33.

Masson, Jeffrey L., and M. V. Patwardhan 1969. "*Santarasa and Abhinavagupta's Philosophy of Aesthetics*." Poona: Bhandarkar Oriental Research Institute.

Massumi, Brian 1995. "The Autonomy of Affect." *Cultural Critique* **31**(31): 83–109.
  2002. *Parables for the Virtual: Movement, Affect, Sensation*. Durham, NC, and London: Duke University Press.
Matoesian, Greg 2005. "Struck by Speech Revisited: Embodied Stance in Jurisdictional Discourse." *Journal of Sociolinguistics* **9**(2): 167–193.
Maturana, Humberto 1997. "Metadesign." www.inteco.cl/articulos/006/texto_ing.htm (accessed May 24, 2007).
Maynard, Senko K. 2002. *Linguistic Emotivity: Centrality of Place, the Topic-Comment Dynamic, and an Ideology of Pathos in Japanese Discourse*. Philadelphia and Amsterdam: John Benjamins.
  2005. *Expressive Japanese: A Reference Guide to Sharing Emotion and Empathy*. Honolulu: University of Hawai'i Press.
Mead, George Herbert 1995 [1934]. "The Relation of Mind to Response and Environment." In *Language, Culture, and Society: A Book of Readings*. B. G. Blount, ed., pp. 95–101. Prospect Heights, IL: Waveland.
Merleau-Ponty, Maurice 1962. *Phenomenology of Perception*. C. Smith, transl. London: Routledge and Kegan Paul.
  1964. "The Phenomenology of Language." In *Signs*. R. McCleary, ed., pp. 84–97. Evanston, IL: Northwestern University Press.
Mertz, Elizabeth 1998. "Language Ideology and Praxis in US Law School Classrooms." In *Language Ideologies: Practice and Theory*. B. B. Schieffelin, K. Woolard, and P. V. Kroskrity, eds., pp. 149–88. New York: Oxford University Press.
Mertz, Elizabeth, and Richard Parmentier, eds. 1985. *Semiotic Mediation: Sociocultural and Psychological Perspectives*. Orlando: Academic Press.
Miller, Daniel 2006. Japanese Voices (Ito, Okabe, and Matsuda's *Personal, Portable, Pedestrian*), in *Current Anthropology* **47**(6): 1050–51.
Mitchell, Lisa in press. *Language, Emotion, and Politics in Southern India: The Making of a Mother Tongue*. Indianapolis: Indiana University Press.
Morris, Rosalind C. 2007. "Legacies of Derrida: Anthropology." *Annual Review of Anthropology* **36**(1): 355–389.
Mueggler, Erik 1998. "The Poetics of Grief and the Price of Hemp in Southwest China." *Journal of Asian Studies* **57**(4): 979–1008.
Mullen, Mary K., and Soonhyung Yi 1995. "The Cultural Context of Talk About the Past: Implications for the Development of Autobiographical Memory." *Cognitive Development* **10**(3): 407–419.
Murray, Stephen O. 1983. *Group Formation in Social Science*. Edmonton, Alberta: Linguistic Research.
Nathanson, Donald L. 1996. *Knowing Feeling: Affect, Script and Psychotherapy*. New York: Norton.
National Public Radio, and Eric Westervelt 2007. "Six Day War: Legality of Settlements Debated." Morning Edition. June 8, 2007. www.npr.org/templates/transcript/transcript.php?storyId=10816818 (accessed December 29, 2007).
National Public Radio, and Ofeibea Quist-Arcton 2008. "Text Messages Used to Incite Violence in Kenya. All Things Considered." February 20, 2008. www.npr.org/templates/story/story.php?storyId=19188853 (accessed June 6, 2008).
Naughton, John 1993. "Cuddling the Crocodile." *Observer*. Manchester, UK.
Nenola, Aili 2002. *Inkerin itkuvirret – Ingrian Laments*. Helsinki: Finnish Literature Society.
Noll, Richard 2004. "News and Notes: The American Reaction to Dementia Praecox, 1900." *History of Psychiatry* **15**(1): 127–128.
Nussbaum, Martha 2004. *Hiding From Humanity: Disgust, Shame, and the Law*. Princeton and Oxford: Princeton University Press.

Obeyesekere, Gananath 1985. "Depression, Buddhism, and the Work of Culture in Sri Lanka." In *Culture and Depression: Studies in the Anthropology and Cross-Cultural Psychiatry of Affect and Disorder*. A. Kleinman and B. Good, eds., pp. 134–152. Berkeley CA: University of California Press.

1997. *The Apotheosis of Captain Cook: European Mythmaking in the Pacific*. Princeton: Princeton University Press.

Ochs, Elinor 1986. "From Feelings to Grammar: A Samoan Case Study." In *Language Socialization Across Cultures*. B. B. Schieffelin and E. Ochs, eds., pp. 251–272. Cambridge: Cambridge University Press.

1988. *Culture and Language Development: Language Acquisition and Language Socialization in a Samoan Village*. Cambridge: Cambridge University Press.

1990. "Indexicality and Socialization." In *Cultural Psychology: Essays on Comparative Human Development*. J. W. Stigler, R. A. Shweder, and G. Herdt, eds., pp. 287–308. Cambridge: Cambridge University Press.

1992. "Indexing Gender." In *Rethinking Context: Language as an Interactive Phenomenon*. A. Duranti and C. Goodwin, eds., pp. 335–358. Cambridge: Cambridge University Press.

Ochs, Elinor, and Bambi Schieffelin 1984. "Language Acquisition and Socialization: Three Developmental Stories and Their Implications." In *Culture Theory: Essays on Mind, Self, and Emotion*. R. Shweder and R. A. LeVine, eds., pp. 276–320. New York: Cambridge University Press.

1989. "Language Has a Heart." *Text* **9**(1 (special issue: The Pragmatics of Affect)): 7–25.

Ochs, Elinor, and Carolyn Taylor 2001. "The 'Father Knows Best' Dynamic in Dinnertime Narratives." In *Linguistic Anthropology: A Reader*. A. Duranti, ed., pp. 431–449. Oxford and Malden, MA: Blackwell.

Ochs, Elinor, Tamar Kremer-Sadlik, Karen Gainer Sirota, and Olga Solomon 2004. "Autism and the Social World: An Anthropological Perspective." *Discourse Studies* **6**(2): 147–183.

Ochs, Elinor, Olga Solomon, and Laura Sterponi 2005. "Limitations and Transformations of Habitus in Child-Directed Communication." *Discourse Studies* **7**(4–5): 547–583.

Opitz, John M. (Amanuensis), Rüdiger Schultka, and Luminita Göbbel 2006. "Meckel on Developmental Pathology." *American Journal of Medical Genetics* **140A**(2): 115–128.

Orwell, George 1946. "Politics and the English Language." In *The Collected Essays, Journalism and Letters of George Orwell*, Volume 4. S. Orwell and I. Angus, eds. Harmondsworth, UK: Penguin.

Pappuswamy, Umarani 2005. "Dative Subjects in Tamil: A Computational Analysis." *South Asian Language Review* **15**(2): 40–62.

Peirce, Charles Sanders 1931–1958. *Collected Papers of Charles Sanders Peirce*. Cambridge, MA: Belknap (Harvard University).

1991[1868]. "Questions Concerning Certain Faculties Claimed for Man." In *Peirce on Signs: Writings on Semiotic by Charles Sanders Peirce*. J. Hoopes, ed., pp. 34–53. Chapel Hill, NC: University of North Carolina Press.

Pendergrast, Mark 1999. *Uncommon Grounds: The History of Coffee and How it Transformed Our World*. New York: Basic Books.

Pennebaker, James W. 1993. "Putting Stress Into Words: Health, Linguistic, and Therapeutic Implications." *Behaviour Research and Therapy* **31**(6): 539–548.

Planalp, Sally 1999. *Communicating Emotion: Social, Moral, and Cultural Processes*. Cambridge: Cambridge University Press.

Plato 1903. "Laws." In *Platonis Opera*. J. Burnet, ed. Oxford: Oxford University Press.

1969. *The Republic. (Volumes 5 and 6 of Plato in Twelve Volumes)*. Cambridge, MA. and London: Harvard University Press, William Heinemann Ltd.

Pocock, John 1985. *Virtue, Commerce, and History*. Cambridge: Cambridge University Press.

Povinelli, Elizabeth A. 1998. "The State of Shame: Australian Multiculturalism and the Crisis of Indigenous Citizenship (Intimacy)." *Critical Inquiry* **24**(2): 575–610.

Probyn, Elspeth 2004. "Everyday Shame." *Cultural Studies* **18**(2/3): 328–349.
2005a. *Blush: Faces of Shame*. Minneapolis and London: University of Minnesota Press.
2005b. "A-ffect: Let Her RIP." *M/C Journal* [online journal http://journal.media-culture.org.au/0512/13-probyn.php] **8**(6).

Putnam, Hilary 1975. "The Meaning of Meaning." In *Mind, Language, and Reality: Philosophical Papers 2*. H. Putnam, ed., pp. 215–271. Cambridge: Cambridge University Press.

Raheja, Gloria Goodwin, and Ann Grodzins Gold 1994. *Listen to the Heron's Words: Reimagining Gender and Kinship in North India*. Berkeley, CA, and London: University of California Press.

Ramaswamy, Sumathi 1997. *Passions of the Tongue: Language Devotion in Tamil India, 1891–1970*. Berkeley, CA: University of California Press.

Reddy, William M. 1999. "Emotional Liberty: Politics and History in the Anthropology of Emotions." *Cultural Anthropology* **14**: 256–88
2001. *The Navigation of Feeling: A Framework for the History of Emotions*. Cambridge, New York: Cambridge University Press.
2003. "The Rule of Love." Paper presented at 102nd Annual Meeting of the American Anthropological Association. Chicago, IL, November 22, 2003.

Reilly, Judy S., Marina L. McIntire, and Howie Seago 1992. "Affective Prosody in American Sign Language." *Sign Language Studies* **75**: 113–28

Robbins, Joel 2001. "God is Nothing But Talk: Modernity, Language and Prayer in a Papua New Guinea Society." *American Anthropologist* **103**(4): 901–912.
2005. "Introduction – Humiliation and Transformation: Marshall Sahlins and the Study of Cultural Change in Melanesia." In *The Making of Global and Local Modernities in Melanesia: Humiliation, Transformation And the Nature of Cultural Change*. J. Robbins and H. Wardlow, eds., pp. 3–22. Aldershot, UK: Ashgate Publishing.

Rommetveit, Ragnar 1998. "Intersubjective Attunement and Linguistically Mediated Meaning in Discourse." In *Intersubjective Communication and Emotion in Early Ontogeny*. S. Bråten, ed., pp. 354–371. Cambridge: Cambridge University Press/ Editions de la Maison de Sciences de l'Homme.

Ronkin, Maggie "Interrogating Power Upside Down: Literal and Hypothetical Worlds in Narration." In *Language and Linguistics in South Asia: Selected Papers from SALA 24*. K. K. Sridhar and S. N. Sridhar, eds. New Delhi: Manohar Publications. To appear.

Rosaldo, Michelle Z. 1984. "Towards an Anthropology of Self and Feeling." In *Culture Theory: Essays on Mind, Self, and Emotion*. R. A. Shweder and R. A. LeVine, eds., pp. 137–57. Cambridge: Cambridge University Press.

Rosaldo, Renato 1996. "Grief and a Headhunter's Rage." In *Anthropological Theory*. R. J. McGee and R. L. Warms, eds. Mountain View, CA: Mayfield.

Rose, Gillian 1996. *Mourning Becomes the Law: Philosophy and Representation*. Cambridge: Cambridge University Press.

Rose, Nikolas 1996. *Inventing Our Selves: Psychology*. Cambridge: Cambridge University Press.

Roseberry, William 1997. "Marx and Anthropology." *Annual Review of Anthropology* **26**: 25–46.

Rosen, Lawrence 1995. "Introduction: The Cultural Analysis of Others' Inner States." In *Other Intentions: Cultural Contexts and the Attribution of Inner States.* L. Rosen, ed., pp. 3–11. Santa Fe, NM: School of American Research Press.

Rosenberg, Daniel V. 1990. "Language in the Discourse of the Emotions." In Lutz and Abu-Lughod, eds., pp. 162–185.

Rosoff, Stephen M., and Matthew C. Leone 1991. "The Public Prestige of Medical Specialties: Overviews and Undercurrents." *Social Science and Medicine* **32**(3): 321–326.

Rotter, Julian B. 1966. "Generalized Expectancies for Internal Versus External Control of Reinforcement." *Psychological Monographs* **80**(1): 1–28.

Rumsey, Alan 1990. "Word, Meaning, and Linguistic Ideology." *American Anthropologist* **92**(2): 346–361.

Sacks, Harvey 1972. "On the Analyzability of Stories by Children." In *Directions in Sociolinguistics: The Ethnography of Communication.* J. Gumperz and D. Hymes, eds., pp. 325–345. New York: Holt.

Sacks, Harvey, Emanuel A. Schegloff, and Gail Jefferson 1974. "A Simplest Systematics for the Organization of Turn-Taking for Conversation." *Language* **50**: 696–735.

Sahlins, Marshall David 1985. *Islands of History.* Chicago: University of Chicago Press.
1992. "The Economics of Develop-man in the Pacific." *Res* **21**(1): 13–25.

Samuels, David 1999. "The Whole and the Sum of the Parts, or, How Cookie and the Cupcakes Told the Story of Apache History in San Carlos." *Journal of American Folklore* **112**(445): 464–474.
2004. *Putting a Song on Top of It: Expression and Identity on the San Carlos Apache Reservation.* Tucson, AZ: University of Arizona Press.

Santiago-Irizarry, Vilma 2001. *Medicalizing Ethnicity: The Construction of Latino Identity in a Psychiatric Setting.* Ithaca, NY: Cornell University Press.

Sapir, Edward 1921. *Language: An Introduction to the Study of Speech.* New York: Harcourt, Brace & World.
1949a[1927]. "The Unconscious Patterning of Behavior in Society." In *Selected Writings of Edward Sapir in Language, Culture, and Personality.* D. G. Mandelbaum, ed., pp. 544–559. Berkeley and Los Angeles: University of California Press.
1949b[1934]. "Symbolism." In *Selected Writings in Language, Culture, and Personality.* D. G. Mandelbaum, ed., pp. 564–568. Berkeley, CA: University of California Press.

de Sardan, Jean-Pierre Olivier 1994. "Possession, Affliction et Folie: Les Ruses de la Thérapisation." *L'Homme* **34**(3): 7–27.

Sass, Louis A. 1992. *Madness and Modernism: Insanity in the Light of Modern Art, Literature, and Thought.* New York: Basic Books.
2007. "Contradictions of Emotion in Schizophrenia." *Cognition and Emotion* **21**(2): 351–390.

Saurette, Paul 2006. "You Dissin Me? Humiliation and Post 9/11 Global Politics." *Review of International Studies* **32**(3): 495–522.

Scheff, Thomas J. 1979. *Catharsis in Healing, Ritual, and Drama.* Berkeley, CA: University of California Press.
2000. "Shame and the Social Bond: A Sociological Theory." *Sociological Theory* **18**(1): 84–98.

Scheper-Hughes, Nancy 1995. "The Primacy of the Ethical: Propositions for a Militant Anthropology." *Current Anthropology* **36**(3): 409–440.

Schieffelin, Bambi B. 1990. *The Give and Take of Everyday Life: Language Socialization of Kaluli Children.* Cambridge: Cambridge University Press.
2000. "Introducing Kaluli Literacy: A Chronology of Influences." In *Regimes of Language.* P. Kroskrity, ed., pp. 293–327. Santa Fe, NM: School of American Research Press.

2007. "Found in Translating: Reflexive Language Across Time and Texts." In *Consequences of Contact: Language Ideologies and Sociocultural Transformations in Pacific Societies*. B. Schieffelin and M. Makihara, eds., pp. 140–165. New York and Oxford: Oxford University Press.

Schieffelin, Bambi B., and Elinor Ochs 1986. "Language Socialization." *Annual Review of Anthropology* **15**: 163–191.

Schieffelin, Bambi B., Kathryn A. Woolard, and Paul Kroskrity, eds. 1998. *Language Ideologies: Practice and Theory*. New York: Oxford University Press.

Schieffelin, Edward L. 1981. "The End of Traditional Music, Dance, and Body Decoration in Bosavi, Papua New Guinea." *Cultural Survival: The Plight of Peripheral People in Papua New Guinea Occasional Papers* **7**(1): 1–22.

Schore, Allan N. 2001. "The Effects of Early Relational Trauma on Right Brain Development, Affect Regulation, and Infant Mental Health." *Infant Mental Health Journal* **22**(1–2): 201–269.

Schubel, Vernon James 1993. *Religious Performance in Contemporary Islam: Shi'i Devotional Rituals in South Asia*. Columbia, SC: University of South Carolina Press.

Schutz, Alfred 1962–66. "Making Music Together: A Study in Social Relationship." In *Collected Papers*. A. Brodersen, ed., pp. 159–178. Phaenomenologica, Volume 2 (Studies in Social Theory). The Hague: M. Nijhoff.

Scott, Frank E. 2001. "Reconsidering a Therapeutic Role for the State: Anti-Modernist Governance and the Reunification of the Self." *Administrative Theory & Praxis* **23**(2): 231–242.

Sedgwick, Eve Kosofsky, and Adam Frank 1995. "Shame in the Cybernetic Fold: Reading Silvan Tomkins." In *Shame and Its Sisters: A Silvan Tomkins Reader*. E. K. Sedgwick and A. Frank, eds., pp. 1–28. Durham, NC, and London: Duke University Press.

Senghas, Richard, and Leila Monaghan 2002. "Signs of Their Times: Deaf Communities and the Culture of Language." *Annual Review of Anthropology* **31**(1): 69–97.

Shakespeare, William 1938a. *Love's Labour's Lost*. In *The Works of William Shakespeare Gathered into One Volume*. New York: Oxford University Press.

1938b *Macbeth*. In *The Works of William Shakespeare Gathered into One Volume*. New York: Oxford University Press.

Shiflett, Dave 2004. "Old Yeller: Misinterpeting Dean's Scream." *National Review Online*. January 30, 2004. www.nationalreview.com/shiflett/shiflett200401300915. asp (accessed April 5, 2008).

Shoaps, Robin 2002. "'Pray Earnestly': The Textual Construction of Personal Involvement in Pentecostal Prayer and Song." *Journal of Linguistic Anthropology* **12**(1): 34–71.

2003. "Shifting Representations of Subjectivity and the Contestation of Loci of Moral Authority in Sakapultek (Mayan) Pentecostal Conversion." Paper presented at 102nd Annual Meeting of the American Anthropological Association. Chicago. November 22, 2003.

Showalter, Elaine 1985. *The Female Malady: Women, Madness, and English Culture 1830–1980*. New York: Pantheon.

Shryock, Andrew 2004. "Other Conscious/Self Aware: First Thoughts on Cultural Intimacy and Mass Mediation." In *Off Stage/On Display: Intimacy and Ethnography in the Age of Public Culture*. A. Shryock, ed., pp. 3–28. Stanford, CA: Stanford University Press.

Sifneos, Peter E. 1973. "The Prevalence of 'Alexithymic' Characteristics in Psychosomatic Patients." *Journal of Psychotherapy and Psychosomatics* **22**: 255–262.

Silverstein, Michael 1979. "Language Structure and Linguistic Ideology". In *The Elements: A Parasession on Linguistic Units and Levels*. R. Cline, W. Hanks, and C. Hofbauer, eds., pp. pp. 193–247. Chicago: Chicago Linguistic Society.

1985. "Language and the Culture of Gender: At the Intersection of Structure, Usage, and Ideology." In *Semiotic Mediation: Sociocultural and Psychological Perspectives*. E. Mertz and R. Parmentier, eds., pp. 219–259. Orlando, FL: Academic Press.

1993. "Metapragmatic Discourse and Metapragmatic Function." In *Reflexive Language: Reported Speech and Metapragmatics*. J.A. Lucy, ed., pp. 33–58. Cambridge: Cambridge University Press.

1998. "The Uses and Utility of Ideology." In Schieffelin, Woolard, and Kroskrity, eds., pp. 123–145.

2000. "Whorfianism and the Linguistic Imagination of Nationality." In *Regimes of Language: Ideologies, Polities, and Identities*. P. Kroskrity, ed., pp. 85–138. Santa Fe: School of American Research.

2001[1981]. "The Limits of Awareness." *Working Papers in Sociolinguistics* **84**." (Reprinted in 2001 in *Linguistic Anthropology: A Reader*. A. Duranti, ed., pp. 382–401. Malden: Blackwell.)

2003a. "Indexical Order and the Dialectics of Sociolinguistic Life." *Language and Communication* **23**(3–4): 193–229.

2003b. "Death and Life at Gettysburg." In *Talking Politics: The Substance of Style from Abe to 'W.'*" M. Silverstein, ed., pp. 33–62. Chicago: Prickly Paradigm Press (distributed by University of Chicago).

2004. "'Cultural' Concepts and the Language-Culture Nexus." *Current Anthropology* **45**(5): 621–652.

2005a. "Languages/Cultures Are Dead! Long Live the Linguistic-Cultural." In *Unwrapping the Sacred Bundle: Reflections on the Disciplining of Anthropology*. D.A. Segal and S.J. Yanagisako, eds., pp. 99–125. Durham, NC, and London: Duke University Press.

2005b. "Ideologies of the Speaking Subject in the Psychotherapeutic Theory and Practice of Carl Rogers." *Journal of Linguistic Anthropology* **15**(2): 258–272.

Smith, Benjamin 2005. "Ideologies of the Speaking Subject in the Psychotherapeutic Theory and Practice of Carl Rogers." *Journal of Linguistic Anthropology* **15**(2):258–272.

Sommers, Christina Hoff, and Sally Satel 2005. *One Nation Under Therapy: How the Helping Culture Is Eroding Self-Reliance*. New York: St. Martin's Press

Speer, Susan A. 2005. *Gender Talk: Feminism, Discourse and Conversation Analysis*. London: Routledge.

Sperber, Dan, and Deirdre Wilson 1986. *Relevance: Communication and Cognition*. Cambridge, MA: Harvard University Press.

Stern, Daniel N. 1985. *The Interpersonal World of the Infant: A View from Psychoanalysis and Developmental Psychology*. New York: Basic Books.

2000. "Introduction to the Paperback Edition." In *The Interpersonal World of the Infant: A View from Psychoanalysis and Developmental Psychology*. D.N. Stern, ed., pp. xi–xxxix. New York: Basic Books.

Stewart, Kathleen 2007. *Ordinary Affects*. Durham, NC, and London: Duke University Press.

StoryCorps.Net 2007. StoryCorps, Volume 2007: Corporation for Public Broadcasting, AT&T, National Public Radio, the American Folklife Center. www.storycorps.net/ (accessed July 26, 2007).

Strachey, James 1965. Editor's Introduction. In *The Psychopathology of Everyday Life*. A. Tyson and J. Strachey, eds., pp. 3–8. New York: W.W. Norton.

Sullivan, Bruce M. 1990. *Krsna Dvaipayana Vyasa and the Mahabharata: A New Interpretation*. Leiden, The Netherlands: E. J. Brill.

    2007. Dying on the Stage in the Nāṭyas; āstra and Kūṭiyāṭam: Perspectives from the Sanskrit Theatre Tradition. *Asian Theatre Journal* **24**(2): 422–439.

Sullivan, Kevin 2007. "Foreign Missionaries Find Fertile Ground in Europe: Singaporean Pastor Fires up Staid Danes." Washington Post Online, June 11, 2007. Washington, DC. www.washingtonpost.com/wp-dyn/content/article/2007/06/10/ AR2007061001267.html (accessed June 17, 2007).

Szasz, Thomas 1975. Back cover. In *I, Pierre Riviere, Having Slaughtered my Mother, my Sister, and my Brother: A Case of Parricide in the 19th Century*. M. Foucault, ed. Lincoln, NE: University of Nebraska Press Review.

Tarabay, Jamie 2006. "Revived Lament Tradition Makes Way for New Grief." Weekend Edition Sunday. National Public Radio (USA). November 12, 2006.

Taylor, Charles 1991. *The Malaise of Modernity*. Concord, Ontario, Canada: House of Anansi.

Thorne, Linda, and Susan Bartholomew Saunders 2002. "The Socio-Cultural Embeddedness of Individuals' Ethical Reasoning in Organizations (Cross-cultural Ethics)." *Journal of Business Ethics* **35**(1): 1–14.

Timm, Jeffrey R. 1991. "The Celebration of Emotion: Vallabha's Ontology of Affective Experience." *Philosophy East & West* **41**(1): 59–77.

Tolbert, Elizabeth 1990. "Magico-Religious Power and Gender in the Karelian Lament." In *Music, Gender, and Culture*. M. Herndon and S. Zigler, eds., pp. 41–56. Intercultural Music Studies, Volume 1. Wilhelmshaven, DE.: International Council for Traditional Music, Florian Noetzel Verlag.

    1992. "Theories of Meaning and Music Cognition: An Ethnomusicological Approach." *The World of Music* **34**(3): 7–21.

    1994. "The Voice of Lament: Female Vocality and Performative Efficacy in the Finnish-Karelian Itkuvirsi." In *Embodied Voices: Representing Female Vocality in Western Culture*. L. C. Dunn and N. A. Jones, eds., pp. 179–194. New York: Cambridge University Press.

    2001a. "The Enigma of Music, the Voice of Reason: 'Music,' 'Language,' and Becoming Human." *New Literary History* **32**: 451–465.

    2001b. "Music and Meaning: An Evolutionary Story." *Psychology of Music* **29**(1): 84–94.

Tomasello, Michael 2003. "On the Different Origins of Symbols and Grammar." In *Language Evolution*. M. H. Christiansen and S. Kirby, eds., pp. 94–110. Oxford: Oxford University Press.

Tomkins, Silvan S. 1995. "What Are Affects?" In *Shame and Its Sisters: A Silvan Tomkins Reader*. E. K. Sedgwick and A. Frank, eds., pp. 33–74. Durham, NC, and London: Duke University Press.

Toomey, Paul M. 1990. "Krishna's Consuming Passions: Food as Metaphor and Metonym for Emotion at Mt. Govardhan." In *Divine Passions*. O. Lynch, ed., pp. 157–182. Berkeley, CA: University of California Press.

Trawick, Margaret 1988. "Spirits and Voices in Tamil Songs." *American Ethnologist* **15**: 193–215.

    1990a. *Notes on Love in a Tamil Family*. Berkeley, CA: University of California Press.

    1990b. "Untouchability and the Fear of Death in a Tamil Song." In Lutz and Abu-Lughod, eds., pp. 186–206.

Trechter, Sara 1999. "Contextualizing the Exotic Few: Gender Dichotomies in Lakhota." In *Reinventing Identities: The Gendered Self in Discourse*. M. Bucholtz, A. C.

Liang, and L.A. Sutton, eds., pp. 101–119. Studies in Language and Gender. New York, Oxford: Oxford University Press.

Trevarthen, Colwyn, and Stuart Daniel 2005. "Disorganized Rhythm and Synchrony: Early Signs of Autism and Rett Syndrome." *Brain Development* **27**(S): S25–34.

Trilling, Lionel 1972. *Sincerity and Authenticity*. Cambridge, MA: Harvard University Press.

Turner, Jonathan H. 2000. *On the Origins of Human Emotions*. Stanford, CA: Stanford University Press.

Turner, Victor W. 1969. *The Ritual Process: Structure and Anti-Structure*. Harmondsworth, UK: Penguin.

Urban, Gregory 2001. *Metaculture: How Culture Moves through the World*. Minneapolis, MN: University of Minnesota Press.

Verma, Mahendra K., and Tara Mohanan 1991. *Experiencer Subjects in South Asian Languages*. Stanford, CA: Center for the Study of Language and Information, Stanford University.

Vincent, Norah 2006. *Self-Made Man*. New York: Viking.

Volosinov, Valentin Nikolaevitch 1973. *Marxism and the Philosophy of Language*. L. Matejka and I. R. Titunik, transl. Cambridge, MA: Harvard University Press.

Waldram, James B. 2004. *Revenge of the Windigo: The Construction of the Mind and Mental Health of North American Aboriginal Peoples*. Toronto: University of Toronto Press.

Wardlow, Holly 2006. *Wayward Women: Sexuality and Agency in a New Guinea Society*. Berkeley and Los Angeles: University of California Press.

Watson-Gegeo, Karen, and Geoffrey M. White, eds. 1990. *Disentangling: The Discourse of Interpersonal Conflict in Pacific Island Societies*. Stanford, CA: Stanford University Press.

Weber, Max 1999[1904]. "The Area of Economics, Economic Theory, and the Ideal Type." In *Essays in Economic Sociology*. R. Swedberg, ed., pp. 242–249. Princeton: Princeton University Press.

Weinberg, Bennett Alan, and Bonnie K. Bealer 2001. *The World of Caffeine: The Art and Science of the World's Most Popular Drug*. New York: Routledge.

White, Geoffrey 1990. "Emotion Talk and Social Inference: Disentangling in Santa Isabel, Solomon Islands." In Watson-Gegeo and White, eds., pp. 53–121.

   2000. "Representing Emotional Meaning: Category, Metaphor, Schema, Discourse." In *Handbook of Emotions,* Second Edition. M. Lewis and J. Haviland, eds., pp. 30–44. New York: Guilford.

   2004. "National Subjects: September 11 and Pearl Harbor." *American Ethnologist* **31**: 293–310.

Whorf, Benjamin Lee 1956a. "Grammatical Categories." In *Language, Thought, and Reality: Selected Writings of Benjamin Lee Whorf*. J.B. Carroll, ed., pp. 87–101. Cambridge, MA: MIT Press.

   1956b. "The Relation of Habitual Thought and Behavior to Language." In *Language, Thought, and Reality: Selected Writings of Benjamin Lee Whorf*. J.B. Carroll, ed., pp. 134–159. Cambridge, MA: MIT Press.

Wickett, E. 1993. "'For Our Destinies': The Funerary Lament of Upper Egypt." Unpublished Ph.D. dissertation, Department of Folklore, University of Pennsylvania.

Wierzbicka, Anna 1996. *Semantics: Primes and Universals*. Oxford: Oxford University Press.

   2003. "Emotion and Culture: Arguing with Martha Nussbaum." *Ethos* **31**(4): 577–600.

Wierzbicka, Anna, and Jean Harkins 2001. "Introduction." In *Emotions in Crosslinguistic Perspective*. Harkins and Wierzbicka, eds., pp. 1–34.

Wikan, Unni 1989. "Managing the Heart to Brighten Face and Soul: Emotions in Balinese Morality and Health Care." *American Ethnologist* **16**(2): 294–312.

Wilce, James M. 1998. *Eloquence in Trouble: The Poetics and Politics of Complaint in Rural Bangladesh*. New York: Oxford University Press.

    2003 Commentary on "The Meaning of Interjections in Q'eqchi'-Maya: From Emotive Reaction to Social and Discursive Action" by Paul Kockelman. *Current Anthropology* **44**(4): 484–485.

    2004a. "To 'Speak Beautifully' in Bangladesh: Subjectivity as Pāgalāmi." In *Schizophrenia, Culture, and Subjectivity: The Edge of Experience*. J.H. Jenkins and R.J. Barrett, eds.. pp. 196–218. New York: Cambridge University Press.

    2004b. "Madness, Fear, and Control in Bangladesh: Clashing Bodies of Power/Knowledge." *Medical Anthropology Quarterly* **18**(3 (special issue on Illness and Illusions of Control)): 357–375.

    2006. "Magical Laments and Anthropological Reflections: The Production and Circulation of Anthropological Text as Ritual Activity." *Current Anthropology* **47**: 891–914.

    2008. "Scientizing Bangladeshi Psychiatry: Parallelism, Enregisterment, and the Cure for a Magic Complex." *Language in Society* **36**(1).

    2009. *Crying Shame: Metaculture, Modernity, and the Exaggerated Death of Lament*. Malden, MA: Blackwell.

Wilce, James, M. "Society, Language, History, and Religion: A Perspective from Linguistic Anthropology." In *The Sociology of Language and Religion: Change, Conflict and Accommodation*, T. Omoniyi and J. Fishman, eds. John Benjamins, in submission.

Wilce, James M., ed. 2003. *Social and Cultural Lives of Immune Systems (Theory and Practice in Medical Anthropology and International Health)*. London/New York: Routledge.

Wilce, James M., and Laurie Price 2003. "Immune Metaphors Our Bodyminds Live By?" In Wilce, ed., pp. 50–80.

Williams, Raymond 1977. *Marxism and Literature*. Oxford: Oxford University Press.

    1983. *Keywords: A Vocabulary of Culture and Society*. New York: Oxford University Press.

Williamson, Judith 1978. *Decoding Advertisements: Ideology and Meaning in Advertising*. London: Marion Boyars.

Wittgenstein, Ludwig 1958. *Philosophical Investigations*. G.E.M. Anscombe and R. Rhees, transl. Oxford: Blackwell.

    1960. *The Blue and Brown Books: Preliminary Studies for the Philosophical Investigations*. New York: Harper & Row.

Woodward, Kathleen 1996. "Global Cooling and Academic Warming: Long-Term Shifts in Emotional Weather." *American Literary History* **8**: 759–779.

Woolard, Kathryn A. 1985. "Language Variation and Cultural Hegemony: Toward an Integration of Sociolinguistics and Social Theory." *American Ethnologist* **12**: 238–48.

    1998. "Introduction: Language Ideology as a Field of Inquiry." In Schieffelin, Woolard, and Kroskrity, eds., pp. 3–47.

Yates, Candida 2001. "Teaching Psychoanalytic Studies: Towards a New Culture of Learning in Higher Education." *Psychoanalytic Studies* **3**(3–4): 333–347.

Zhang, Everett Yuehong 2005. "Rethinking Sexual Repression in Maoist China: Ideology, Structure and the Ownership of the Body." *Body & Society* **11**(3): 1–25.

INDEX

223

STUDIES IN THE SOCIAL AND CULTURAL
FOUNDATIONS OF LANGUAGE

Editors

Judith T. Irvine
Bambi Schieffelin